Weight Control
The Hi-Way

"The key to the lock that holds someone's weight problem in place and a map to the secrets they need to find their way out".

A Global Weight Control Solution
Using The Human Intelligence (Hi) Common Platform
To Successfully Achieve Long Term Weight Control
For The Spectrum Of Weight Problems

By

David John Sheridan

In this book we are using material from:

PALM Solutions
Strategic Lifestyle Management Solutions
& Lifestyle Management Platforms

And

The Human Algorithm® Project
The Human Intelligence (Hi) Common Platform

Combined into the Application: Weight Control The **Hi-Way**

Introducing the Global Communications Platform:

The Human Intelligence
Common Platform   ©™

Copyright © 2015 David John Sheridan

Published by Sheridan Publishing

All Intellectual Property Rights & Applications are reserved.

ISBN: 978 0 9932355 0 4

DEDICATION

To What Can Be!

CONTENTS

	Acknowledgments	i
	Introduction	Pg 1
1	Mind, Body, Attitude & Human Intelligence (Hi)	Pg 7
2	Understanding And Getting Hi	Pg 10
3	Let's Be Imperfect People And Relax!	Pg 18
4	Where Are You On The Dieters Scale?	Pg 24
5	The Most Successful Diet In The World	Pg 36
6	Eat What You Want; Just Accept The Consequences!	Pg 41
7	Food Addiction; Fact Or Myth?	Pg 48
8	Consuming More – The New Normal	Pg 58
9	Permanently Changing Your Life Profile For Food, Etc.	Pg 66
10	Your Tendencies For Gaining Weight	Pg 71
11	Genetic Realities	Pg 76
12	Finding Your Seed Of Belief	Pg 81
13	Chaos, Chaotic Behaviour And Chaotic Situations.	Pg 86
14	Why Is It Easier For One Person Than Another To Achieve Their Goals?	Pg 89
15	The Reality Of Failure	Pg 96
16	The Role Of Habits In Your Problem	Pg 100
17	The Role Of Relationships In Your Problem	Pg 106
18	The Role Of "A Lack Of Understanding" In Your Problem	Pg 112
19	The Role Of Symptom Solutioning In Developing And Maintaining Your Weight Problem	Pg 115
20	The Role Of Food In Your Problem	Pg 120
21	The Role of "Processed" Foods In Your Problem	Pg 126

22	The Role Of Exercise In Your Weight Problem	Pg 138
23	The Role Of "Influencing Factors" In Your Problem	Pg 151
24	Confusing Problems	Pg 155
25	Body Dysmorphia And Social And General Dysmorphia	Pg 158
26	Coping With Discomfort	Pg 163
27	Are You A Secret Eater, Boozer, In Denial...	Pg 165
28	How Long Does It Really Take?	Pg 167
29	Life Improvement Programmes; Why?	Pg 171
30	Balancing Lifestyle, Wealth, Health And Well-Being!	Pg 174
31	A Different View Of Diet, Weight Loss And Exercise Classes	Pg 180
32	Putting It All Together	Pg 184
	Book Part 2 – Introduction	Pg 186
1	The Stepping Stones Quest	Pg 195
2	Preparation & Practice – The Real Key To Success!	Pg 199
3	Focus On The Right Things!	Pg 206
4	Preparation & Practice – Steps 1 to 5	Pg 214
5	Preparation & Practice – Steps 6 to 10	Pg 223
6	Preparation & Practice – Steps 11 to 15	Pg 230
7	Preparation & Practice – Steps 16 to 20	Pg 234
8	Preparation & Practice – Steps 21 to 30	Pg 239
	A Summary Of The 30 Steps	Pg 247
9	Adding More Pieces To Your Life Map	Pg 249
10	Getting A Foothold On The 2nd Stepping Stone	Pg 258
11	Understanding The Difference Between A Diet And A Weight Management Process	Pg 261
12	Frequency – Food Flow Rate	Pg 265

13	Nutrition	Pg 271
14	Calories	Pg 277
15	Using The Dieters Scale For Calories	Pg 279
16	An Alternate View Of Calories	Pg 281
17	Processed Foods	Pg 285
18	Calories And Portion Control	Pg 288
19	Using Volume To Control And Manage Calories	Pg 292
20	Burgers, Fries And Pizza	Pg 296
21	Improving The Burgers, Fries And Pizza's Diet	Pg 300
22	Getting The Body Stable And Prepared To Go On The Diet Proper	Pg 304
23	Achieving Stability And Moving On To The 3rd Stepping Stone	Pg 306
24	Weighing Yourself – How Often?	Pg 310
25	The Common Purpose	Pg 313
26	Locking Things In Place	Pg 315
27	Creating Your Slim Land Identity	Pg 320
28	Moving Into Slim Land	Pg 323
29	Don't Get Mugged By Poor Hi	Pg 325
	About the Author	Pg 326
	Licensing	Pg 327

ACKNOWLEDGMENTS

To a challenge that has been hard;
To an elusive foe that hides itself well;
To a master of disguise that occasionally lets you glimpse their true nature;
To a fickle companion who constantly tries to leave;
Who am I speaking off?

The Purpose and Direction that leads on to Success!

Other books by the Author include:

Self Esteem For Imperfect People

How To Motivate Yourself; to do something positive!

The Perfect Life Diet For Imperfect People With Weight Problems

How To Move From Fat Land To Slim Land In 3 Steps!

An Introduction To The Human Dynamics Matrix

And the children's book:

The Magic Mustachio And The Tale Of The Bear That Loved Pies

Introduction

Weight Control The Hi-Way

When we cut through all the stuff that surrounds dieting, slimming, losing weight, gaining weight, burning fat, exercise, high protein foods, low fat foods, low sugar foods, low carb diets, fad diets, fad foods, weight loss products, surgical interventions, meal replacements and calorie controlled products; what is it that it all comes down to?

Achieving And Maintaining Successful Weight Control

In one form or another it is about this simple process and the consequences of getting this wrong.

If we get it wrong we change our weight and change the shape of our bodies. We alter our health and we change our ability to do things.

If this persists for too long, then many of the changes that occur with our bodies become permanent or difficult to change.

The reality is that a Weight Problem takes time to develop; and it will develop as a result of a series of events, spread out over a period of time. It's usually a slow process that occurs so slowly that we don't notice the little changes that occur.

Often a Weight Problem will have been there, in one form or another, for many years. It's only when it gets to certain stages that someone begins to pay attention to it and have problems with it.

A common approach that many people take is that they try to undo the consequences of a Weight Problem by going on a diet. After all; diets are about losing and controlling weight.

So it should be simple; you have a weight problem, so just go on a diet!

If it were that simple then we could finish this book here.

In reality the normal cycle of putting on weight and then going on a diet, often doesn't really help the weight problem in the medium to long term.

For most people with weight problems there are missing pieces of information, knowledge, wisdom and structure; that are required to fix the weight problem long term; and to achieve the sought after Weight Control that gives them the results they really want.

With this book I want to help you find and use those missing pieces that can really make the difference between being successful with weight control and not being successful. We will call these missing bits Human Intelligence or **Hi** for short.

Most people understand that their body has certain things that it requires to operate and maintain good health. If they don't give it those things, then it will eventually move into a different state of health.

And they understand that if they abuse their body through excessive or inappropriate consumption, then eventually that will show in their body.

By the time it shows in their body; it will have taken their body time to adjust to that excessive consumption; and to show it in the form of fat and a changed body shape.

Part of the adjustment that their body will have made is in how it processes and manages the excessive or inappropriate consumption. This change will then become their normal State.

For simplicity let's call this change their Fat Land identity.

When someone gets to the stage where they have a Fat Land identity, going on a conventional diet does not allow their body to change from being in the Fat Land State; to being in the Slim Land State. Instead; it just adds to the complexities that their body has to deal with and causes stress.

It also puts them under mental and emotional stress; and that in turn puts them under dietary stress.

From my point of view, a normal diet, with all the expectations that goes with it, is the wrong thing to do for most people with a Weight Control problem. One reason is that those diets tend to be about losing weight quickly and not about Weight Control.

This is an important point to understand. Diets are usually about losing weight quickly and consistently. Weight Control is about achieving a weight and then maintaining that weight within a range. They can appear to both be going in the same direction but they are actually going to destinations that are miles apart.

Time is one of the key components to successful Weight Control. If you do not have enough time to apply to the right Weight Control solution, then you are not going to achieve and maintain the results that you want.

Often people want to achieve results in a few weeks or months; and they expect those results to carry on into the future. The reality is that this is not possible for most people who have a Weight Control problem; because their bodies simply cannot adjust; and maintain that adjustment, in so short a period of time. It takes longer!

At this point let me say something loud and clear:

It is my belief that virtually all Weight Control problems can be successfully dealt with; and be changed into successful long term Weight Control!

Successful Weight Control really is an achievable result for almost everyone but it has to be done with good quality Human Intelligence (Hi).

Has anyone ever said to you that being successful with a diet is as much about the state of your mind, as it is about the diet itself?

What you may need to change first is that view that the Weight Control problem and "You" are somehow not connected to each other.

You are the foundations on which the Weight Control problem is built.

So this means that "You" are the foundations on which the Weight Control solution will also be built.

And what we want to do is to build a very strong Weight Control solution with "You" at the centre of that successful result.

To help you achieve that; I am going to come at the Weight Control problem from another direction with this book. The direction of applying better Human Intelligence (Hi) to the Human Behaviours and the Human Activities that are part of a Weight Control problem; so as to achieve more positive results with Weight Control.

So what is Human Intelligence (Hi) and why is it important with Weight Control?

When you are better informed about Human Behaviours and Activities you can manage them better and achieve better results. When the Human Behaviours and Activities are your own; then you can achieve better results.

This is important for people with weight problems because it is often what is hidden and unknown in their Behaviours and Activities that drives the development and then the maintenance of their weight problem.

For example; a diet may give you an eating plan. How does that eating plan help you to see and understand the emotional triggers that make you want to throw the diet out of the widow when you are stressed? It doesn't.

But if you could understand, and then manage, and then modify those emotional triggers; you can then change the nature of your weight problem!

So what we need is a way of bringing the behaviours and activities that are hidden below the surface; and the behaviours and activities that are on show above the surface – Together!

We need to join the right things together and get them working in a better and more productive way; rather than a bad and destructive way.

And this is what Human Intelligence (Hi) can help us to do. It can help to illuminate the things which are causing us to fail and help us to improve things.

> Better Human Intelligence (Hi) can help us to see, understand and then modify the Patterns of Behaviours and Actions that help create and maintain a Weight Problem.

So what are the difficult pieces of a weight problem that normally get left out of a diet and which lead on to failure?

In my view it is the following:

> Emotions/Feelings, Actions/Reactions (Behaviour), Our Psychology (how we process and manage), Relationships, Legacy Issues, Human Dynamics, Problem Dynamics, Hidden Influences, Unknowns, and other factors and components.

And they get left out for some very good reasons. First of all, they are usually very difficult to deal with and it can take a great deal of time and effort to do so.

What I wanted to do was to find an effective way of being able to work with all of these difficult bits and the weight problem; but do it in a simple format.

The Hi Common Platform gives us that simple format.

> The Human Intelligence (Hi) Common Platform is a new way of working with Human Behaviours and Human Activities; to reveal the secrets and unlock the codes of those Human Behaviours and Activities; so as to help people achieve better outcomes with those Human Behaviours and Human Activities.

In this book you are seeing an Application of Hi-**Way** *lite*; a simplified user friendly version that does not require the user to have any specialist skills, training, education or knowledge.

To use this method effectively you just need to use some simple tools that I will show you and that are very easy to learn. You can also take these tools and use them in other areas of your life. So they are transferable, which is good.

I have done most of the work for you by focusing **Hi-Way** *lite* into the; Weight Control the **Hi-Way** Application. That you can use to achieve and maintain long term Weight Control.

This Application has been designed to work across the entire spectrum of weight problems. It will work with simple and easy to deal with weight problems and with very difficult and hard to deal with weight problems.

All you have to do is use it and work with it until you reach your goal.

This will work with any diet, any dieting approach; whether formal or informal.

As part of this Approach I will help you to look at any diet in a different way and see whether that diet and what you want to really achieve are compatible.

Having a diet or weight control process that is compatible with your weight control abilities is a critical factor. We will see what that really means and how you can really go about achieving and managing this. This is an example of having and using good **Hi**.

Failure is often a prerequisite of success. Why should being successful with Weight Control be any different?

Weight Control The **Hi-Way** has been designed to work with dieting failure. It doesn't matter if the diet you tried is wrong or it just doesn't work. We can work with that situation and move beyond it. It is simply another step on your journey to successful Weight Control.

Weight Control The **Hi-Way** is a combination of The **Hi** Common Platform and PALM Solutions Strategic Lifestyle Management structures and Lifestyle Management Platforms. By combining these projects we can supercharge the Weight Control process and deal with it properly. Dealing with it properly doesn't mean dealing with it fast.

Speed is usually one of the things which causes dieters to fail; they try to achieve far too much, too quickly and often too easily.

Weight Control The **Hi-Way** has also been designed to work with chaotic behaviour, destructive behaviour, low self-esteem, low confidence, bad relationships, difficult relationships, controlling relationships and abusive relationships.

These are all reasons why people end up with a weight problem and lose control of their lives. All of these can be gradually dealt with and changed. All you need to start with is a direction to go in. I want this book to give you that direction!

In part this book is a workbook. In part it is also a reference book. In part it is a guide book. In part it is an education book. In part it is a map. In part it will be a record. In part it will be a compass. In part it will be the key to the lock that holds your weight problem in place and a map to the secrets you need to find your way out.

To achieve this I have written the book in different parts. In the first section of the book I am going to focus on introducing you to a different way of looking at and understanding a weight problem. Then we will look at the Common Components that make up weight problems.

After these sections we will move on to moving from Fat Land to Slim Land and how to take us residence in Slim Land. This section will focus on Weight Control and how to achieve successful long term weight control and have a better quality of life.

By using Weight Control The **Hi-Way** you may find that you will be challenged and that you want to quit. That is all part of making progress. We want you to become dissatisfied with living in Fat Land and motivated to start living in Slim Land.

Do you think that anyone who is successful at something didn't have times when they wanted to quit; and didn't have times when they thought that they could not keep going and succeed?

This is normal when you are doing something different from what you are used too. Changing your life and how you live your life can be difficult; stick with it!

Stick with it and you will find that you will make progress but maybe not quite in the way you thought you would in the beginning.

Chapter 1

Mind – Body – Attitude
&
Human Intelligence (Hi)

I am going to start this book with a quote from one of my other books.

> A Weight Problem is a set of conditions looking for a better way of being managed, so as to produce a more successful result.

From The Perfect Life Diet for Imperfect People with Weight Problems by David John Sheridan

This simple quote sums up what a weight problem really is and what we really need to do to solve it.

If you remember nothing else from this book; you should allow yourself to remember this simple quote. This is good Hi.

It is when we lose sight of this simple point of view that we begin to think that a weight problem can be deal with by a diet or a quick fix of one type or another.

In reality every weight problem involves: Your Mind, Your Body, Your Attitude and other factors.

How you understand them and how they influence and affect your problem is what most people get wrong.

I invented the Human Intelligence (Hi) Common Platform to help people understand how things like their Mind, Body and Attitude influence each other. I did this so that they would be able to increase their Human Intelligence (Hi) of their own Behaviours and Actions; and how these influence and control their weight problem.

As a result of increasing their Human Intelligence (Hi) they can find and use "that better way" of managing their own individual set of conditions that created, and which helps to maintain, their weight problem.

We are not talking about a temporary fix to a weight problem. We are talking about resolving and removing the problem from your life!

And of course, because this is a book, I will help you with the process of increasing and using your new Human Intelligence (Hi) by using **Hi-Way** *lite*.

Part of what I will do is to help you understand that a weight problem differs from one person to another. It is not that each person's weight problem is so unique that it cannot be resolved; it is that each person will require more of one thing that another.

So this means that any solution to a weight problem needs to be flexible and dynamic (be able to work with changing conditions) to increase its success rate.

I also want you to understand that weight problems can be graded into different types, with different levels of complexity and difficulty. The reason that we need to do this is that we want to match the type of weight problem to the right type of weight solution and time scale.

This grading isn't done by the BMI index or by measuring inches of fat. It is done in another way.

To do this grading I created something that I called The Dieters Scale. You will be introduced to this as you go through this book and you will use this with many of the different aspects of your weight problem.

> *I first introduced The Dieters Scale in my book: The Perfect Life Diet for Imperfect People with Weight Problems. And I used it again in another book of mine called: From Fat to Slim in 3 Steps!*

One of the major reasons why so many people with weight problems fail to achieve successful Weight Control; and the resolution of their weight problem is:

> That they do enough of the wrong things at the beginning of the weight loss process to make it very difficult for them to succeed.

Let's use this as an example:

Imagine that you were in the middle of America and you wanted to go somewhere that was in the North of America. But instead of heading North you tried to get there by going in a South Westerly direction. You are simply going the wrong way!

And this is what many people with weight problems do: They go on the wrong journey to achieve the successful results that they want. Often it may seem to them as if they are on the right path but they never achieve and maintain the results that they really want.

That is an example of bad Human Intelligence (**Hi**) at work. Often this isn't really the fault of the person. They have been exposed to so much bad Human Intelligence (**Hi**) through marketing, the media and bad information; that they simply believe that they can achieve a fantastic body by eating low fat something or other.

The reality is that if any part of your life is not how you want it to be; then the Human Intelligence (Hi) for that part of your life can be improved and you can do something positive towards helping yourself achieve what you really want to achieve.

Now another thing about Human Intelligence (Hi) is this. Knowledge without the right actions; is like being able to read but never reading. It becomes pointless!

My advice about this book is that you read it all the way through first.

Then read it through again and work out what type of weight problem you have and what type of weight solution you should be using; and what length of time it may take to really achieve Weight Control.

Answer the questions and write down your answers. It is surprising how quickly we forget what we have really achieved. Your written answers will help to remind you.

Then begin your journey from either the Green Zone, the Amber Zone or the Red Zone. These will indicate the length and difficulty of the journey you will have; as you move from one zone to another to reach your prize.

You will be starting your journey from Fat Land and you will have a Fat Land identity when you begin.

The journey is about moving from Fat Land to Slim Land and developing a Slim Land identity along the way.

You cannot live in Fat Land and Slim Land at the same time. You will continue to wake up and find yourself back in Fat Land if you do this.

If you fall off a Stepping Stone on your journey; don't worry. Simply begin the process again and learn from what you did before.

Don't try to jump over Stepping Stones. It never works.

The classical mistake that people with weight problems make is that they try to move too fast; and they try to take short cuts. All this does is weaken the structure that you are trying to build. Then it falls down.

Chapter 2

Understanding And Getting Hi

This book has two sections that are intended to do different but complimentary things.

In the first section of the book I am going to give you my view on different aspects of weight problems.

There are some chapters where I will go into some detail, and perhaps more detail than many of you will want. I will do this to try and dispel a lot of misinformation that exist around dieting and weight control; and to try and get you looking at and understanding things differently.

I will also do it because many people really need to know more about the structures and components of weight problems and what really needs to be done to fix them long term.

This will be new information that you will not have been exposed to before and that few people really know and understand. I have personally developed this material.

Try to think of this process as laying a foundation of knowledge and correcting wrong information.

The reason that I am doing this is that I want to build your Human Intelligence (Hi) so that you can use that Human Intelligence (Hi) to understand and manage a weight problem better.

> Remember that a weight problem is about behaviours and actions, and if you can understand them better; you can improve and change them.

You can use this book as a reference book. It will help you to help understand the structure of your weight problem now and as it changes. So keep referring back to the book.

In the second part of the book I am going to take you on the Journey from Fat Land to Slim Land; and take you through the process of changing from a Fat Land identity to a Slim Land identity.

Fat Land and Slim Land are metaphors for the weight problem that you don't want to have and the slim person that you do want to be.

It is the same for the Fat Land identity and the Slim Land identity. With the Fat Land identity people will be living, feeling and behaving in ways that they don't want.

With the Slim Land identity they will be living, feeling and behaving in ways that they do want.

The journey that I will talk about is the process of getting from Fat Land to Slim Land; and the time that it takes to change from the Fat Land identity to the Slim Land identity.

Throughout this book I will be attempting to increase your Human Intelligence (**Hi**) related to successful Weight Control and living a better life.

Let me give you some background to my work.

I first began working professionally with people who had weight problems in the early 1990's.

I set up a small clinic working with a number of people who had long dieting histories and problematic lives.

The people I worked with had all tried multiple diets and different types of weight control and exercise programmes. Some of these were main stream solutions and others were not. Some of them had gone to quite extreme lengths to lose weight.

At the time I was also working with people in the area of drug and alcohol addictions.

The medical team I was attached to were dealing with the very problematic and chaotic people who required a clinical detox to break the addiction cycle.

As I was working with these different groups of people I could see patterns and structures within their behaviours.

I also saw that there were patterns and structures within their abilities to understand and manage their problems better.

I found that these patterns and structures were the same across the different conditions of drugs, alcohol, weight and other problem groups.

I realised that as well as having common factors in these conditions. That when we looked at other problems that involved people, that these common factors continued. The common factors include self-esteem, confidence, self perception, etc.

And over time I began to look at other types of problems where people were involved. This included businesses and social structures at both small and large scale.

Over time I undertook more training and became involved in different businesses.

I trained in Finance and in Business Consultancy. As I spent more time talking to people and working with people who provided solutions to problems; my belief that there was room for new approaches for understanding and working with problems grew.

I could see that there was room to change, to improve and to develop new ways of understanding and working with problems that involve people.

The trouble is that when you begin to connect different conditions together, you come up against different groups who specialise in those conditions, and this creates resistance to new ideas and approaches.

What you find is that Experts in different fields don't like "Outsiders" having and expressing views that may affect their specialisations.

Even when the Outsiders views may help them; you still encounter resistance and even hostility.

It's just the way that the systems, groups and the people behave when they are faced with new thinking and challenging ideas.

People with weight problems can also behave like this.

As a result of my curiosity; I had began a process of trying to understand the structures of problems and solutions. This was working at a very in depth level.

What I was interested in was getting to the DNA level and understanding it from that level upwards. I was looking at the Architecture or problems and solutions; and the natural designs that occurred.

I wanted to understand what it was about those structures that contributes to and influences Success and Failure. I wanted to understand this because if I could; then I could understand how to influence structures by applying Strategic Influences.

Because of my curiosity; I had began working on new ways of looking at and understanding the actual structure and nature of problems and the solutions that they required.

I did not know that it would take me this long or that so much hard work would be involved.

This book has been written as a result of those many years of hard work and experience; and the Weight Control the **Hi-Way** Application was also produced from this work.

Over the years that I have been doing this; I have developed an eye for the Patterns of Success and Failure in Human Behaviours and Human Activities.

Those Patterns of Success and Failure are not as obvious as we may think they are.

> Often Success is achieved by contra thinking and contra behaviour: Going against the tide of popular opinion; rather than allowing yourself to be carried by it.

Some of what I say in this book may go against the tide of popular opinion. These are my views and they are the result of my experiences and observations. Until I have evidence to the contrary; I will stick with them.

It is my intention that this book is going to be different from the other diet, weight reduction, and diet and exercise books that you may have read and heard about.

In this book we are going to be looking at and working with weight problems by understanding what weight problems really are; and understanding what they are not.

Because you live with a weight problem, you might think that you already know what a weight problem really is; but in truth I doubt that you really do.

You have probably had what most people with weight problems have had:

> You have had the experiences of living with a weight problem and trying different things to deal with that weight problem.

Living with a weight problem is different from understanding the problem, so that you can effectively deal with it.

Let me us this as a comparable example:

> We are all capable of eating a great meal, but just because we can eat a great meal; it doesn't mean that we now know and understand how to cook a great meal.
>
> This is because they are different experiences and require different knowledge and skills.

It's the same with a weight problem. Because you know how to live with a weight problem; it doesn't mean that you know how to fix a weight problem.

One of the problems with Weight Problems is that they are not straight-forwards.

For a start we have different types of people, different types of bodies, different ages, different sexes, different abilities and different resources.

Then we have the pressures that people bring to the Weight Problem.

They want to lose weight quickly, easily, with no exercise, with exercise, change their shape, be toned, have a younger looking body, etc.

Then there are the "Other Problems" that everyone has.

This is the complicated mix of personal, domestic, work, social and other problems that populate the lives of people with weight problems; and everyone else!

People with weight problems are not unique when it comes to "Other Problems".

All of us have this entourage of "Other Problems" which annoy and frustrate us as we move through life.

In fact we all have the same problem of:

>How do I have a better quality of life and live the life that I really want to live?

So we will look at the physical, emotional, psychological and social components of a weight problem.

At the same time we will be looking at how to effectively deal with these, so that you can have a better quality of life without all the dieting pressures and disappointments. *You may not think that you have any of these, but trust me; I haven't come across anyone with a weight problem who doesn't.*

What I am going to do within this book is try and help you Understand your weight problem and Understand how to deal with it more effectively.

Don't think of this process as giving you all the answers and providing you with a quick result over a short period of time. Think of this as the beginning of the end of your weight problem; and the start of a new Life Opportunity for you.

To help me do this, I am going to put weight problems into "A Spectrum of Weight Problems".

A Spectrum is simply grouping all the different types of weight problems together and putting them side by side in a line and looking at the way that they line up and fit together.

This process helps us to see weight problems in different ways; and it helps us to see commonalities, relationships and differences between the different parts of the Spectrum of Weight Problems.

This is important when you want to work with weight problems and resolve, improve or manage them in a better way.

You see; certain aspects of a weight problem are common regardless of what type of weight problem you have. Whether this is someone being too fat or too thin.

These common aspects include things like Self-Esteem, Self-Perception, Self-Expectations, Confidence, Motivation and general Unhappiness.

Other aspects of a weight problem are unique to where the weight problem is on the Spectrum of weight problems.

For example: If someone is too fat then they would need to lose weight and someone who is too thin would need to gain weight. Obvious right!

However; both the person who is too fat and the person who is too thin can both have a problem with vitamin deficiency and malnourishment. Not so obvious!

The Spectrum of Weight Problems we will be working with will include the entire Spectrum of weight problems.

At one end of the Spectrum we will be looking at weight problems from the position of those who are very overweight and considered to be Morbidly Obese.

The Morbidly Obese are the very large people who can spend most of their lives in a bed or room because they are too large to move around without assistance.

In effect they have become physically disabled by their weight.

And we will be looking at those who are beginning to edge out of the normal weight range and move into the more problematic ranges of weight related problems. This group of people is increasing in number as each year passes.

At the other end of the Spectrum we will be looking at weight problems from the position of those who are very underweight and who have problems associated with being very underweight. This would include Anorexia.

Why: You might ask should someone overweight be interested in someone who is underweight?

The reality is that these people also have problems with Weight Control. The same dynamics that are affective overweight people can be affecting underweight people as well. Think of it as different sides of the same coin.

I won't focus too much directly on those who are underweight. Most of my focus will be on people who are overweight. However; it is my intention that those who are underweight will be able to read this book and see that the things which apply to overweight people can also apply to them.

Understanding this is good Hi.

As well as considering the weight problems themselves, we will also be looking at what leads to weight problems and what sustains weight problems.

Weight problems do not exist in a vacuum and we know that there are issues which contribute to the development of weight problems; and to the maintenance and further development of weight problems.

We also know that weight problems cause or contribute to the development of additional problems. Which can include physical, social, emotional and psychological challenges.

Within this book and within the scope of what I want to achieve with it; I am recognising that each person will have their own Back Story.

A person's Back Story is their own unique mix of things that have taken them to where they are now, and which helps them to stay where they are, and which helps prevent them from achieving what they want from life.

In my experience that Back Story often tends to hold great strengths, which if employed correctly, can help the person out of the shadow of a weight problem and into the sunshine of a better quality of life.

> *It always seemed strange to me that so many diet and exercise experts fail to understand the Back Story of people with weight problems or that there even is a Back Story behind a weight problem.*

In this book I will introduce you to a process that I developed called:

The Dieter's Scale ©™

This is a simple and easy process that helps you to begin looking at and understanding your weight problem in a different way.

The Dieters Scale will help you to better understand why and how many of the things that you have tried in the past have not worked, will not work or could not have worked.

In The Dieters Scale I use Green, Amber and Red Zones for simplicity.

These Zones will help you understand the different ways in which different things can impact your life and affect your weight problem.

Through the use of these Zones, we can begin to understand the real shape and structure of your weight problem; and the real shape and structure of the solution that you need to improve and change your life.

I also have an unusual approach to diet structures. I will not give you a strict diet to follow or say that you cannot eat this or that.

I will make suggestions about your dietary practices that I know have helped people in the past and that still will do so today.

We will look at different things; such as the role of exercise and how I think many people would be better off approaching exercise in a different way.

I will also look at the other ways of measuring your weight that I think are often much more productive than constantly looking at your weight on a scale.

In this book I will be looking at the best and most effective diet in the world and seeing how you can use this to help you with your weight problem. This is not going to be what you are used too or what you would expect!

Throughout this book I will be looking to help you better understand what a weight related problem is and what it isn't.

And then we will look at how to improve, resolve or better manage weight related problems; so that we can have a positive influence on a weight problem.

Overall; I will see if I can help you to adjust your perceptions, understandings and thinking around weight related problems and help you to become a more successful person. A Person who is:

    Living a life without dieting pressures and disappointments.
A Person who has improved their Hi and who is using better quality Hi.

Chapter 3

Let's Be Imperfect People And Relax!

In this book and others I use the phrase:

Imperfect People

So who or what do I mean by Imperfect People?

When we are dealing with an issue such as a weight problem; Image, Self-Perception and our Comparative Perceptions (Us compared to others) are very important, powerful and often used.

It doesn't matter whether Our Perceptions are accurate or not. The reality is that we have the Perceptions that we have; whether they are serving us well or serving us badly.

If we don't understand this then we will just assume that how we see things and how we feel about things is correct; even when it is completely wrong.

Why is this a problem?

Often people with weight problems have faulty perceptions. This is poor **Hi**.

And the poor **Hi** (your faulty perceptions) helps to create and maintain the weight problem.

This is because our perceptions help to shape our Confidence, Self-esteem, Self worth and other aspects of our mental and emotional image of ourselves; and that affects our eating and consumption.

If our thoughts about ourselves are negative and detrimental; it simple re-enforces our negative image of ourselves and our behaviour. We will live up or live down to what we expect of ourselves.

Look at it another way. On the one side you have the weight problem. And on the other you have the "Life Problems" that we may find difficult to deal with and to cope with. And in the middle of this; there is "You" – The real "You" caught between them.

Weight Problem – You! – Life Problems

If we are not able to understand and deal with our own Life Problems. Then how can we really deal with a weight problem that is part of that reality or which comes out of that reality? This is being in a position of poor **Hi**.

So how do we begin to deal with this?

I created "The Imperfect People" concept to help people to better understand and deal with the impact that our faulty perceptions; and our misunderstanding of things has upon our Lives and the things that we do.

It is designed to help you when you are stuck in the middle between the weight problem and the Life problems.

It's a way of being able to understand and deal with things without having to beat yourself up or feel bad.

When things go wrong: Instead of desperately trying to find answers or blaming yourself and beating yourself up; why not try something else?

Try allowing yourself to be:

>An Imperfect Person.

You see the reality is:

>THAT NO-ONE IS PERFECT!

Over the years I have met and talked with many very attractive and beautiful women. From models, to high profile singers, to royalty and those very lovely and beautiful women who populate everyday life.

Being a man I am interested in women but I have also met men who are the same mix.

I have met very attractive and very handsome men from all walks of life; high profile performers, politicians, academics and people from wealthy and privileged backgrounds, as well as self-made millionaires.

In every person there are flaws. Some of which are real and many which exist just in the mind of the person themselves.

However; the ability to Compare Apples and Pears and see Peaches, is part of the make-up of every person.

As a result; when we see someone who is slim and attractive; and we feel overweight and unattractive; are we concerned when the slim attractive person says that they don't like their smile?

Or do we find ourselves saying something like:

>What have they got to complain about!

> With a figure like that and looks like that; I wish that I had problems like they do.
>
> Now if they had my...

I am sure that you can fill in the rest of that?

How often have you heard people with weight problems say things like:

- If only I was taller.
- I am big boned.
- I have a slow metabolism.
- I only have to look at food to put on weight.
- It's my allergies.
- It's my medication.
- If only I could get sick and stop eating; think how much weight I could lose.
- Some people stop eating when they get upset, I wish I could; all I do is eat.
- I don't have time to eat properly.
- It's genetic!

And so on and so on. I am sure that you could add to this list?

Another thing that happens to people with weight problems is the Perception Distortions that they will experience and focus on.

Let me explain.

How often have you heard people say things like:

> If only I could deal with problem (X) first. Then I am sure that I would be able to sort out my weight problem; as I would feel so much better and I would then be able to do it.
>
> Or; it can be the other way around. If only I could sort out my weight problem first. Then I am sure that I will feel so much better and then I will be able to sort out problem (X).
>
> And if they do manage to sort out problem (X) first or lose the weight first. How often do they then continue on to the next stage of actually sorting out the other problem?

In reality it is often the case that when they do feel better, it leads them to the conclusion that; perhaps things weren't as bad as they thought they really were.

They begin to doubt the validity of their previous experiences and they do nothing.

Because they have not acted the window of opportunity soon closes; and they find themselves back in the same position as before. This is a position of poor Hi.

How often has this happened to you or someone you know?

Another thing that we do; is that we have the ability to see and focus on that which we are worried about or self-conscious off.

Let me explain.

When you are looking at yourself in a mirror or you happen to catch your reflection in a window; what do you notice?

Do you notice that spot on your face or do you see a great looking person and think how great they look?

- Are you noticing with a Critical Negative View or with a Critical Positive View?

The point I am making is that Other People may seem as if they are perfect or are capable of being perfect people; but the reality is that we are all Other People to someone.

When we make the Comparison to ourselves and our situation, Other People may seem as if they have perfect lives or that they are perfect people.

But in reality there is no such thing as the Perfect Person. They don't exist!

So this means that we are all Imperfect People.

Because we are Imperfect People we can give ourselves a break, cut ourselves some slack, take the pressure of ourselves: And begin the process of achieving the Life we really would like to be living and experiencing. Better Hi.

Part of the process of developing better Hi when we are dealing with a weight problem; is that we have to accept:

The Reality of Failure.

In my experience Failure is part of the Reality of Successfully dealing with difficult problems that involve Weight. And Failure is something I will refer to a number of times throughout this book.

It might seem strange to you to think that Failure with your weight problem is a good thing; but it is if it is dealt with in the right way.

You see a weight problem becomes entangled with your life and how you live and manage your life.

When something goes wrong with your Life, then it will affect your weight problem.

It is at times of crisis, difficulty and hardship that people often fail with diets.

It is also at times of great joy and happiness that people fail with diets.

It is also when anniversaries come around each year and someone remembers something or someone; that people fail with diets.

And it is also true that when things are going really well and someone is achieving all the things that they want; that people fail with diets.

The reality is that failure is part of the process of success and we will deal with that later on in this book.

Another thing that we can do, as Imperfect People, is to Compare Apple and Pears and see Peaches.

This means that we can use our Insecurities; our Self-Doubts; and our Desire Not To Be as We Are; and we can use all of those things: To convince ourselves that many different things which we know, hope or fear could be true; are actually true!

We can suffer from:

- Selective Hearing.
- Selective Seeing.
- Selective Understanding.
- Selective Insights.
- Selective Self-Perceptions; just to name a few!

And this process makes us Vulnerable! This often gives us Poor quality Hi.

It makes us vulnerable at many different levels. And some people will realise the extent of their vulnerability and others will not.

For many; their ability to convince themselves of whatever they want to believe, will be being used to fuel Negative Self-Perceptions and Negative and Destructive Behaviour. Bad Hi.

All of this stuff is all part of the Back Story of different people. And all this stuff may seem gloomy and difficult; and even impossible to deal with.

The reality is different!

All of this stuff has the seeds of great outcomes buried inside of it.

You see this stuff can be turned around and focused on Positive things rather than Negative things.

If you actually realised the amount of effort, time and resources that it takes to have an unsatisfactory life; you would be surprised.

What I am interested in is changing the focus of all that negative stuff and making it work for you; rather than against you. Helping you to improve your Hi.

So what do I want you to take away from this chapter?

It is this:

I'm an Imperfect Person;

And I have the ability to improve;

And I have the ability to have a better life;

And Being an Imperfect Person; Is OK!

Better quality Hi.

Chapter 4

Where Are You On The Dieters Scale?

To help you increase your Human Intelligence (**Hi**) of your weight problem; I want you to begin to get an idea of the structure of your weight problem.

I am not talking about just your physical weight; I'm also talking about the other components that help to create and maintain a weight problem.

We are going to achieve this by using The Dieters Scale ©™.

The Dieters Scale has 3 different Zones. These are coloured Green, Amber and Red for simplicity. I have chosen these colours for this Application because most people will be familiar with traffic lights.

We could use more or different colours and more Zones; but for now we want to keep things as simple as we can.

By answering a few questions we can begin to see and understand how your weight problem is structured.

So what we are going to do in the first part of this book is to look at 6 questions; and then put the answers into the appropriate Zones in The Dieters Scale.

That means that you will end up with answers to these questions that will be in either the: Green Zone, Amber Zone or Red Zone.

As we move from Green to Amber and then to Red, the problems get more complicated and require more time and effort to sort them out.

It's this simple process that lets us begin to see your weight problem in another way; a more realistic way.

Some of you may find that your answers don't fit in just one Zone and that they cross Zones. This is fine as problems do move across Zones as they increase or decrease. Just write down what you think is correct.

What this simple process will show is that the different problems, difficulties and challenges that we all face in life, will tend to be located in one or more of these 3 Zones. This then means that we can use this simple process to create a Map of our problem and use that Map to help us fix it.

You will get the idea as you go through the questions.

Question 1

Most people would know what is considered to be their ideal weight, given their physical build, age and other relevant factors, or they can easily find this out.

Their ideal weight will be within a range between weight (X) and weight (Y).

Now you might not agree with this ideal weight; so if you don't then let's do this:

> Find out what that ideal weight is and make a note of it.
>
> Then work out what you consider to be the right weight for you; and then write down what you consider to be your right weight.
>
> Now if there is more than 1 stone or 7 kilo's difference, between the figure that you prefer and the weight that is considered right for you; write down:
>
> Why you believe your figure is correct and why the other one is wrong?

Once you have done this, keep this, and you can refer back to it at another time.

Either way, we should now have a weight that you believe is the ideal weight for you; and you have written that weight down.

So the next thing we need to know is:

What is your actual weight now?

There is no point cheating with this as I am not going to see the information. You don't have to hide it, be ashamed of it, worried about it or be afraid of it.

The truth is that the "real weight that you are" just gives us a starting point to work from that is accurate and that we can rely upon.

So check your weight and write down the real information. You should then have two pieces of information:

1. Your actual weight.
2. The weight that is considered to be your Ideal weight.

The reason why we want this "Accurate Information" is to help us place you in the right position in The Dieters Scale.

So now we want to take one weight away from the other. This is done by taking No.2 away from No.1.

For those who are overweight this will produce a positive figure; and for those underweight this will produce a negative figure.

Whatever that figure is; it will be the figure that we will use.

In the following graphic you will see that we have 3 sections and they are marked Green, Amber and Red. Underneath each of these colours is a weight.

So let's get you into the right Zone.

There are some examples below the graphic.

Green Zone	Amber Zone	Red Zone
1 Stone (7 Kilo's)	3 Stone (22 Kilo's)	More!

Weight Control The **Hi-Way** - The Dieters Scale ©

If the figure you have is 1 stone, or less, choose the Green Zone.

If the figure you have is between 1 and 3 stone; then choose the Amber Zone.

If the figure you have is more than 3 stone; then choose the Red Zone.

It's simple really, isn't it!

For those of you who are underweight we will use the same process.

If you are 1 stone, or less, underweight choose the Green Zone.

If you are between 1 and 3 stone underweight then choose the Amber Zone.

And if you are more than 3 stone underweight then choose the Red Zone.

So write down what your answer is for this:

Green, Amber or Red Zone?

Now we will look at your Frequency of Dieting.

Question 2

What I am interested in here is Your Dieting History and how often you will have dieted.

Some people will begin their Dieting History early in their lives and others will begin it later in life.

Generally speaking the older you are; the longer Your Dieting History is likely to be.

The longer Your Dieting History is; the more diets you are likely to have been on.

The more times that you will have dieted and/or been on a diet; then the more of your life that will have been spent dieting.

You will also have more dieting experiences and knowledge of how you manage the dieting process.

We will use The Dieters Scale to see where you are with Your Dieting History.

Green Zone	Amber Zone	Red Zone
2 Diets or less	2 - 4 Diets	Always Dieting

Weight Control The Hi-Way - The Dieters Scale ©

If you have dieted 2 times or less in your life, then you will be in the Green Zone.

If you have been on or followed between 2 and 4 diets in your life then you will be in the Amber Zone.

If you are always on one diet or another or you have been on more than 4 diets, then you will be in the Red Zone.

Now some of you might try and cheat on this one and say that you have been on something like "The No Food Diet" all your life; but the reality is that you know what I mean and you know what the truth of the matter is. You don't need to cheat!

So write down what your answer is for this:

Are you in the Green, Amber or Red Zone?

Question 3

Now we will look at your ability to stick to a diet and to achieve the desired weight that you went on the diet to achieve.

What we really want to know is: Have you ever done it?

Have you been able to stick to diets and achieve the desired outcome with your weight; through that dieting process?

Green Zone	Amber Zone	Red Zone
Easily Stick to Diet	Keep to It a bit!	No Chance!

Weight Control The Hi-Way - The Dieters Scale ©

If the answer is that you have easily been able to follow and stick to the diet, without cheating, and you stuck with it and achieved the result you wanted:

> Then you should choose the Green Zone.

If the answer is that you have started diets with all the best intentions:

- But you have struggled.
- You found it difficult.
- You cheated a lot and you got fed-up and bored.
- But you did manage to lose weight and you did feel better being on the diet:
> Then you should choose the Amber Zone.

If the answer is that you look at diets and you think that they are great. But when you start them:

- You just can't be bothered.
- You immediately want to eat all the food that is forbidden to you.
- You have no motivation for this; even though it was your idea and you give up:
> Then you should choose the Red Zone.

Some of you might be carefully reading the text at this point and seeing if you can place yourself in the Zone below where you really should be.

The reality is that you are where you are. The only person that you are going to try and fool here is yourself. And as you are an expert on you; that won't really work very well, will it? So put down the right Zone!

Question 4

Next we will look at Exercise and the role that exercise has in your daily life and how it influences your weight.

As part of being Human we need to move and do things with our bodies.

We need to use energy to exercise; but to the body exercise is work. As a result the body will be very efficient with the energy that it uses, to do the work that it needs to do.

- The reality is that Exercise is not a very good weight management tool. In fact; it is a rubbish way of trying to lose weight.

Exercise is about maintaining the bodies' abilities to perform certain task and to function well. Understanding this is good Hi.

If we fail to maintain the bodies' abilities then we experience consequences.

Those consequences can be short term; as in being generally unfit, a lack of energy, poor sleep, tiredness, poor digestion, etc.

Or; they can be medium and long term consequences such as poor posture, skeletal problems, cardiovascular problems, sleep problems, poor balance and co-ordination, etc.

I personally like to think of exercise as an investment in my life which gives me immediate and long term benefits. This is good Hi.

So let's see where you are in your life with genuine exercise, on the Dieters Scale.

Green Zone	Amber Zone	Red Zone
I am Fit I Exercise!	Occasional Exercise	Don't!

Weight Control The Hi-**Way** - The Dieters Scale ©

So: If you are fit and you exercise regularly then you should select the Green Zone.

Regular exercise would be about 3 hours a week (up to about 6 hours) of planned and reasonably demanding periods of exercise, where you break a sweat doing it.

This will be a part of your normal everyday life; and you will be maintaining this ongoingly; and you will have done so for some time.

If you fall into the occasional exercise zone then you should select Amber.

If you occasionally exercise then you won't have a regular weekly programme that you have followed for a long time; or for a reasonable period of time, of say 6 months or more.

Occasional Exercisers may exercise when they feel particularly out of shape; or when they are following another diet programme; or for some other reason like having a medical check-up.

They may do things like have the occasional swim or walk. *Please note that going to the swimming pool and standing around having a chat; is not the same as having a good swim.*

The Red zone is for those who know that they are unfit and don't care about it; or who will get around to it one day.

These are the people who would love to take a pill to be fit; or if they could get someone else to do it for them, they would.

They know all the arguments for getting fit and they have been told to get fit by their doctors; but they really can't be bothered yet. They will wait until they really need to do it.

On the other hand; they could be people who just don't know about and understand the real benefits of exercise and keeping fit. They may just be uneducated about this area of life and have never engaged with this before.

So are you a Red Zone person?

> Some people are very active but overweight; and some people are underactive and slim.
>
> You should not confuse being overweight with being unfit and you should not confuse being slim with being fit. These are generalities that can apply but do not always.
>
> Generally, in my experience, Obese and Morbidly Obese people will be unfit.

Question 5

The next thing we will look at is Stress!

Stress comes in all shapes and sizes; just like people do.

What one person finds stressful another might find to be a challenge. Life is just funny like that!

So what we are interested in is the total level of stress in your life, regardless of where that stress comes from or originates from.

Now stress is a funny thing in many ways. Stress is something which we can Self-Report on and it is something which others can Inform Us Of.

The Self-Reported stress is the stress which we ourselves are aware of and which we respond to. It might be working long hours, putting up with things we don't want to, not getting the things we want out of life, etc.

Generally, Self-Reported Stress is the stress that we are aware off and which we may want to keep private. It can also be the stuff that we talk about to our best friends and try to cope with ourselves.

"The Inform Us Of" stress is when other people notice that we are stressed and they tell us about it.

Often this can be that someone is "Snappy" with other people; when someone is drinking or smoking too much; or when someone is constantly eating or snacking.

These are often talked about as "Stress Indicators".

To keep things simple we will bring all the different stresses that you experience together for this exercise.

Green Zone	Amber Zone	Red Zone
No Stress!	Quite Stressed	Always Stressed

Weight Control The Hi-Way - The Dieters Scale ©

So: if you have no Self-Reported stress and no Inform Us Of stress then you would be in the Green Zone.

Very, very few people who have a weight problem do not suffer from one type of stress or another; they just might not recognise it.

If you have the occasional thing which stresses you out, but you are not normally stressed by very much; then you would also be in the Green Zone.

Now my experience of working with people who are very highly stressed is that after a while they stop seeing or recognising stress. It can become like wallpaper; it's there but they no long really see it.

The Amber Zone is for those people who are quite stressed and very busy with life. When you experience stress you will be doing things like:

- Eating far too much; even for you.
- Drinking too much alcohol.
- Taking medication to cope.
- Having more arguments than normal.
- Having trouble sleeping.
- Feeling tired all the time and unable to relax.
- Frequently feeling dissatisfied with your life.

The Red Zone is for those people who are stressed all the time.

You will know that you are in the Red Zone because you won't know what it's like to really relax and be enjoying life.

So which Zone are you in: Green, Amber or Red?

Question 6

The next thing we are going to put into The Dieters Scale is the Negative Experiences that cause us to feel bad about ourselves and to develop Negative Habits.

This includes:

Being Negative; Putting Yourself Down; Negative Self-Talk; Other People Putting You Down; and Other People Being Negative Towards You. You putting other people down.

For example: You may have a friend who turns on you when you are doing well and they begin to undermine you until you get back to the position where they are the one who is on top. This gives you lots of Negative Feedback which amounts to a high Quality and high Quantity Negative Feedback.

For example: Something small could have a big impact on you; but you feel that other people might find it small and insignificant. It's is your view of this that matters and not other peoples.

What we are interested in is the Quality and the Quantity of the Negative Experiences that you have, or that you feel that you have, on a daily or regular basis.

Green Zone	Amber Zone	Red Zone
Very Little	Quite A Lot!	All The Time!

Weight Control The **Hi-Way** - The Dieters Scale ©

So: If you have a very small amount of Negative Experiences or Negative Self-Talk; then you would be in the Green Zone.

If you experience quite a lot of Negative Experiences or Negative Self-Talk; then you would be in the Amber Zone.

If you have quite a lot of Negative Interactions with other people; then you would be in the Amber Zone.

If you experience a continuous process or ongoing experiencing of Negative Experiences, Negative Feedback or Negative Self-Talk; then you would be in the Red Zone.

If you have a continuous process or experience of Negative Interactions with other people; then you would be in the Red Zone.

So which Zone are you in: Green, Amber or Red?

We could continue to take different parts of someone's life and use this process to build a larger Dieter's Scale Map and a more accurate picture.

However; we will stop at the 6 that we have and see what that is telling us.

In the next graphic I have brought the 6 different questions together into a simple graph.

Green Zone	Amber Zone	Red Zone
1 Stone (7 Kilo's)	3 Stone (22 Kilo's)	More!
2 Diets or less	2 - 4 Diets	Always Dieting
Easily Stick to Diet	Keep to It a bit!	No Chance!
I am Fit I Exercise!	Occasional Exercise	Don't!
No Stress!	Quite Stressed	Always Stressed
Very Little	Quite A Lot!	All The Time!

Weight Control The Hi-Way - The Dieters Scale ©

If you were to put your answers into the relevant boxes in The Dieters Scale above; what would this show?

        Do you have a mix of all three zones?

        Are all your ticks in one zone?

        Are your ticks in two zones?

What I would expect you to see, if you have been honest with your answers, is something like the following:

If you are OVERWEIGHT with a long dieting history, then your ticks should be predominantly in the Amber and Red Zones.

If you are UNDERWEIGHT with a long dieting history, then your ticks should be predominantly in the Amber and Red Zones.

If you are between the two extremes of being very underweight and being very overweight, then I would expect that you would have a mixture of two or all three Zones.

Personally; I find that The Dieters Scale is a useful tool that can provide us with information that can be very helpful.

If I added more questions to The Dieters Scale, we could bring in more components to increase the general overview of the weight control problem. We will do this in the second part of this book.

Looking at and understanding the real nature of the weight control problem, by breaking it down into Zones also makes the problem less formidable.

So what do I want you to take away from this chapter?

We have looked at The Dieters Scale and this gives us 3 Zones that we can use to understand things in another way. Those Zones are Green, Amber and Red Zones.

You have completed 6 simple questions and these provide a brief and simple indicator of where your answers were in those Zones.

Dependent to your answers; you may have been in 1 Zone or all 3 of them.

If you have a weight problem then you will have tried different diets and probably been to organised classes for weight control.

So let me ask you to think about this:

> You now know that we can put people's weight problems into one of 3 Zones and this helps us to understand that they are at different levels of complexity.
>
> So when we see people from the Green Zone in a diet class with people from the Amber and Red Zones; and they are all applying the same solution to their problem; is it any wonder that the long term success rate is very low?
>
> Would we really expect someone with a Red Zone weight control problem to be able to use a Green Zone Dieting Solution to solve their problems?

Is it the case of square pegs and round holes? Could it be that they just simply don't go together!

Could this be a reason why we have a growing problem with weight and weight related issues?

Chapter 5

The Most Successful Diet In The World!

What is the most successful and the best diet in the world?

The reality is: That it depends!

> What is it that you want to achieve from the diet; both in the short term and in the long term?
>
> Do you want to keep going on diets or do you want to get yourself on the right path for a successful life in the future; where you have cracked the weight control problem?

Being someone who designs solutions for problems; I thought that a much better way to approach this question was to actually design the most successful and best diet in the world; for every person.

I am not interested in designing bad solutions. So I want to design:

> A Great World Class Solution.

So let's create a structure for the Most Successful and the Best Diet in the World; that will get you on the right path and be able to keep you there!

And this is what I came up with:

The best diet in the world is one that fits into your lifestyle today; and into the lifestyle that you want to have in the future; without undue pressure and demands.

The best diet in the world isn't bothered by the occasional dietary indiscretion; because it allows for it to happen.

The best diet in the world is one that you can stick too; without undue pressure and without feeling that you are being deprived of the things that you like.

The best diet in the world is the one that helps you achieve the weight control that you really want to achieve; and it is able to help you maintain weight control over the longer term.

The best diet in the world is personal to you. It becomes like comfortable clothing.

The best diet in the world is not temperamental. It is robust, strong and full of vitality.

The best diet in the world is easy to follow and does not have a rigid structu that you have to slavishly follow.

It does not rely upon points, calorie counting, prepared meals or having a very limited diet.

The best diet in the world does not make false claims about weight loss and play tricks with your body.

The best diet in the world knows that you want to live for a long time and have a high quality of life; for the rest of your life.

The best diet in the world helps you to understand and work with your own Personal Tendencies; so that you can achieve and maintain the life that you want.

The best diet in the world does not ban any foods; but it does require moderation at times and that you take responsibility for what you consume. There is no such thing as a "Free Lunch".

The best diet in the world recognises that you are an Imperfect Person and accepts that you will have to learn and adapt; and that occasionally, you will make mistakes that you will both have to put right.

The best diet in the world will become like a brother, sister or best friend; always there to help and support you for the rest of your life; but not there for you to abuse and misuse.

The best diet in the world wants to become your new best friend, but you have to make a decision about how much time, effort and money you are willing to put into developing and maintaining that friendship.

The best diet in the world is something that you "Do" on a daily basis. Not something that you talk about doing.

The best diet in the world doesn't expect you to be a Perfect Person and achieve quick lasting results. It knows that weight control and weight management are for life and not for a fling.

The best diet in the world knows that you are not Perfect and it still wants to have a lifelong relationship with you.

The best diet in the world recognises its own limitations and that it does not exist in isolation to the other parts of your life, that touch and are touched by food, and by eating habits.

Do you want the best and most successful diet in the world?

In reality the best and the most successful diet in the world is made up of different components which can be individually adapted for each person.

This means that you can build this diet by creating the different parts and working with them in the right ways.

There are no rigid time restraints with this diet. This makes it easier to do.

No part of it is too difficult or over demanding of you, your abilities or your lifestyle. This makes it easier to do.

Nor are there any demands for you to lose or gain weight quickly. This means less stress and pressure for you.

There are no ongoing measurements saying things like; this week you must lose (X) amount of weight; this week you should be so many inches slimmer when we measure various points of your body; or that you must drop a dress size; or any other dietary pressure point. This makes it easier to do.

In this diet there is "Reality" which is grounded in the reality of your lifestyle; and the reality of the different aspects of your life, behaviour, habits, psychology and emotional responses. This means that it matches you better. This makes it easier to do.

There are challenges and expectations that are part of the process of having and using the best diet in the world. That is because you want to achieve something and you want to improve, resolve and better manage different aspects of your life. It actually aligns itself with your real goals and the things that you can really do. This makes it easier to do.

The best and most successful diet in the world is about mutual co-operation between you; the diet; and the lifestyle management processes you are using. All these parts work together; rather than against each other. This makes it easier to do.

The best and most successful diet in the World is about:

- Doing things when the time is right.
- In the right way.
- And with the correct application of actions.

All of this is what I do when I am working with someone on a Life Improvement Programme; where Weight is the focus of the Programme.

So we will use this book to put you onto the right path and give you the right direction to go in. We will be using The Best Diet in the World as our model.

When I am working with someone with a problem; it often happens that the person I am working with does NOT see the full picture of what is happening at the time.

It is with Hindsight that they begin to appreciate the work that we have been doing and the progress that they have made. So why are you going to be any different?

In my opinion and experience Real Success with Weight Control is NOT achieved by someone following a diet or exercise plan that claims they could lose 14 pounds (6kg) in 14 days and get fit in 6 weeks (or variations of this).

Nor is it achieved by Diet Pills or Surgery which limits someone's ability to Consume More or which limits the effects of increased consumption.

They don't work because:

Quick and simple solutions to complicated and difficult problems rarely work well.

Normally, in my view, the simple diet and exercise approaches can work best for those who would genuinely be all Green Zones on The Dieters Scale.

> *People who are in the Green Zone not just for our 6 questions but for additional ones as well.*

These are the people who tend to have a small to moderate weight problem; and if they focus just on the weight problem then they can change it.

However; should they not be able to maintain the weight loss, then this should be viewed as an indicator that other factors may be in play and influencing the problem. And that their weight problem is not as Green as they believe it is.

Those who have Amber Zone and Red Zone problems will usually fail with the simple diet and exercise approaches. They will need the Best and Most Effective Diet in the World to succeed; the diet that is right for them now and in the future.

For someone with an Amber or Red Zone problem; it would be normal that their diet structure would change as they began to better manage their problem. At each change their diet would still meet all the right conditions.

Understanding this is good Hi.

So what do I want you to take away from this chapter?

The simple reality, in my view, is that the weight control process that focuses on food is doomed to failure for most of the people who use that process; because the process can only give them a part of what they really need.

In the short term it can satisfy their need to feel as if they are doing something and taking charge of the problem. But the tools that they are using are inadequate for the task.

A weight problem is about more than food for most people and dealing with this successfully requires a different structure.

Those who fall into the Amber and Red Zones of The Dieters Scale will usually find that they will really struggle, and continue to fail, when they follow these food focused weight control plans.

A weight problem isn't simply about your diet; it about your Lifestyle Management and the other things which are going on for you.

One way to look at a weight problem is:

> That part of your life is telling you that it is time to change how you are living.
>
> Because what you are doing, and how you are doing it, is not giving you what you really want and what you really need.
>
> In effect: The weight problem becomes a Life Barometer.

Chapter 6

Eat What You Want; Just Accept The Consequences!

To deal with weight problems effectively:

People need to accept that it is they who are experiencing the problem;

Therefore, they are part of the problem;

Therefore, they need to be part of the solution;

Therefore, they need to be Pro-Active in achieving the results that they want.

Because if they wait on other people to do it for them:

Things will have a Tendency to become worse, rather than better.

So to achieve what they want; they need to begin to be Pro-Active!

Understanding this is good **Hi**.

Being Pro-Active means taking Positive Actions to deal with something, rather than waiting for things to happen to you and hoping that they sort themselves out.

You generally have more control by being Pro-Active.

It is the practice of Being Pro-Active that is behind:

Eat what you want; just accept the consequences.

Let me unpack this for you a little more!

When I work with people who have problems with their weight they usually:

- Expect me to provide them with a diet.
- Weigh them.
- Tell them all the things that they can no longer eat.
- And tell them what they should now eat.

I don't do this because by the time I normally see people; they have already been through the weight loss process a number of times.

By the time they get to me I find that they have a lot of experience with diets, and all the different things that goes with dieting; including failing with diets.

They have a lot of Experience about what they will actually do and what they won't actually do. All of this is good Hi and we want to try and use this.

So what I want to work with from their Experiences are:

- The Experiences that They Are Aware of.

- And the Experiences that They Are Unaware of.

Let me tell you why I want to do this. With weight related problems there is a Human Dynamic which I see repeatedly.

A Human Dynamic is a process, structure, behaviour or activity; which has a consistent form or pattern to it that involves or relates to people.

So it is something that people do often; in a predictable way.

The Human Dynamic I am referring to is this:

Someone decides that they want to do something about a problem. Often the problem has escalated and may be out of control.

However; when they look at the problem they want to sort out, they find that it is not just one problem; it's a number of different things.

While trying to improve this one problem, they try to leave the other problems alone. Their reasoning is that they don't want to rock-the-boat in case it upsets too many things at once; and they won't be able to handle it.

What is Motivating them to sort this single problem out now, is that they don't like the Consequences that the problem is producing; and how it is Affecting things.

So they find themselves in the position where they want changes to occur; but just with the single problem they are focused on; and nothing else.

They think that if they can deal with that single problem, that they will then be able to cope better with all the other stuff that is going on around them. And they will often say that they will deal with all that other stuff later on but not now.

Sometimes people manage this trick but most of the time they don't. It ends up failing.

The reason it ends up failing is that the structure of the basket of problems is such that when you move one thing; it causes other things to move as well.

How does this relate to weight control?

The people who are in the Amber and Red Zones on The Dieters Scale will have a problem with their weight; and they will have a basket of other problems as well.

Their version of this is:

> "I will go on a diet" and as a result of going on a diet I will feel better about things and then I will be able to...

Over time the process of "going on a diet" becomes a part of the persons Coping Mechanisms when things get tough. This is because the process of "going on the diet" gives them a boost and it makes them feel better.

The adoption of this (dieting) as a problem solving strategy occurs because it can partly work for a period of time. And because it partly works, just for a while, it continues to be used.

Why does this matter?

It matters because eventually it fails; and then it begins to fail easier and more often. But in the process of using this strategy someone can end up with the habits of the classic Yo-Yo Dieter; without knowing why?

Understanding this is good **Hi**.

Let's continue to unpack this!

This Yo-Yo Dieting Dynamic is, in effect, the Human Dynamic which underpins many dieting and exercise approaches.

That is that people keep trying to apply a solution where the demands of the problem exceed the capability of the solution.

So let's have a look at the structure of that dynamic.

> The person experiencing a weight problem will deal with the obvious problem (their weight); and hope that it creates enough momentum/motivation to improve other things in their live as well (all the other problems that affect their weight and which are caused by their weight).

The tragedy of this approach is that there is a time in the development of a problem when you can apply a solution that will work; however it is not always desirable or convenient to do so at that time.

If you wait and don't apply the solution at the right time; then the window of opportunity closes and the structure of the problem changes. As a result it becomes more complicated and more difficult to deal with.

Once the structure of the problem has changed; the structure of the solution also needs to change. Because it now has to deal with a more complicated and difficult problem.

As it is with this Human Dynamic; so it is with weight related problems.

> The nature of the weight problem changes as you move from one Zone to another Zone; and so the nature of the solution that the problem requires; also changes. They need to keep pace with each other!
>
> If they don't keep pace, then you end up trying to apply a Green Zone solution to an Amber or Red Zone problem.
>
> If the structure of the problem and the structure of the solution don't match; then it is square pegs and round holes.
>
> Understanding this is good Hi.

What complicates things for most people is that problems don't usually develop in isolation. They usually bring other problems, challenges and issues with them; but this usually happens so slowly that they don't tend to notice it.

When problems develop they tend to blend together and I liken this process to a spider spinning a web.

And we know that if you pull on one part of the spiders' web that you can feel the tug somewhere else.

This means that by the time something becomes a big enough issue for someone to want to sort out, it touches, influences and is influenced by other things as well. Just like a spider's web.

So as the problem grows and moves from the Green Zone, to the Amber Zone and to the Red Zone; you end up in a position where you don't just have one thing which needs sorting out; you have multiple things. The spiders' web.

Understanding this is good Hi.

I also call this spiders web "a Basket of Problems" as this is also a good description.

And for most people dealing with a Basket of Problems becomes overwhelming!

They don't know where to start, how to do it or what they should be doing.

This is when it becomes easier to deal with the obvious problem and hope that it has a knock-on effect with the other problems. And it is this that takes us full circle.

Because we are all Imperfect People we will look for easy solutions if we can find them.
However: Easy doesn't mean Effective!

When I work with people we look at the Basket of Problems that someone has.

When we do so it is not uncommon to find that one part of the problem mix is in the Green Zone; another part of the problem mix is in the Amber Zone; and another part of the problem mix is in the Red Zone.

> So dealing with these types of problem can be complicated and difficult; but you have to remember that we are dealing with this over time and in a planned way.
>
> What we are looking to do is to take a difficult and complicated problem; and turn it into a problem that is easier and simpler to deal with; and simpler to resolve.
>
> Breaking the problem down into Zones helps you to understand it better and to manage it better.

So let's focus this back onto the subject of this chapter.

Eat what you want; just accept the consequences.

In a later chapter of this book, I will take you through a breakdown of the different things that are going on when someone goes on a diet.

Amongst those things are an increase in stress, the removal of coping strategies and the introduction of new behaviours.

So there are plenty of new and different things going on for the person when they diet; and we know that they are going to have difficulties dealing with it all. They can be overwhelmed by it.

My view was that rather than do what other people are doing with weight problems; why not do something different?

So I said to myself:

- So why not give them back some Control?

- Why not give them back some Choices?

- Why not use this process to help them understand Their Own Behaviour?

- Why not use all the Experience that they have in positive ways?

- Why not take away some of the Stress and make it easier?

So I took the approach:

> That I would not give them a diet plan.
>
> I would not tell them to exercise.
>
> I would not tell them that they could NOT eat certain foods.

There were a number of other things as well but I will not go into those here.

All that I asked them to do was to accept that if they eat any food or consumed any drinks, that they accepted the potential disappointments and consequences of their actions.

I gave them the Freedom to make their own decisions and the Permission that they were free to eat what they chose to eat.

> Why pretend that you love "healthy food" when all you want to do is eat burger and chips?

The reality that I am accepting here is that by the time I am seeing people; their metabolisms are messed up.

> Their eating habits are all over the place and their bodies have lost reference to the Normal State that they are attempting to achieve through dieting.

So if we do what is normally done through the dieting process; our chances of success are actually low.

By changing the approach that we take; we actually increase our chances of achieving a successful outcome.

It may be Counter Intuitive but the chances of Success are higher!

This is good **Hi**.

Within this process I am accepting a truth that I have seen many times.

It can actually be months before the person brings themselves to the point where they have a diet structure in place that they Can and Will be able to follow.

It doesn't matter that it takes this long because when we get there, we are in a very strong position; and we can begin to work on and build on a different foundation.

A foundation that can support the work we need to do.
As we go through this process it ceases to be about dieting and it begins to be about Weight control, Life Improvement, Life Development and Management.

So Weight becomes just one of the components of a Life Improvement Programme and the importance of it reduces over time; to the point where it isn't a problem anymore.

This is the Smart Way! And it's great Hi.

So what do I want you to take away from this chapter?

If you have a weight problem, then you are the arena where the problem is going to be played out.

As you are the arena, then you can exercise control over different things.

> What you consume is one of those things over which you can exercise control.
>
> When you do exercise control – good or bad; just accept that whatever the consequences are; you will accept them.
>
> Your decisions and choices will have an effect which is either Positive or Negative.

You can deal with your weight problem in the way that the problem requires you to; or you can just keep doing the same things and hope that you get lucky.

The problem with luck is that you can't rely on it, and when you do need it; it is seldom around.

Dealing with the problem as it requires you to; is the Smart Way to do things. As you will waste less time, less effort; and the disappointments you avoid are huge.

This is good Hi.

Chapter 7

Food Addiction - Fact Or Myth?

In this chapter I think it is worth taking the time to explore something which I am hearing more and more often. The subject can be a little complicated so I will break this down into different parts to try and make it easier; and to provide you with the information you need. What I am hearing is:

"I'm addicted to food".

Now I can see the attraction of having "Food Addiction" as an explanation for many of the weight problems that people have.

I can also see that there would be a dramatic increase in the number of people who would claim that it is not their fault that they have a weight problem; because they are Addicted to food.

One of my questions would be: Would this be a good thing for the person with a weight problem?

As a result of the food addiction claims, it would not be long before their weight problem would become a Medical Condition. Just like alcohol and drug addiction is.

As a medical condition there would be the view that there must be a medical remedy to fix this Medical Problem.

I can see that the preference for the medical remedy would be in the form of a pill, or procedure, which quickly and simply cures someone of their weight problem or it reduces the affects to an acceptable level.

And once the remedy is applied; the view of many would be that they should never have another problem with their weight, regardless of their eating habits and behaviours; because they have been treated and cured of that problem!

If they do put on weight after the treatment, they will want to blame the treatment and not their behaviour.

Now if people were really addicted to food then I would not have a problem accepting this; but I would want proof in each case. After all; you would not operate on someone without making sure that the operation was necessary; would you?

The pertinent questions for this chapter are:

1. Is Food Addiction real?

2. Will the label of "Food Addict" help or hinder someone's attempts at dealing with a weight problem, in the short and long term; or is it just an excuse?

I will give you my take on this and we will see what it produces.

What I am going to do is to break the Food Addiction question down into sections and go through them.

Let's begin with Physical Addiction to a substance.

We will begin with this because simply put:

> If there is No physical addiction to a specifically identifiable substance, as a result of the consumption and/or use of the substance; then there is No Addiction.

No Addiction means that something else is going on.

Physical Substance Addiction

To understand Physical Substance Addiction, I am going to use the categories of Drugs and Alcohol to illustrate the processes involved. I will focus just on alcohol to make is simpler.

> Food Addiction would follow the same processes as addiction to drugs and alcohol; as we are talking about the Consumption and Use of a Substance by the body, to which it becomes directly or indirectly physically addicted.

Just about everyone is familiar with and has had some exposure to Alcohol, so you should be able to follow me.

I am going to break the addiction problem down into 2 inter-related areas that go hand in hand and which occur at the same time:

1. Physical Exposure to Alcohol – *The actual physical Consumption and physiological effects/affects produced as a result of consuming alcohol. How you physically feel and what you physically experience when you drink alcohol.*

2. Psycho-Social Exposure to Alcohol (The emotional, psychological and behavioural reasons for using alcohol) – *Also called Socialising. Basically this is being exposed to the use, effects and consequences of other people consuming alcohol and your own use of alcohol in social and other situations.*

As our starting point: Let's begin with a person who has never used, taken or consumed Alcohol of any type in their lives before. This person would be an Alcohol Virgin.

> Therefore their Physical Exposure and Psycho-Social exposure to Alcohol is Zero!

So let's create an Alcohol Drinking History for this person and follow it through to see how they become clinically addicted to alcohol.

An Alcohol Drinking History is like the Dieting History for someone with a weight problem. It shows how you got to where you are with the problem that you have.

Let's create the drinking history and say that the person never consumed alcohol before they were 18 years of age.

So; at 18 their initially use of alcohol is Social. They only consume it at parties.

As they become older their Social use of alcohol increases and they begin using alcohol more frequently. They also go to more places where alcohol is being consumed; and they begin to keep and consume alcohol at home. They also try different types of alcohol and develop preferences for certain drinks.

Throughout this period the person maintains their work, home and social life without problems.

At this early stage there are no problems with alcohol; or as a result of their consuming alcohol. They may have put on a bit of weight but nothing serious.

In the person's body there have been no obvious changes due to their consumption of alcohol.

So there is no sign of Clinical Addition to the substance of alcohol. And many people stay in this position. Our person won't because they will develop a problem. At this stage we would say that they are in the Green Zone.

Gradually, over time, the person increases their consumption of alcohol and the frequency and amounts that they consume increases.

At first it is within the normal range, let's say 18 units of alcohol per week (2 bottles of wine).

More time passes and different life problems occur.

To help them deal with the different aspects of life, which can be both Positive and Negative, the person consumes more alcohol.

And this increased consumption becomes a daily occurrence. They are now using alcohol to celebrate, commiserate, to deal with a bad day, a family row, work pressure, etc. Alcohol has become an integral part of their life.

As a result of their ongoing behaviour, their consumption increases from 18 units per week to 40 units, then to 60 units. This is Amber Zone territory.

Due to the different pressures of life they continue to use alcohol and their consumption increases to 80 units.

At 80 units they are consuming about 1.3 bottles of wine per day.

And let's say that this increases further to about 100 units per week; which is about 1.5 bottles of wine per day. *Many people out there are currently drinking at this level and above. I have come across cases of over 80 units/day.*

At 100 units per week the person has now moved into Red Zone territory.

Now let's say that this person continues drinking at this level for a reasonable period of time; let's say 3-5 years.

What will have happened during the time that the person has been consuming alcohol at these higher levels is:

1. That the person's body will have first become accustomed to the alcohol.

2. Then: As it becomes accustomed to the alcohol; it builds up a Tolerance to it.

3. It is important to understand that it doesn't matter what type of alcoholic drink the person consumes. This is because alcohol is the common component across all the alcoholic drinks; and it's this that the person becomes addicted to.

   So this common factor, that can be clearly identified, would need to exist across foods. For example: Simply saying fat ignores the reality that there are many different types of fat. It would need to be a specific single fat at specific levels. This would be the same for any other substance.

The tolerance the body develops to alcohol allows the person to consume more.

So, someone who is used to drinking a lot of alcohol can seem to have less visible signs of that consumption, than someone who is new to drinking alcohol.

The newbie gets drunk quicker!

With the consumption of all the Addictive Substances, there is a point at which a line is crossed; and this line varies from person to person.

As we cross this line, the body adjusts to a State where it is normal for the body to have alcohol in it. So it becomes unnatural for the body not to be under the influence of alcohol and processing alcohol.

This line is a point at which things can change for the person in a number of different ways. Some of these changes can be permanent.

These Changes can influence all their further usages of alcohol; either directly or indirectly.

Once someone crosses this line; there can be changes within organs, such as the Liver, and different physiological and psychological changes can occur.

Some of the changes can be permanent and some temporary. As the person moves across that line, Addiction and Dependency become blended together and appear as one and the same thing; but they are not!

Let's move on from having crossed the line!

So now the body's normal state is that it should have 1.5 bottles of wine each day. It has moved from Green Zone being the normal to Red Zone being the normal.

And because so much alcohol is consumed each day, the body has adjusted in different ways; in order to manage and process the alcohol that the person is consuming each day.

> *Now what we also need to understand is that alcohol does have calories but it doesn't have nutrition. It also has a large amount of water.*
>
> *The alcohol itself is actually potentially toxic to the body. The body can cope with a small amount of toxic material but changes can occur when it has to deal with a lot of toxic material; especially over time.*

At this stage, 100 units of alcohol per week (Red Zone), this person would be considered to be a heavy user of alcohol or a heavy drinker.

This is because their Body and their Psyche have got used to having 1.5 bottles of wine each day. And in preparation for the consumption of the wine; the body has prepared itself to deal with the alcohol it receives each day.

What you will also find is that the consumption of alcohol follows a pattern and it will have a timing attached to it. For example; consumption only takes place in the evening and the body will adjust to these timings as well.

In preparation for receiving the alcohol, it will automatically adjust the body's chemistry and processes; so as to convert and manage the alcohol and what else is contained within the wine.

If the body doesn't get the alcohol it expects, at the time it expects it; it will now protest and this is out of the conscious control of the person.

At this point; if we now take the alcohol away from the person, they will experience problems.

And this shows the addiction process:

> How the body copes with the withholding of the substance.

So what is it that has happened?

By removing the alcohol from the body, we deprive the body of something that it is expecting and which it has prepared itself to handle. It has become conditioned to having the alcohol and its functions now don't work properly unless the alcohol is present.

For alcohol addiction this will produce a number of symptoms that can be unpleasant; and some can be dangerous.

If we re-introduce alcohol back into the body the withdrawal symptoms will stop.

So we could replace wine with vodka for example and the withdraw symptoms would stop.

The key ingredient here isn't the wine or the vodka; it's the alcohol content of the wine and the alcohol content of the replacement drink. So they are not addicted to wine, wine is simply the preferred drink that delivers alcohol to their body.

Physical Clinical Addition is actually a fairly easy process to understand and deal with. For example;

Physical Clinical Addiction to alcohol can be dealt with in about 7 days.

Within 7-days the body goes through the withdrawal from alcohol addiction and is no longer clinically addicted to alcohol.

Medication may be used during the withdrawal period to make the withdrawal process easier and to prevent the potentially dangerous fits which can occur.

However; this does not mean that the person's problems that they have with; and which are associated with alcohol, have ceased. It just means that their body is no longer clinically addicted to the alcohol.

So the person may have dealt with the clinical addition to alcohol but the problems, difficulties and challenges that faced the person in life, when they were drinking; still exist when they are not drinking.

So this is one of those spider web problems. In the case of alcohol addiction we still have the Dependency to deal with and this will contain the Psycho-Social exposure to alcohol and other life problems that exist.

Removing the alcohol now provides an opportunity to begin to deal with these without alcohol consumption and intoxication getting in the way of the solution.

The Habits and Behaviours Associated With the Addictive Behaviour

It can be around the time at which the clinical addiction is being dealt with that other problems can occur; such as switching addiction from one substance to another, or to another type of behaviour. (The same thing can happen with dieters)

Switching addiction is problematic because someone may appear to have dealt with the original problem; but what is really happening is that they are seeking another quick way of managing things.

At a surface level it can appear that the person is dealing with the problems well; and they can often appear to be making remarkable progress using the new coping structures.

Whereas in reality; they are likely to have just found something else to focus on for a while; and this can act to absorb stress; for a while.

> I have seen this a number of times and seen people crash and return to previous behaviours with a vengeance; both with alcohol and with their weight.
>
> As a therapist you have to watch out for this and deal with it with the person; if you can; and if they will work with you.

A failure to deal with the Psycho-Social components adequately, often leads the person back to their previous behaviour or to behaviour of a similar type and degree.

Now relate this to dieting. Can you see the similarities that many dieters (especially those in the Amber and Red Zones) will experience?

This is good **Hi**.

Post Addiction

This later part; Post Addiction (afterwards), should be familiar to many dieters! I have written it to include food rather than alcohol. So let's see what you make of it.

>The Psycho-Social behaviour is usually the part of the problem that takes the most time and effort; and it can be very complicated and difficult to deal with.
>
>This is the spider's web part of the problem.
>
>The Psycho-Social components have to be dealt with in the real world of the person; and in real time.
>
>In the dieters real world, they would have had Psycho-Social exposure to Foods over a period of time; often many years and decades.
>
>Some of that exposure to different foods and food related behaviours would be Positive and some would have been Negative. And some of it would have become Messed-up and Corrupted.
>
>Throughout this process they would be learning, copying and experimenting.
>
>Where they have no clear directions they will have made up their own behaviours; and established their own internal mechanisms for managing Life issues by using the various behaviours and actions around foods.
>
>This will be in the eating, preparation, obtaining, volume, quality, taste, texture, visual appearance, associations, places, rituals and smells.
>
>Into this mix we also have to add the sense of physical satisfaction; and the feelings and emotions when consuming foods.
>
>
>*So a diet can be thought of as a form of rehabilitation of habits. And if that rehabilitation does not go far enough, it will prove ineffective. And this tends to prove true for many people with weight control problems. The rehabilitation of their weight control does not go far enough.*
>
>*This is why so many people fail on diets; even when they put lots of positive effort into trying to succeed.*
>
>Remembering this is good Hi.

Are You Ever Free? – A note about Addictive Substances

Once someone has been addicted to alcohol. Their bodies processing of alcohol, even in very small quantities, can trigger connections and associations which can lead to the person going back to drinking alcohol and using their previous behaviours.

Now it doesn't matter what liquid or solid is consumed by the person; it is the active Alcohol content in what they consume, that is taken in and processed by the body. And it's this substance that matters!

So wine, beer, spirits, alcohol based mouth wash, alcohol based perfumes, puddings with alcohol in, etc; all have the base component (ingredient) of Alcohol in them; which will be picked up and processed by the body if it is consumed in any way.

Links to addiction can also be triggered by things like muscle memory, sound memory, smell memory, places, behaviours, situations, etc.

This is also true about drugs and other addictive substances.

So although someone may deal with their clinical addiction, something within them has changed as a result of becoming addicted.

In my view; that change remains in place like a Sensitivity or Scar, which can easily be disturbed. It is my view that once someone has become addicted to a substance that they should avoid that substance.

Another way to think of this is that the person was in the Red Zone when they were addicted. As a result of dealing with the addiction they have now moved back to the Green Zone.

However: They now have a connection between these Zones that can quickly and easily take them back to the Red Zone. It's like a short cut.

In my view; this connection will remain.

Understanding this is good **Hi**.

Hidden Substances In Things We Consume

Now there is another component to complete this section; which is:

> Substances that we may consume without knowing that we are consuming them.
>
> And having consumed them over time; we have become used to having them in our bodies.
>
> If we then stop taking the substance, we may experience a reaction to the fact that this substance has been removed.

This type of problem has occurred over the years with things like Tranquillisers.

People took the Tranquilisers under medical supervision only to find that they had extreme physical and sometimes psychological reactions when they changed medication or stopped taking the medication.

Over time it was discovered that components within the medication had addictive qualities that were not appreciated or understood at the time.

Is it possible that this could occur with foods?

In reality almost anything is possible. That however does not make it probable.

Let's look at what I think is more likely and what I think makes more sense for people with weight problems.

Consuming More – The New Normal

Chapter 8

Consuming More – The New Normal

Now we know that foods have components such as sugars.

In normal quantities sugars do not present problems for most people.

In larger quantities sugars create a problem for most people.

For the normal functioning of the body we need to consume sugars in different forms, along with fats and other materials. It is actually healthy to eat the right amounts and types of fats, sugars and other materials. This would be Green Zone consumption with a balanced diet.

We know that we can "Over Provide" our bodies with substances (such as Food) which then causes our bodies to process them; and manage the consequences of that consumption.

Once we put food or drink into our body it has no choice but to process it one way or another.

If we Over Provide on a regular basis, then our body will also go through an adjustment, where it needs to be able to handle Above Normal Amounts of food.

If you keep this up for a long enough period of time; you will adjust the Normal State of the body from one of handling Normal Amounts of food (Green Zone); to one of having to handle Larger than Normal Amounts of food or consumed items (Amber or Red Zones).

So for the person who Over Provides their body with food or with a certain type of food; their New Normal becomes one of Consuming More!

And as a result of Consuming More:

> They move out of the Green Zone and into the Amber and Red Zones for Food Consumption. And in the process they reset their bodies Normal Condition to another state. You change it from a Green Zone State to an Amber or Red Zone State.

Once you have change the bodies Normal Condition to one of Consuming More, and you then take away the increased consumption; such as what happens when someone goes on a diet, certain things are bound to happen.

> When you remove the Increased Consumption; your body then has to go through an adjustment period while it adjusts to the severe reduction in food.

During this period you may well feel very uncomfortable, as if you are missing something fundamental from your life. It can be unpleasant.

You may feel as if your life is in turmoil.

You may well feel hungry all the time and even completely ravenous.

Of course you would; because you have ceased to do what has become Normal behaviour for you; and you have done something "Not Normal" for you.

You have moved out of the Over Supply Range; which is normal for you.

And you have moved into the Under Supply Range which is not normal for you.

At the time of dieting you are changing something fundamental to Your Lifestyle in a drastic way by going on a diet. It is not just food that is altered; it is behaviours and actions as well. These behaviours and actions are the Psycho-Social things that we mentioned with the alcohol addiction; The Spiders' Web.

In reality; when people diet, they are attempting to do two physically demanding things at the same time: Which are actually somewhat Contradictory.

They want to:

Change their eating habits and change their practices with food from one Zone to another Zone; usually quickly. They try to jump from the Amber or Red Zones into the Green Zone.

And at the same time they want to:

Reduce their food intake. Stop putting on weight and begin Losing weight; usually quickly.

And what they are trying to do with this process is; they try to jump from a +Amber Zone or +Red Zone (Consuming too much) into a (-) Amber or (-) Red Zone (Consuming too little).

Over supply is Positive + and Under supply is Negative (-).

So this means that they want to *Change their bodies Normal State by rapidly reversing and changing their normal practices with food by introducing new foods and new behaviours.*

Putting these two things together simply compounds the difficulty of the process and reduces the probability of success.

If you then throw exercise into the mix; and that someone is attempting to change the embedded behaviours that have developed over time. Their stress is now going to be very high; or it soon will be.

Then if we ask the question:

> How have they previously responded to stressful situations?

The answer is that they will usually have been using the consumption of food and other behaviours related to food; to control their stress and anxiety. And as part of their dieting process, they have tried to remove these from their life.

So the stage is now set for failure and they are probably not long into the new diet.

We are also now in a position where we can see another Human Dynamic playing itself out that I mentioned earlier:

> The Yo-Yo Dieting Process; once again!

What you need to understand about the Yo-Yo Dieting Process is that the repeated dieting, and all that goes with it, just compounds the problems, challenges and difficulties that both your body and your mind have to deal with.

Yo-Yo (or Repeat Dieting) helps to move you from the Green Zone, into the Amber Zone and then into the Red Zone. It then will move you deeper into the Red Zone.

All the other Components of the weight control problem and the Lifestyle Management challenges are also affected. You are pulling on the Spiders Web.

Bad behaviours get re-enforced. More chaos can be introduced. Someone's loss of control can be increased. And a general lack of a clear purpose and direction can descend on someone's life.

So is this Food Addiction or is it something else?

Personally I do not think it is Food Addiction or substance addition as I currently understand it.

This is similar to Addiction to a Substance but is not the same as it. When Dependency and Addiction occur together (as they often do) it can be hard for someone to tell the difference; but there is a difference.

Here is my reasoning why I don't think that the label of Food Addiction is appropriate.

There is no single substance or single group of substances that the person is consuming on a regular enough basis, or in quantities which have the profile to form an addiction.

Being hungry and requiring nourishment, sustenance and nutrition might make us ravenous and cranky; but this is easily satisfied by many different types of food with different components in them.

Satisfying hunger in this way is not the same as satisfying the addiction when alcohol is removed. Only alcohol can satisfy the addiction.

Having a high fat, high sugar diet and then reducing or changing that will cause us to notice a difference because of our palate. Our taste preferences are altered as our usage of food changes. We get accustomed to the different taste, flavours, textures and smells and these become our new Normal.

In this process, it would be my view, that we are dealing with Psycho-Social components which have become interwoven with the Over Supply of food and the culture, habits and structures around food.

Needing to use food to satisfy Psycho-Social behaviours and different needs; is what I would call Dependency; rather than addiction.

I think that it is a Problem Mix where food and food related behaviours have become Over-Used in different ways; and that has created problems which have compounded over time.

One of those problems is that the body has adjusted its Normal State from being one of dealing with less food (Green Zone); to a Normal State of dealing with Consuming More; or an Over Supply of food (Amber/Red Zone). And as a result of this the person's Normal State moves out of the Green Zone and into the Amber or Red Zones.

If we compare the process that I used earlier with Addiction to alcohol, and compare this to the Consuming More State; it will be similar but different in a significant way.

A Food related example would look like this: It may begin with, for example, that someone is not very confident, is shy, nervous, feels like they don't fit in, are unhappy, etc.

They find that eating and the behaviour around food and eating, helps them to feel better and to have some form of control when faced with certain situations, feelings or emotions.

This process can lead to the release of hormones within the body that produce the "feeling better" affect.

The person then has an altering relationship with Food which, over time, leads on to changes with their Use and Consumption of Foods. "I eat and I feel better!"

> And over time this behaviour becomes over used and then problematic through the consequences that it produces.

As this Food related process is developing and becoming problematic; other things in their lives are changing as well, such as their physical appearance.

So in my view it becomes Dependency and a Psycho-Social problem rather than an Addiction problem.

Let's put this into the context of the Green, Amber and Red Zones from the Dieters Scale that we looked at earlier.

Someone would begin their relationship with food in the Green Zone, then progress towards the Amber Zone as their normal food consumption changed; and then they would move into the Red Zone as their normal food consumption changed once more.

Not only would they move through the different Zones for food consumption, they would also move through the different Zones for Relationships, Work, Confidence, Self-Esteem, etc.

As a consequence the overall Pattern and structure of someone's Life alters gradually over time!

And this is what ends up needing to be changed:

> The Pattern and structure of someone's Life!

Note

We can become addicted or biased towards the release of certain hormones in the body. And an example of this can be from behaviour that tends to become extreme.

Examples of this are behaviour like Base Jumping, very high levels of Sex, Gambling, and Dangerous Activity with very high risk factors, etc.

People who do these activities say: They love the High or Rush that they achieve.

Once again these activities can begin innocently; but then become corrupted as a means of achieving and providing more than they are able to give; and they can become abused.

Consuming Less and Less

In the previous example I have used Increased Food Consumption which focuses on people who are overweight.

For those who are Underweight, I think that the same processes apply but we are working with the other end of the Spectrum of Weight Problems. Think of this as the other side of the same coin.

Eating less becomes their New Normal.

Their Normal State is changed from eating in the Normal Range (Green Zone) to eating Outside of the Normal Range.

Eventually someone with a Negative Weight Control problem will move from the Green Zone and take up Residence in the (-) Amber Zone; and then in the (-) Red Zone; just like someone overweight does.

As they progress through the Zones; the scale, complexity and difficulty of their problem mix is going to increase. Their Spiders Web becomes more complex.

When it comes to the time to change eating behaviours from Consuming Less to Consuming More; the same uncomfortable processes occur.

Most people will take years to develop their problem mix to a point where they are Properly Motivated to finally do something Positive about it.

So it stands to reason that to be able to successfully address such problems so as to Improve, Resolve or Better Manage them; that it will also take time and effort to achieve this.

In my view this same information applies across the spectrum of weight problems.

> A diet can be thought of as a form of rehabilitation of habits. And if that rehabilitation does not go far enough, it will prove ineffective. And this tends to prove true for many people with weight control problems. The rehabilitation of their weight control does not go far enough.
>
> Remembering this is great Hi.

Changing how we Feel!

Whether we are looking at substances which are introduced into the body, like alcohol, drugs and food; or whether we are talking about substances that the body produces as a result of behaviour, such as; having a really good time, Sex, or extreme sports.

What we are really concerned with is:

> The process of Changing how we feel through an activity or experience.

If we are looking to change how we feel or experience something, then we are looking at:

> Altering our moods.
> Altering our emotions.
> Altering our feelings.
> Altering our behaviours.

All of these can lead on to:

> Substance addiction.
> Behavioural Dependency.

It is my view that everyone can live a better and more positive life: If they want to and they are prepared to do what is required to do so.

I think that many people with weight problems are actually making a very strong request for help when they go on a diet.

Unfortunately they often try to put too many conditions on the help that they want.

I invite you, as someone who diets, to make this the beginning of a new style of Living and Being.

A New Start; where you can deal with the realities of Life without turning to food to provide the help, comfort and support that you need.

Instead you will use the new tools and structures that are available for you, to help you have a better quality and more successful life in the future.

Go on: Go for it!

If we accept the fact that we want to improve our lives, feel better about our lives and how we live them; then we can address this in a more Positive Way.

It is often when we are being Passive that we develop Negative Habits; rather than Positive Habits.

To be a successful person we need to be Pro-Active.

Anyone, at any age, regardless of any life factors can become Pro-Active.

This is good **Hi**.

So what do I want you to take away from this chapter?

We can look for exotic justifications for our problems but the reality is that the causes of our problems are usually more mundane and simple:

> We are not using food and the consumption of food in the right way, for the right reasons, at the right times.

As well as the behaviours related to food, there is a basket of other issues which also develops; The Spiders' Web.

These other issues can become more complicated and difficult to understand than the weight problem itself.

And the longer that all this goes on for; the more difficult it becomes to deal with it all.

Eventually people lose sight of the things that have happened in the past and just begin to focus on the Consequences that they are experiencing today.

As a result; they then become focused on dealing with the consequences of the problem and not the causes.

As a result; the consequences can continue for many years because the causes remain to fuel to consequences.

When you deal with the causes; you disempower the consequences.

This is good **Hi**.

Chapter 9

Permanently Changing Your Life Profile For Food, Etc.

I am including this chapter because I want people to understand something about how we create and influence the structures of our own lives. This is important to someone who has a weight control problem that they want to change.

The structures of our lives are created through our previous Life Experiences; and how we have Processed, Internalised and Used those experiences.

Some of the experiences we have had can affect us more than others; and some can affect us in ways that we don't clearly understand.

So this means that if we have Processed and Internalised those experiences; and the knowledge from those experiences in the wrong way, or in ways that do not help us, that we need to be able to change them so that they stops harming us; or so that they begin to help us.

In effect; how do we deal with the bad data that we have acquired?

There is a process which is involved in this; and that we all use; but which we don't all know about; or get right.

I hope that this explanation will help you to understand about the Internalisation Process, how it actually affects you and just how powerful it can be.

I am going to use the device of a book and the structure of a book to do this.

So think of your Life Experiences being put into a book and creating chapters and pages in a book called:

Your Life Profile – This is really me!

So what is "Your Life Profile"?

An easy way to think of it is like this.

Imagine that when you are born you are given a book. And this book is going to tell your Life Story; but in a different way to normal.

Instead of looking in at your life from the outside world perspective; this book is about how you experience and interact with the world from the Inside Out. It's you looking out at and interacting with the World.

So this book contains your Inner World Experiences and Perspective of things.

This book contains the experiences, knowledge, insights and other important things; which together create the structures of your life and which shape you as a person.

As you go through your life, you will experience new things which can affect you and which help to create the person you are at that time.

As a result of those new experiences, new chapters are created in your book and new pages are added to those chapters.

For example:

>Going to school creates a new chapter.

>Adolescence creates another. During Adolescence; as our bodies are developing, we become self-conscious and we are vulnerable to comments and observations made by others.

Each of these significant episodes creates their own chapter which helps to inform how comfortable we are with things like showing our bodies to others.

Then there are the chapters on Relationships which we develop as we become older.

And the chapters on our various life experiences; the holidays we have enjoyed, the places we have lived, the people we have met.

Then there are the chapters on Loss: The people and things which we lose as part of the process of living.

Now if we experienced difficulties in life with things like Bullying, relationships and other traumatic experiences; then different things can happen.

Certain Life Experiences become a part of our past; but they continue to cause ripples throughout our lives that still connect with us today.

The result is that these experiences remain present in our lives because of these ripples and they become a part of our Life Structure; even though they may have happened many years previously.

>So these experiences can bridge the past, the present and the future. This means that they can have a high level impact on our life structures and on our behaviours and actions.

Your Dieting and the different Positive and Negative experiences you have had with dieting and food, also create their own chapters and pages.

Eventually you will have lots of different chapters that tell the story of your Life history and the different behaviours and different activities associated with it.

Now the place where all these different chapters of Your Life Profile are stored is in your Mind, your Body, your Spirit and in your Lifestyle. They now help to shape and control who and what you are and what you do.

As you use and misuse a new substance or behaviour it creates a new chapter or it adds new pages in the index of the book called:

Your Life Profile.

Many of the chapters in Your Life Profile will merge together and form the foundation for who and what you are as a person; and for what you will do in the future.

However; not all the chapters will merge together. Certain Chapters in Your Life Profile are going to be different from the others.

We will call these the Special Chapters.

The Special Chapters

The Special Chapters are different because they can cause something to change at a Fundamental Level in your life.

These changes can be both Positive and Negative in the results they produce.

What I want to focus on at this point is the one that troubles us: The Negative.

> Now what you need to understand here is that although this is Your Life Profile; you are not always in charge of this thing.
>
> It will operate on its own and with or without your Cognitive Support (Your awareness of giving support or permission to thoughts or actions that you take).

In fact: Your Life Profile develops chapters which tell it how to operate and what to do when you are Confused, Uncertain, Unhappy, Undecided, Nervous, etc.

Think of these chapters as being like a Hand-Book or Instruction Manual that is referred to at certain times.

And the more Your Life Profile refers to those Special Chapters, the more influence and control that they have; and the more you will follow them without question.

And Yes! This includes the chapters that you have for Diets and Food.

Now what you have to realise is that once a chapter has been created; it can't be removed. It is there, it exist, it has happened. It's part of your history.

So for a dieter; you cannot remove your dieting history and the behaviours associated with it.

For someone who has become Addicted to Drugs and Alcohol; their Chapters on these substances cannot be removed and they will always exist.

So how can we begin to change this to achieve more Positive and Productive outcomes?

The next part is one of the most important things for you to understand:

> Once something is in Your Life Profile it cannot be removed.
>
> However; you can write New Chapters.
>
> And you can write New Special Chapters!
>
> And you can change how you use the existing chapters and the new chapters.
>
> So you can change which instruction manuals will be used to create and maintain the structure of your life.

And that is what this book is all about.

It's about Writing New Special Chapters in Your Life Profile so that we can use them to change your future.

And this is where many people make mistakes!

Instead of writing New Special Chapters, what they actually do is they write more pages for the existing ones; usually the Negative ones.

This just makes the existing ones bigger and more influential; and this then causes them to repeat the same behaviour and achieve the same results.

So going from one diet plan to another diet plan will add new pages and new chapters to the Weight Control and Diet Plan Index in Your Life Profile.

The result is that you make the Weight Problem section bigger and more influential.

My question to you is:

Are you ready to write New Special Chapters for Your Life Profile that influences and affects your weight problem in a Positive and Beneficial way?

Or:

Do you want to continue to re-enforce all the things which do not work, which harm you long term and which make you Unhappy?

So what do I want you to take away from this chapter?

Your dieting history and your problems are written into Your Life Profile.

At the start of each day, you have a choice to continue to write more pages into the existing chapters of Your Life Profile or not.

To deal with a long term weight problem and the associated issues; you need to write new Special Chapters and new positive pages in Your Life Profile.

We can all do this with the right help and support.

Understanding this is good **Hi**.

Chapter 10

Your Tendencies For Gaining Weight

When I have worked with people who have problems that involve their weight; I have found that many of them have become conditioned to weighing themselves and measuring themselves; often in a self conscious way.

The frequency with which they do this doesn't take account of normal physical variability and the effects of this variability upon measured weight and size.

Measuring too often and in the wrong way is a Counter-Productive Process which produces ongoing Negative Re-enforcement. This is not good for someone who has a problem with their weight.

However; the marketing and sales of diet products and diet solutions needs us to focus on a benchmark that they can successfully use to get us to buy their products.

And a quick and easy benchmark is your weight and your size.

And they know that you are going to be sensitive to one or the other, or both of these, when you have a problem with your weight.

Now I am not saying that the Diet Industry is to blame for your weight problem or for how you measure your weight.

However; your Psycho-Social Education will have been exposed to lots of information from these areas and they will have influenced you; whether you realise it or not. For example:

Think of how many newspapers and magazines you have looked at where Looks and Appearance mattered?

How many television programmes, news reports and films have you seen where Looks and Appearance mattered?

How many conversations have you listened to or taken part in where Looks and Appearance matters?

All of this adds to your Psycho-Social Education. And it can make you more and more Sensitive to your weight, your looks and how you feel about these things.

This can drive you in the direction of quick solutions and to develop a false understanding of the realities of weight loss.

The process of weight loss is often treated as being a simple linear process, as is illustrated in the following graphic.

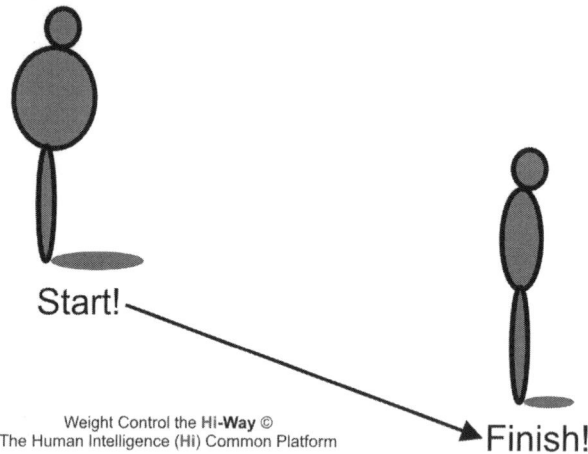

I think that a better way to view the long term dieting process is illustrated in the next graphic.

Achieving weight control is a process which involves Positive and Negative moves with your weight; over time. And over time your weight begins to stabilise into a weight range which is acceptable.

If you work with this natural process you can achieve much better results.

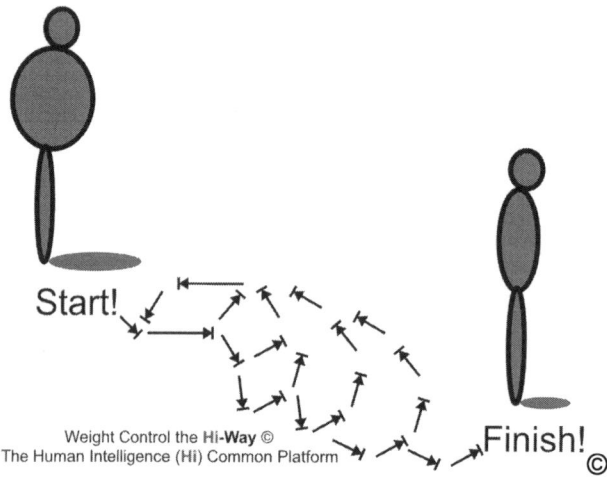

So what advice do I give to the people that I work with on a Life Improvement Programme that focuses on Weight Problems?

In reality; sustainable weight gain and sustainable weight loss is measured over months, years and decades. Not in days and weeks.

A more accurate way to think of weight control is:

> That we acquire and have Tendencies to either Gain weight, Lose weight or Maintain weight.
>
> And we may move from one Tendency to another.
>
> And at any one time, we are normally going to be living in just One Tendency as regards our weight.
>
> We will be Living In the Tendency for:
>
> - Increasing weight.
> - Losing weight.
> - Maintaining weight.

If we are Living In the wrong Tendency for what we want to achieve; then we need to move to another one.

> Moving into another Tendency takes time and effort. It is not a fast process and it requires consistent behaviours over a period of time for it to happen.
>
> So when someone goes on a normal diet they try to rapidly move from one Tendency Zone to another.
>
> For example: They want to move from a Red Zone Tendency to a Green Zone Tendency in a matter of a few weeks.
>
> This just adds to their stress as it is not possible to achieve this.

When I work with someone on a Life Improvement Programme that is focused on Weight Control:

> I help them to move from the Tendency for fast short term results, to the Tendency for sustainable longer term results.

We do want to achieve some short term benefits; but our eyes should be on the future prize: Focused on the person living the life that they really want to live!

When we do this we take account of the fact that the person is going to live for many years (baring illness and accidents).

Working with Tendencies is a longer term game.

As well as working with the persons Tendencies related to their weight; we also work with their Tendencies in other areas of their lives such as their Self-Esteem and Confidence.

I do this because weight problems do not exist in a vacuum; they exist in real life.

I mentioned earlier that:

> Nature has given us methods by which we can tell if we are growing in the wrong direction.

So I like to use these methods. And in reality they are simple and easy to use.

As we begin a Life Improvement Programme, I would want to know personal details such as someone's actual weight.

After that I am not really interested in their actual weight until we reach certain milestones; and then only to have accurate information.

I am more interested in:

- How easy the person finds it to move about?
- How their clothes are fitting them?
- Do they feel better as they get up and sit down in chairs and use other furniture?
- Are they feeling healthier?
- What are their Emotions doing?
- How are they Feeling about themselves.
- What they are doing that feels different?
- How are they sleeping?
- Are they looking in mirrors?
- And other aspects of their behaviours related to food and the consequences of having a problem with their weight.

If we do things like this, we don't have that same pressure that we experience with a regular weigh-in.

I also discourage people from regularly weighing themselves at home. Even though, in the early days, people still tend to continue to do so.

Other issues that we will address on a Programme include things like:

- Cyclical weight gain.

- The physical realities of weight gain and weight loss.
- Genetic realities.

I find that this approach takes us in the Right Direction and it helps us to develop the right Tendencies that help us achieve the Right Long Term Outcome.

This is good quality Hi.

So what do I want you to take away from this chapter?

Weighing yourself too often means that you are Living In the wrong Long Term Tendency and using the wrong chapter in Your Life Profile.

To moving to the Right Long Term Tendency takes time and you many need to write some new chapters in Your Life Profile to help you with this.

Weight problems are as much a Mind problem as a Body problem. And as such both of these need to be worked with.

This is good quality Hi.

Let's see if any of this is familiar to you?

I have seen people:

Use weighing scales; measure the circumferences' of different parts of their bodies; put themselves into wraps to squeeze themselves into different shapes; and try to squeeze themselves into different sized clothing (often with the help of sturdy undergarments).

Stories of people not eating before going for a weight-in and then gorging themselves afterwards are common.

Stories of people going to the toilet and taking laxatives and diuretics before a weight-in are common.

Stories of people taking off their clothes before a weight-in are common.

These are just simple examples of what lengths people will go to, so that they can be told that they have achieved some form of success with weight loss; or look as if they have lost weight to other people.

This is poor quality Hi.

Chapter 11

Genetic Realities

"Is your mind writing cheques that your body can't pay?"

When you were born your genetics were provided to you through your parent's genetic mix. This mix provided you with your own unique genetic profile.

Within your genetic profile you have scope for variations in different areas.

Things like how tall we grow will be influenced by our genetics and access to food, medical treatment and exercise.

For example: If someone with good food, exercise and health grows to 6 feet tall; they cannot reduce their size to 5 feet tall or grow to 7 feet tall.

Once we have used the genetic tools that we were born with and we have developed and exploited their Potential; it is usually not possible to change things.

The Potential is the range within which something can develop and grow. For example:

> We can build larger muscles; learn to run faster, run further, lift more, etc. And each of us has the Potential to change; up to our own limits.

Our Physical Weight and size is also one of those things where we have scope for variation.

> Our weight can vary over a Potentially wide range. From thin to large.

> We can survive over this wide weight range; and we can even go to extremes of it for long periods of time.

Now some people naturally have the genetic ability to be slim and some people naturally have the genetic ability to be large.

A great number of us fit somewhere between the two.

The reality is that if you have the genetic ability to become large and you feed that ability; then you will become large.

Once you have become large and your body has adjusted to Being Larger.

Then this is: The New You.

You will have changed the profile of your body to a new profile.

You may not like the result when you look in the mirror but this has not happened overnight; you would have worked at developing it over a period of time.

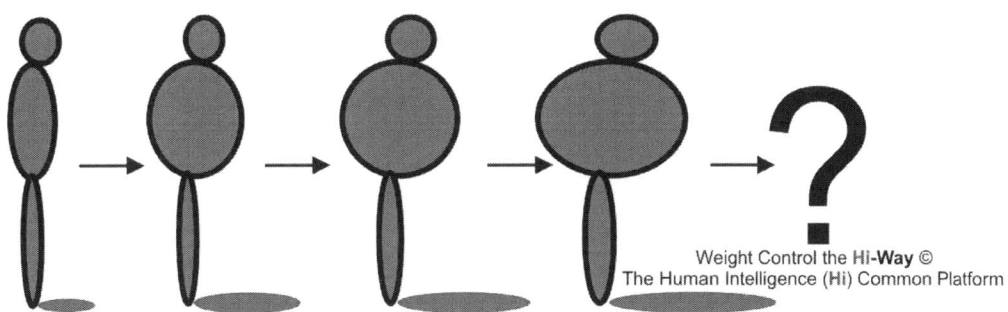

Weight Control the Hi-**Way** ©
The Human Intelligence (Hi) Common Platform

If you don't like what you have created and you want to change it. What you then have to do is work with the profile of the New You and the Potential for changing that new profile.

So if you want to change what you now have into something more desirable. Then you need to use the same process that you used to create the new profile; to change it.

And this is what we are attempting to do with this book. Use the skills that were used to create the problem; to help create the solution.

The different Potentials for change that are available to us includes:

> Physical improvements.
> Psychological changes.
> Behaviour changes.
> Emotional improvements.
> Perceptual changes.
> Environmental changes.

So you see that we have a lot of different Potentials that can be exploited.

What we need to be clear about though is: What we really can achieve and what we really can't achieve.

To help understand what this means let's do something stupid. Let's take an example from the Animal World to explore this. Let's take a large African elephant.

An elephant is one of those big grey things with tusk, a long trunk and big ears. Oh yeah; it has one of those stupid little tails at the back.

Now imagine that our elephant is being a normal elephant and it becomes as big as its genetics and its access to food and water allows it to become; Large right!

Then imagine that one day our elephant comes across a Rhino running through the grass and thinks: Wow!

Our elephant thinks about how elegant that Rhino is. How slim and attractive and fit it is by comparison to how the elephant sees itself.

>Elephant big: Rhino slim and elegant.

Our elephant then thinks: I want to be just like that Rhino!

Now we all know that the elephant is never going to be just like that Rhino.

They are different species, have different body types, are different sizes, have different capacities and have different capabilities.

If the elephant compared itself to another elephant, then it may be able to do something; but to a Rhino!

So now let's say that the elephant sets about becoming just like the rhino that it so admired.

It is in this process of trying to become the rhino that:

> The elephant's mind is now writing cheques that its body cannot pay!

So why is this relevant? It is relevant because people do this same sort of thing, in all walks of life, in all forms of activity and in all fields of endeavour.

A great example is when you watch children playing.

> They want to be the super hero that flies through the skies.

> They want to be the monster that comes from the seas.

> They want to be the doctor that operates and saves the day.

> They want to be the policeman, spaceman, fireman, etc.

However; no sane adult would actually let the child perform a real operation, try to arrest a real criminal, tackle a real fire or get on a real rocket into space.

As adults; we can see the difference between the healthy imaginings of a child; and the reality of doing these things.

However; sometimes these things do take a turn for the worse, and sometimes with fatal consequences when children actually begin to believe that they can fly or that they can jump from tall buildings. And in this process:

The child's mind begins to write cheques that their body cannot pay. And catastrophic outcomes can follow.

Of course adults and teenagers know better!

- They are not going to have unrealistic expectations; are they?

- They are not going to look at themselves in the mirror and see a fantasy image of themselves; are they?

- They are not going to look at other people as if they are some form of super hero; are they?

Of course they are!

Except they are not looking at children playing in a park; they are looking at themselves through the perspective of their own insecurities, fears, anxieties, tiredness, frustrations, wants, needs and desires.

This process of comparing and wishing to be like someone else; is almost guaranteed to give those with any form of imagination; a platform for Self-Deception and Self-Deprecation.

A platform where we can see ourselves, our life, and ourselves within our life; in some distorted shape, size and perception.

And it is this that takes us to the point where:

We lose the ability to see the Comparative Realities of what we really can achieve; and we begin to lust after those which we cannot.

And so many people don't realise that this Human Dynamic exist or that they have, in fact, become caught in the fantasy world that they thought they had left behind as children.

Except this is not a children's world; it is the world of Being Human.

And this is a world that we can negotiate and navigate in successful ways.

Let's see if we can stop our minds writing cheques that our bodies cannot cash.

Let's focus on writing cheques that we can cash!

> I developed The Human Intelligence (**Hi**) Common Platform to help me negotiate and navigate through this world.
>
> To help me see that which is not so obvious but which has real world consequences for us all at different times.

So what do I want you to take away from this chapter?

Have the wisdom to know the difference between what you can really change and what you can't change.

Have the courage to change what you can and to live with what cannot be changed.

Focus on where you want to go with your life and not where you have been.

Stop allowing your mind to write cheques that your body cannot cash!

This is good **Hi**.

Chapter 12

Finding Your Seed Of Belief!

I am going to let you into a secret.

> Successful weight control is often about who wins the battle for the Mind Space of the dieter; and how that Mind Space is used.

Let me give you some background to what it is that I am trying to do when I work with people.

In the early 1990's: When I worked with people who had long term weight problems, I found that all the people that I saw had problems with sleeping.

They either found it difficult to get to sleep, have a good quality of sleep or both.

At the time I had trained and practiced as a Hypnotherapist.

However; I did not agree with how people were marketing Hypnotherapy and the claims that they were making for it. *(I still don't today)*

Personally; I just seemed to view Hypnotherapy, and the potential benefits that it could provide, in a different way to my Peers. And I just could not make claims that I did not support or believe in.

So I went my own way with the Principles of Hypnotherapy and how to use it. I knew that Hypnotherapy could be used in beneficial ways but I just did not believe in the quick fix claims and I still don't.

To me, too many of the problems that people were claiming could be cured, improved or resolved by the use of Hypnotherapy were not credible or sustainable.

I knew that people could feel better through its use; but to claim that you were able to change, often quite substantial things, by simple suggestions through one or two Hypnotherapy sessions: I just did not see the evidence for that and I still don't.

My view has always been, and still is, that if an Alternate Therapy approach or any other form of solutions is as good as people claim it is; then it will have Predictability of Outcome and this can be measured in some form.

And when I work with Weight related problems and other types of problems, this is what I am interested in: Predictability of Outcome, and:

> The Processes for successfully achieving it.

Predictability of Outcome means that you should be able to say:

- That if I have a person with (X) condition/situation.
- And I apply (Y solution) in this way.
- Over this period of time.
- Then I would expect to achieve (Z) Outcome.
- To a percentage degree (%) of success.
- If the person does their bit along the way.

So let's get back to my secret.

When it comes to problems, I have always been interested in the Predictability of the Outcome; because this leads on to achieving an increased probability of success.

And when I was working with people who had weight problems; I knew that I was working with people who had a long dieting history.

These were people from different backgrounds, who had lived in different countries and who had a wide range of ages.

Some had been successful or were currently successful in their careers and others had normal occupations and incomes.

Most of them were women.

And I knew that they had tried many diets and programmes and many had achieved successful results from them.

But!

Despite being successful with various diet plans, weight control programmes and programmes that provided calorie controlled meals, meal replacement and dietary products. None of these people had been able to maintain their weight; and then build upon the success that they had achieved with those dieting and weight control processes.

They had all gone back to their previous weights and some had gone a long way past.

What these people really wanted to achieve but didn't actually realise it was:

> They wanted to; Be Happy In Their Life!

Being successful with your weight but not being happy with your Life; is not really the type of success that most people want. It's not substantial enough.

They want both of these things together! They want:

1. To be in control of their weight and to be successful with managing it.
2. To Be Happy in their lives!

You see; being happy in your life means living the life that you want and that you are happy living. Or; that you are moving in the right direction to achieve this and that when you get there; you can sustain it.

So let's get back to my secret.

At that time, in the 1990's, I had spend several years working with Alcohol and Drug problems with a Charity and also with a multi-disciplinary medical team that ran a Community Alcohol Programme (CAT). I had also trained as a Counsellor.

I could see from my own experiences that there were Commonalities between Alcohol, Drugs and Weight problems and many other conditions.

Over a period of time I was able to identify common issues across the range of different problems.

These common issues included: Self-Esteem, Confidence, Self-Perceptions, Motivation, etc.

I called these common issues: The Basket of Common Components.

This is because they tend to be Common Components of the structures that make up difficult and complex problems that involves Human Behaviours and Activities.

So to recap: I had all these people who had weight problems and also problems with sleeping. And I had this tool called Hypnotherapy.

To me, Hypnotherapy was a tool that could be used better in the mid to long term, in a progressive way; rather than in the short term or very short term.

So I began developing a way to use it this way.

Because of the availability of audio equipment I decided that I would write, record and mix an audio programme for the people with weight problems.

So I created and produced a 6 cassette programme that I had designed to be used over a 3 month period.

It probably took me about 6 months to do this.

My plan was that I would use this audio programme to help establish a better sleeping pattern for the people I was working with.

I also wanted to use the audio programme to help them with relaxation and to give them something different to focus on.

What I also wanted to do was to begin working with the common basket of problems through the audio programme and the one-to-one sessions we were having. So there were a lot of different things going on.

And this is my secret!

There was something that I observed and picked up on when I was working with and interviewing people with weight problems.

That thing was:

   That they Hoped that the New Diet approach would work;

   But they actually didn't really Believe that it would.

And as a result of their previous experiences and their inability to maintain result long term:
               They had lost their Seed of Belief.

So I began a process of helping them to Discover their Seed of Belief. The Belief that this time: It could work and that it could be different!

I did not tell them that we were doing this and I had very good reasons for not doing so. I won't go into those here.

I found that the audio programme helped change people's sleeping habits. Once people sleep better they also feel better. This then helped to facilitate the work that we then needed to do.

The results I experienced were that those who persisted with the programme went on to change their relationships with their weight, food, and to change and improve other aspects of their lives.

The process helped them to find hope and belief and themselves; and that they could achieve the changes and improvements that they wanted.

More importantly these changes were significant and sustainable.

Achieving this was not an easy process for me. There was lots of hard work with little reward over many years.

At that time I was still to invent, innovate, create and develop the material which I am now making available through my books and programmes.

What I was doing, without realising it, was, that I was laying the foundations for the work that I would do in the future.

So what do I want you to take away from this chapter?

That there is a difference between Wanting something and Knowing that you can obtain it, achieve it and maintain it.

I want people with weight problems to know that they can obtain the results that they want; but these results are part of a Package. You can't obtain the results without that Package.

The Package that Successful Weight Control and Freedom From Dieting is a part of is:
>Being Truly Successful In Life!

It is Moving towards Living the Life that you really want to live; how you really want to live it.

You can't achieve that result from a diet; as a diet by itself is simply not up to that task.

Understanding this is good Hi.

Chapter 13

Chaos, Chaotic Behaviour And Chaotic Situations.

When we have Chaos, Chaotic Behaviour and Chaotic Situations around for long enough:

> They become NORMAL.

As this Normalising of Chaos happens our own behaviours adjust; and our lifestyle begins to support what has become the New Normal for us. This is just the same as it does for a weight problem; when it changes from someone living in Slim Land to someone living in Fat Land.

As things change, the range of the chaos being experienced by the person moves from the Green Zone, to the Amber Zone and then into the Red Zone; as it escalates and they lose more and more control.

If we referred back to the chapter where we looked at The Dieters Scale and the way that we used the Green, Amber and Red Zones; and we now relate that to this subject.

We find that:

> People in Chaos, when they participate in the Chaos, do not Live in the Green Zone.
>
> What they are doing is Living in the Amber or Red Zones.
>
> The Amber and Red Zones have more difficulties associated with them, and more Stress, and they are More Demanding.

So Chaos, Chaotic Situations and Chaotic Behaviour can all be graded into Zones. And we may need to work our way back from the Red Zone to the Green Zone in order to sort out the chaos properly.

In my experience there are very few, what I would term, "Real Chaotic" situations; where we cannot achieve Control, Stability and Better Management of the situation.

What I find is that as people gradually lose control of situations that Chaos moves in. And it can then become a justification for the person's inability to better manage the situation; and the poor results that they are achieving.

It becomes a case of: Don't blame me; it's the chaos, and I can't do anything about that!

The view that I take is that Chaos is a result of other things; and when Chaos becomes established, it can then in turn be the cause of other things.

So the symptom can turn into a cause in its own right; and that then goes on to produce other symptoms.

Fixing these types of problems takes a little time and Strategic Planning.

What I have also found to be true is:

> If Chaos is a constant part of the problem; then Chaos becomes predictable.
>
> Once Chaos is predictable it then becomes understandable.
>
> Once it becomes understandable; it then becomes manageable and able to be improved or resolved.

So if we have someone with a weight problem who claims that they cannot do something because other things outside their control are constantly changing; or that they never know what is going to happen from one day to another; then the reality is that they are living in the Amber or Red Zones with chaos.

And you will find that their weight problem will also be living in the Amber or Red Zones; and other aspects of their life will also have drifted in this direction. This is because chaos doesn't tend to exist on its own. It tends to have other companions.

Because we are Imperfect People, we can get ourselves into the situation where:

> Through our own behaviours we find ourselves in situations which are Chaotic.
>
> We then blame the Chaotic situations for our behaviours and for How we are living our lives.
>
> Therefore; the Chaotic situations continue and so do the Negative Consequences which can compound.
>
> Over time the degree of difficulty in the situation is also likely to increase; and more areas of the person's life will become affected and move into the chaotic Amber and Red Zones.

Once someone becomes Established in the Amber and Red Zones it becomes their New Normal State.

And when we want to change this by improving things; we will get all the problems and difficulties that go with changing someone's Normal Behaviour from one State to another.

This shifting of Zones from one to another and establishing the new Zone as the new Normal; is a key structure that repeats again and again with both the problem itself and the individual components of a problem.

As more and more of the person's life moves into different Zones; then their life structures changes and becomes more complicated.

Understanding this is very good **Hi**.

From my perspective:

> I have never seen a situation which could not be changed; if the people involved are willing to do what it really takes to improve, resolve or better manage the situation.

I would also say: Don't be afraid of Chaos. See it for what it is and deal with it as the problem requires you to do so.

So what do I want you to take away from this chapter?

Chaos, Chaotic Situations and Chaotic Behaviours are Problems that have a set of conditions, which are looking for a better way of being managed, so as to produce a more successful result.

David John Sheridan

Chapter 14

Why Is It Easier For One Person Than Another To Achieve Their Goals?

The enthusiasm has been building for a while.

Mentally you have been preparing yourself to go on another diet.

In preparation you have put on another few pounds as you eat those things which you know you are going to miss; and that you are not going to be able to eat whilst on the diet.

You may even begin limbering up and starting to do a few simple stretching exercises in preparation for getting fit.

> Eventually "The Day" arrives and you're off!
>
> It's like change-over day at a holiday camp.
>
> Your places in the kitchen become off limits.
>
> Food items may have been moved and hidden; by you.
>
> The off limits food is replaced by the Good Stuff.
>
> All the healthy stuff is there for you to eat and lose weight.
>
> Your daily schedule changes.

In preparation for the weight loss that you are expecting, you may even have been out and bought or ordered new clothes; in "The New Size" that you are going to be.

You may have called it "An Incentive". Something to help you focus and get through the difficult times that you know you are going to face.

This may even be an emotional experience for some; like meeting a good friend who has been away for a while and that you are glad to see.

You may even have enlisted the support of others like you; friends who have the same wants, needs and desires.

Fellow travellers of The Diet Road.

For those who are in the Green Zone it is more of an even battle.

Those few extra pounds (kilo's) of weight soon give way to the diet plan and the exercise.

The reward of being slimmer, and feeling fitter and healthier is fantastic. Wow what a buzz!

So how long will the person in the Green Zone keep this up?

Eventually they will reach "A Point Of Balance".

A point at which they will weigh up the benefits of being slimmer, and feeling fitter and healthier. And they will weigh this up against the visits to the gym, the disruption to their social life, the inconvenience and costs of their new diet, and the effort to keep this going.

And all the way along The Diet Road different people will reach different "Points of Balance" where they decide whether they will continue in the direction they are heading or not.

When we look at those in the Amber Zone.

Well these are more experienced with the dieting process than those in the Green Zone.

They know what to expect and they will also go through their Preparations.

The Amber Zone people will have more "On The Line".

Their physical health issues may have been a motivator for the new diet. Or it may have been Doctors Orders.

This may be "The Opportunity" to sort out their life and the different issues that are "Uncomfortably" there.

So they begin.

How soon the first crisis or mini-crisis hits depends upon the support structure that the person has managed to put in place.

Do they get over the first crisis or do they want to change the rules of the game, just this once; and cheat?

As they move forwards; when do they hit the second mini-crisis, then the third?

Will they hit a forth?

If they continue along The Diet Road they will also come to a stage where they hit "A Point Of Balance". The point where they weigh up whether it is worth it and decide whether they will carry on.

And then we can ask about those people in the Red Zone.

Have they been pushed into another diet?

Is it that they simply must do it and that the consequences of failure are so great that they simply can't be considered?

Is it the last chance for (X)?

And increasingly nowadays:

> Is it time for surgery? As I just can't stop myself; and with the help of surgery I am sure that I could. I just need that extra something which makes a difference!
>
> But I can't get the surgery unless I can lose a bit of weight.

And the same process will occur for the person in the Red Zone; they will also hit a "Point of Balance" where the scales of Gain and Effort are weighed and they decide either to continue along The Diet Road or go back to their old ways.

So how can we understand what is actually going on here; across the 3 Zones?

The reality is that each Zone is in a different place and each Zone represents a more difficult and complex range of problems. So if we think of this as a journey; then the journeys from the Amber and Red Zones to the Green Zone are longer and harder.

This means that the people who are in the Amber and Red Zones will hit more "Points of Balance" than the person in the Green Zone; and they will be challenged more often about giving up or keeping going.

I like to use a simple way of understanding this problem.

The simple way I use is:

> You can't walk far when you are deep in a hole!

When we begin our lives there is no weight problem, but the tools that we need to develop one are there in our environment.

And as we develop within that environment we begin to pick up tools that will help us with developing a weight problem; and the other problems that will go with it.

And at some stage we begin to use those tools.

As we use the tools that we have picked up; we will find that Over Time we begin to develop a weight problem and we begin to dig a hole for ourselves.

The tools we use include; low Self-Esteem, poor Confidence, Relationships, Fear, Lack of Direction, etc.

Those who remain in the Green Zone, and develop a Green Zone weight control problem, don't dig their holes too deep.

So when they want to deal with all of their weight related problems, it is easier for them to move out of the hole that they have created.

They might trip getting out but they can get out of the hole reasonably easy.

If they fail to move out of the hole then they will stay in it.

If life continues in the same way; then they are in the right place to progress to the Amber Zone.

If we now consider the Amber and Red Zones.

People in the Amber and Red Zones will have gone and dug through the Green Zone.

And as a result; the hole that they now have to get out of is bigger and deeper.

Because the hole is deeper, it's simply more difficult to get out of it!

You can see that as the hole gets bigger, that more tools are in the hole.

Each tool represents another issue that relates to the weight problem. These will be either directly or indirectly related issues.

Once you are in the hole, if you put down one tool you can easily pick up another one. So throwing away one tool doesn't work because there are plenty of other tools to hand. And you can't throw them far when you are in a hole anyway; so picking them up again is easy.

So thinking that you can get out of the hole by throwing away one diet tool and grabbing another diet tool, just gives you another way of staying where you are and making the hole bigger.

Once you are in deep enough, then you really are: "In The Hole".

And when you try to get out of the hole, you soon bump into the sides. You can no longer walk out of the hole or easily get out of the hole like the person in the Green Zone. You have to climb out!

In effect; the hole you have created now defines the dimensions of your life!

So this is why I say:

> You can't walk far when you are deep in a hole!

To get out of the hole they have dug for themselves; People tend to try and use the tools that they have and which they are familiar with.

However; they have got into the habit of using these tools in particular ways; which produces certain results.

So: Grabbing the tool of a new diet while you are deep in the hole produces predictable results.

It may be a new diet but it probably won't be giving you anything new or getting you to do anything new; that is substantial enough to make a long term difference.

Remember the saying from earlier:

> A diet can be thought of as a form of rehabilitation of habits. And if that rehabilitation does not go far enough, it will prove ineffective. And this tends to prove true for many people with weight control problems. The rehabilitation of their weight control does not go far enough.

Remembering this is good Hi.

Someone who is on the thin end of the weight spectrum will tend to have the same problems as those in the Amber and Red Zones that are overweight.

So what do I want you to take away from this chapter?

As you move from one Zone to another Zone; the nature and structure of the problems that you have changes.

It will have taken you time to dig the hole; and as it got deeper you would have shored it up (you build a framework which stops the hole from collapsing in on top of you).

What you used to shored up the hole are all the different things which support and help to maintain the weight problem.

Very often the best thing to do, is to Prepare and Practice for what you are going to do; but do this in a different way to how you will have done it in the past.

If you are caught in the problem; it will probably be very difficult for you to do this on your own.

> You need to do a combination of changing your tools and the way that you use the tools that you have.
>
> You also need a different plan to the one that you have been using and which has lead to you being in the hole and staying in the hole.
>
> This is what I am attempting to do with Weight Control the **Hi-Way**.
>
> Understanding this is good Hi.

Chapter 15

The Reality Of Failure

There are certain activities where failure is part of the process of success. This includes:

> All Sports.
> All Business.
> All of the Sciences.
> All of Literature and the Arts.
> All Politics.
> All Wars.
> Peace.
> Medicine.
> Relationships.
> Religion.
> Life.

And yet; Dieting and Weight Control are meant to be Failure Free!

All the evidence seems to suggest that this is an untenable and completely unrealistic position.

> Failure Free Dieting and Weight Control is a Myth on the same level as Unicorns and Little Green Men from Mars. *(My apologies to Unicorns and little Green Men from Mars; if you are reading this.)*

Having the expectations that you must not or will not fail on a diet, puts you under so much pressure that you cannot really succeed.

So rather than waste our time focusing on something which is unachievable; let's scrap it!

Let's accept that you are going to fail! Then let's get beyond it.

You see Failure, in the Right Context, is actually Good!

It says that you are an Imperfect Person who has a problem with your weight and you are working on it.

What I want to do is to get you looking at and working on failure in the right way.

> I use people's failure as a way to understand what was actually going on for them when it happened: Because something is always going on when you fail on a diet.

Then we try to make the failure provide a benefit that we can use in a Positive way.

I use different tools to help myself, and the person that I am working with, to understand what motivated or produced that failure.

And then we look to deal with it differently when it happens again.

What we want to do is create New Special Chapters in Your Life Profile that you can begin referencing and using.

These become New Special Chapters that have you dealing with failure in ways that are more beneficial.

And these New Special Chapters have you experiencing a better and more successful life.

I think that a better way to think of Weight Control and Dieting is as indicators for:

Being Successful In Life!

Or

Not Being Successful; Yet!

Being Successful In Life!

This means that you are living the life that you want, in the way that you want; or you are on your way to doing so, by taking the Actions that you need to take to get there.

Not Being Successful: Yet!

This means that you have begun a process of Becoming Successful In Life; and you are beginning to put the structures in place that you will need to achieve your goals.

Remember:

Your weight is only part of your Sorrow or your Joy!

And that's the way to go about this; asking yourself the question:

Are you working on your Sorrow or are you working on your Joy?

If you begin doing this, then I would say that you are beginning to find the Right Path to achieving a Successful Life that is free from the pressures and disappointments of dieting and weight control.

So what do I want you to take away from this chapter?

Not making mistakes and Being Perfect all the time is not something that people are good at.

Basically: You can't achieve it and if you can; you can't sustain it.

So it becomes an impossible task; like catching and keeping smoke.

I prefer to think and act in this way:

> I will achieve Excellence when required and be good enough when appropriate!
>
> I will Allow myself to make mistakes and learn from the mistakes that I make.
>
> Failure is often the difference between what I can achieve and what I have achieved.
>
> By seeking Excellence when it is required, I can often eliminate failure.
>
> Having the wisdom to know the difference between the times when Excellence is required and when Good Enough is appropriate; is achieved by Experience.
>
> Experience is achieved through Doing, Succeeding and Failing.
>
> So failure is part of the process of Succeeding!
>
> Understanding and using this properly is good **Hi**.

WHAT'S COMING NEXT!

In the Chapters that follow I am going to look at the Role of certain Common Components that are associated with Weight Control problems.

These are what I would call Lifestyle Management Problems that are common to all of us at different times.

I am not suggesting that you have these problems but I do think that it is worth exploring them in this way. This may help to give you insights or an understanding of things which can help you.

These problems exist across the entire Spectrum of Weight Problems.

Understanding that these issues may be relevant for you is good Hi.

Chapter 16

The Role Of Habits In Your Problem

As people, we could not survive without habits.

Habits get us out of bed in the morning, they get us to work and they help us all get along with life.

In every area of our lives we develop habits. This includes:

> Lifestyle, Wealth, Health & Well-Being

Often, because habits are so ubiquitous, we fail to even recognise them as being habits.

Another way of looking at and understanding habits is to think of them as Learned Behaviours; which is exactly what they are:

> Learned ways of doing things, which often become automatic.

In fact; most of the time we just drift along in the stream of life and allow ourselves to be moved around by our habits; without really thinking about it.

What we all get affected by is:

> The Habitual Nature of our Lives.

So how would I define a Habit?

If we consider the world that we occupy as a human being, we see that it has different areas which include:

- Emotions/Feelings.
- Psychology (how we process information).
- Actions/Re-actions (how we respond to different things).
- Human Dynamics (situations in which we find ourselves).
- Other factors.

In each of these areas we are capable of developing and maintaining habits.

Habits are like Short-Cuts.

Rather than have to keep working out how to process, manage or resolve an issue; we do it a few times and then it becomes automatic.

It becomes automatic because at some level it makes sense at the time.

Once it makes sense and it becomes something that we use as part of our make-up as a person; it becomes part of us.

Once it becomes part of us, we often tend not to consciously think about what we are doing, why we are doing it or how we are doing it. We just do it!

In fact; thinking about it becomes a chore!

> As Human Beings; we are built so that we do things which we repeat in an automatic fashion. And so much of our lives are repetitions of actions which we repeat.

Now let's consider Habits as Learned Behaviours and use The Dieter's Scale to understand them better.

On the Dieter's Scale we have Green, Amber and Red Zones.

As we move from the Green Zone to Amber and then to Red, the nature of the problem changes and becomes more complicated and difficult.

Also the Behaviour that occurs within the Amber and Red Zones tends to be less and less Desirable.

So let's use this scale and apply it to habits and Learned Behaviours.

For most people; a lot of our habits will be in the Green Zone. And many of these will serve us very well and be really useful to us. But not all of them!

As we move into the Amber Zone; these will be habits that can cause us problems and difficulties.

And even though we may be aware of this, we have not changed the habits so as to take them out of the Amber Zone.

In reality: We end up living with them until we have to change them.

As we move into the Red Zone; these will be those habits that cause us most difficulty; one way or another.

Once again we have not changed these habits, so as to take them out of the Red Zone. And once again we end up living with them until we have to change them.

Now one of the things that we need to understand about habits is this:

> Just because we have developed a habit, it doesn't mean that we know all about it and how to change it.
>
> Often we don't and we can't!

You see; with habits we often lose Perspective!

That old saying: "Can't see the wood for the trees" applies to habits.

You need to remember that the habit has become automatic and that thinking about it becomes a Chore.

So dealing with it, on your own, becomes difficult. And if it is too difficult; we will tend not to deal with it until we really have no choice.

So we put up with it, hoping that it will sort itself out.

This then leads us to the question:

> How can I do something Positive about my Bad and less desirable habits?

The truth is that often we can't see what it is that we are doing and we can't understand why we are doing it.

If we can't see it properly or understand it; how can we change it?

We need to think of a habit and habitual behaviour as being one and the same thing.

Then it becomes easier to work with.

If we were to sit down and look at the behaviours that you don't like and which you find problematic.

We would find that we can put them into either the Green, Amber or Red Zones.

This would give us a scale for measuring the Problematic Habitual Behaviour and we would expect to handle them differently; according to the Zones that they were in.

For example: We would expect that a Green Zone habit would be easier to deal with than an Amber Zone habit.

Now if you decide to take on the hardest and most difficult habit first; then you are taking on the most difficult habitual challenge without any preparation or practice.

So it might be best to tackle something easier to begin with.

> What you need to remember is: Little steps add up to large distances.

In reality; Habits are a necessary part of being human. So you are not going to eliminate habits from your life.

> What we want to do is to change our Tendency (that word again) from developing and using Bad Habits; to a Tendency for developing and using Good Habits.

> So how do we go about doing this?

Remember earlier in this book we had the chapter about Your Life Profile?

Habits are part of Your Life Profile. Habits are what make you use one chapter in Your Life Profile over another.

So what we want to do is to change or modify some habits. And we want to eliminate, reduce or stop using other habits. We also may want to create new habits.

To achieve this we need to be Specific.

- What do we want to change?
- Why do we want to change it?
- What result does this habit produce that we don't want?
- Why are we using this habit in this way?
- How long have we been using this habit?
- Which Zone is this habit in: Red, Amber or Green?

By doing this we can begin to create the Comparative Understanding that we need to change Habitual Behaviour from one thing, to another thing. The Undesirable to the Desirable!

Once we begin consciously thinking about these aspects, we can begin to get a proper feeling and understanding of what we are dealing with; and things become less scary.

The next step is to put "A Plan" together for how we are going to change it.

This Plan would include:

> What steps are we going to take?
> When are we going to do them?
> How do I want to change this habit? (What's the desired result?)
> How long do I think it will take?
> Can I do this on my own or do I need help?

Now something that you need to understand is this:

> Habits don't always exist in isolation.

So what you might find is that dealing with your problem habit is not as simple as you think.

You see; Habits can develop out of other existing behaviour.

And just like Rabbits; habits can breed habits.

If one bad habit develops out of another, then it just becomes more complicated.

I liken this process to a "Spiders Web".

A Spiders Web is created when we have different habits which connect together and support each other.

When it is like this, it can be very difficult to know where to begin and what to do for the best.

The best thing to do is to start somewhere and see what happens. If it is the wrong place, then learn from the experience and start on another.

You will soon find out whether this is something that you are able to do on your own, or whether you need to find some help with it.

You know that you have found the right help and that you are doing the right things; when you begin to get the right results.

> Later there is going to be a chapter on "Symptom Solutioning" and this will help you understand why so many people do the wrong things when they try to deal with a problem or change a habit.

So what do I want you to take away from this chapter?

Habits exist for all sorts of reasons and purposes.

A habit can be a:

>Change agent.
>Tolerance tool.
>Survival tool.
>Relationship tool.
>Stress tool. Etc.

A habit has no emotions. It will allow itself to be put to any purpose whether it is good or bad.

Understanding this is Good **Hi**.

As people, we have the ability to modify and change habits, remove them and create new ones.

As we do so; we can change, modify and improve:

>Your Life Profile.

Understanding this is Good **Hi**.

At the beginning of every day:

You have the opportunity to write the Life Profile you want to have; you are not stuck with the one that you currently have.

Get into the habit of Living a Better Life and Improving Your Life Profile.

Understanding this is Good **Hi**.

Chapter 17

The Role Of Relationships In Your Weight Problem

There are many different and good books about Relationships.

So I am not going to go into all the different aspects of relationships that there are.

Instead; what I am going to focus on are the aspects that I want to highlight as being relevant and appropriate to Weight Problems.

I am going to point out:

"The Tips Of Possible Iceberg's"

Icebergs are things that are partially visible above the surface but that may have a lot hidden beneath. And it's what's hidden that may be contributing to the development and maintenance of someone's problem with their weight.

In my experience where there are significant problems; such as a weight problem. Then there is often a problem, or problems, with relationships around somewhere.

If there is a family then it is not unusual for the Mother to become a "Dogs Body" and have to give up their own identity and personal activities for the family.

Sometimes this role is undertaken by the Father.

Sometimes this role is undertaken by another member of the family or even a friend.

> Sacrifice and Compromise in relationships can cause serious problems at times; especially when it goes too far or goes on for too long.

I have worked with a number of people who have found themselves in this type of situation.

Eventually they begin to lose "Themselves" in the process of looking after and looking out for others.

Their own personal rewards in life continually get put to the back of their priority list. And eventually all of this becomes normal. They no longer have any priority status.

They can reach the position where their Needs don't really count or matter; and eventually they only matter for what they can do for others. They become Facilitators of other people's lives but not their own.

Over time, even in the best relationships, Resentment begins to creep in when someone isn't being sufficiently valued; or doesn't feel as if they are.

Resentment is one of those things that can fester over time and begin to creep into other areas of life and affect other aspects of life.

Aspects such as Sex, Closeness, Trust, Confidence, Self-Esteem and Self-Worth can all be affected.

So a "Giving Person" can find themselves in a relationship where there is too little in the relationship for them. How do they then begin to deal with that when they may have been in that position for years?

This then brings us to Love.

Things can get terribly complicated by Love and Affection. Love of children, love of parents, love of partner, love of position, love of pets, love of home, etc.

How do we deal with things when Love and Affection complicate a problem?

Then there is Guilt.

Oh, we can feel terribly guilty when we have negative thoughts about our loved ones.

And how do we handle those guilty feelings?

Then there may be the feelings that we have when we are not getting enough Attention.

> Well we are part of this relationship and we should be treated like a Valued person; shouldn't we?

Do you feel like you are asking the other person to choose between you and your children; or their children; or their sick or old parent; or is someone actually putting you in that position?

> The reality is that NO-ONE is immune to Relationships; Good ones or Bad ones.

Of course, there are the people who will tell you that:

"It doesn't matter"

That there is:

"Nothing Wrong!"

But what are the costs to them of Burying or Disconnecting from their Feelings and their Needs? Who will pay for this in the future?

And then there are the Selfish Ones. I am talking about the Truly Selfish Ones.

Not the ones who are being Bullied by someone else; and as part of that bullying process they are being told that they are Selfish; as they are punished in some way that pleases the bully. No these people are often the victims of the truly selfish ones.

I am talking about the ones who are likely to be on the other side of this equation; those that might do the bullying and be doing the putting down of others.

These are often the ones where No-one and Nothing that they have is good enough.

These are the people who can so easily cause harm to others and also to themselves; if they have sufficient self-awareness.

What do you do if you find yourself on the wrong side of a selfish relationship?

Then there are those who are simply: Just Cruel and Nasty.

Those people who relish and enjoy the pain and suffering of others.

Those who make it a point to destroy relationships, ruin friendships, destroy confidence, kill happiness and ruin other people's lives. Why?

Relationships can give us happiness; and they can make us unhappy as a result of what we do and what we expect or want from them.

However; there is a secret with relationships, regardless of whether the relationships are good or bad.

The secret is:
> That we often have more control in any Relationship situation than we understand.

So many times I have had to help people to manage their relationships in different ways; as part of the process of helping them resolve, improve and better manage other life problems; such as their weight.

So let's not pretend that Relationships are easy all the time or that there are easy fixes for all relationship problems; because there are not.

Sometimes it comes down to hard choices and difficult courses of action.

That old saying:

> You can choose your friends but you cannot choose your family, is true.
>
> However; you can choose how you want to manage both of these and the level and type of involvement that you want to have with them.
>
> This is how you achieve the Control.
>
> Understanding this is good Hi.

The process of starting to Manage Relationships and change them can often begin from the position of:

"Being On The Back Foot".

That is to say that you are out of position, off-balance, really down, tired out, worn out, completely confused, befuddled, under resourced, beaten-up, scared and afraid, desperate, lonely, etc.

The reality is that we all have to begin from wherever we are at; wherever that may be: Good or Bad.

Because wherever we are at, is it:

The Starting Point!

Sometimes it's family relationships that are the problem and other times it is friendships that are a problem.

Sometimes its work related relationships that are the problem.

Sometimes we are lonely and at other times we long for solitude.

Sometimes we want physical closeness and at other times we want emotional connections.

Sometimes we just want the recognition from another person that we exist. And that we have not become insignificant and irrelevant to the world.

And at times like these a simple conversation with another human being can make a difference to us.

Relationships, or the absence of Relationships, will form Chapters in Your Life Profile.

Many of our relationships also have Habitual parts to them. Some of these will be beneficial and some may not be.

With each Relationship we have the choices of:

- Continuing to write the same things into our Life Profiles.
- Changing what we write.
- Deciding to stop writing that chapter.
- To begin writing another chapter; that tells our story in a different way.

All of us, without exception, have relationships with People and Things.

Some of us have fewer than we want and some of us have more than we want.

All of us, at some time or another, don't have the Right Types of relationships.

All of us Want and Need something from another person, at one time or another because we are Human!

This requires Interactions at a personal level.

Understanding this and understanding that we can really do something about it is good **Hi**.

So what do I want you to take away from this chapter?

When someone has put up with difficulties in a relationship for a long time, and things have come to a head (often because the weight problem has began to get dealt with properly), they can often feel compelled to take drastic action and make life changing decisions.

The reality is that relationships do break-up; but they should break up for the right reasons and not the wrong reasons.

> Avoid The Knee Jerk Nuclear Option with Relationships!

In my experience the drastic action can often be the wrong action, at the wrong time, for the wrong reasons.

Before anyone makes any drastic long term decisions; such as to end a marriage, move home, change locations or give up a career. I normally like to try and take the Steam out of a situation and bring some long term thinking and clarity into the situation.

This is not always possible but it usually works.

> By delaying critical life decisions until such time as we can see them clearly and without built up resentments; we can generally make better ones.
>
> This is good **Hi**.
>
>
> Don't think that any significant relationships that you have (or don't have) are not influencing your behaviours. They will be; you just may not be seeing it or acknowledging it.

As part of fixing a long term weight problem we need to address Influencing Factors; and relationships are often Influencing Factors.

Understanding this is good **Hi**.

Chapter 18

The Role Of "A Lack of Understanding" In Your Problem

A large part of what this book is attempting to do is to help you achieve an understanding of a weight control problem, by taking an alternative view and an alternative approach to dealing with it.

I am trying to move your thinking away from the conventional and the so called "Easy" approaches that people usually try to take.

> The "Easy Thing" to do with a weight problem is to focus on a diet and an exercise programme.
>
> The "Harder Thing" to do is to move away from this position; and look at the things that are behind and driving a weight problem forwards; and keeping it going.

One of the problems with the "Harder Thing" is that most of the time the person with the weight problem doesn't actually understand the different Human Dynamics that are part of their problem; and which are influencing them towards having a problem with their weight.

> In effect: What they have is a lack of Understanding and a lack of Comprehension about the problem itself. And about what is actually required to sort it out properly.

This is not their fault and it is usually not a wilful thing; it is just the reality of the structure of the problem itself.

Understanding this is good Hi.

The lack of Understanding and the lack of Comprehension occurs, in a large part, because of the way that the problem itself evolves.

Weight problems normally evolve over reasonable periods of time; and things associated with a weight problem generally happen gradually and at a slow pace.

Weight problems and the associated issues that develop; integrate: And they become blended together over a period of months, years and decades.

The progression is slow; and because it is slow the person misses it.

> Because of the slow progression of the problem; they lack the perspective to see the real differences between how life "Is" now and how life "Was" before.

So as they are losing something; they fail to see it going and to understand the full impact of losing it.

To be able to remedy the weight problem we need to address this process, and to do so, we need to go through a New Learning Process.

Some of this New Learning Process involves filling in the gaps that exist in your life experiences and understandings; as these will affect your Lifestyle Management.

Much of the work that is required would be considered to be Experiential Learning.

Experiential Learning is Learning by Doing and Experiencing; while having someone to guide you.

To show you how effective this process is:

> Your weight problem developed as a result of this process!

> It just happens that it went wrong because you had the wrong **Hi**.

In order to get to where you are now:

> You Experimented and learned and adapted your behaviours.

And what we want to do is to use that same process to Evolve your weight problem into a more Positive Outcome; rather than the Negative Outcome that you have.

This book is going to be part of that process for you. This is why I am explaining these different things in the level of detail that I am. You may not understand all of it but if you can understand enough to make a difference to you; then you can make Positive Progress.

This process can be a difficult thing to facilitate with another person. I developed the **Hi** Common Platform and other tools to help me with this process.

It helps both the facilitator and the person with the problem to understand the different Human Dynamics which are involved and that need to be worked with.

It helps us to see things with the Correct Perspective and Understanding; so that we can then deal with them effectively.

Understanding this is good **Hi**.

So what do I want you to take away from this chapter?

Many problems develop because of the lack of the right type of education, life skills, structures and Hi. Weight problems are the same!

> We use what we have in order to understand and work with the life problems and the life challenges that we encounter.
>
> And if we don't have what we need; then we try to find it elsewhere or adapt and use what we do have. Often this leads to a weight problem and other problems.

Somehow or other, those gaps in someone's Life Education need to be filled in with the right type of Education, Information and Hi.

And in that process the faulty material needs to be corrected, modified or removed.

> If the degree of your problems falls into the Green Zone, then this should take less time and have less difficulties attached to them; than someone whose problems fall into the Amber Zone.
>
> If the degree of your problems falls into the Amber Zone or Red Zone; then this will take more time that the person who falls into the Green Zone.

The greater the degree of your Weight Problem, and the Associated and Related Problems; the greater the time and Experiential Learning that will be required for the restructuring of the framework of your life.

I have worked with people who had very difficult weight problems and associated issues. With very difficult problems there is something that occurs from time to time.

What this is, is that you do all this great work; and then you find out that there was another layer to the problem that never came to light before, and that you were never aware of; we find an iceberg hidden in the problem!

This occurs because these other problems were the foundations on which the weight problem and the other issues which developed; were built. At this point you then have the opportunity to tackle these issues.

Because of all the great work that has occurred; it now becomes possible to finally deal with the huge iceberg that you could not see before.

Once this is deal with; the person truly is free!

> Understanding this is good Hi.

Chapter 19

The Role Of Symptom Solutioning In Developing And Maintaining Your Weight Problem

No-one ever just wakes up one morning to find that they have a weight problem.

They might suddenly wake up to the realisation that they have a weight problem and the scale of it; but the problem would have been there for some time.

The reality is that Weight Problems take time to develop and there are processes that allow and cause it to happen. We will now look at one of the Patterns of Behaviours and Actions that help to create and maintain a weight problem.

> The real causes are ignored and you focus on the symptoms.

Let's look at Diet Clubs, for example:

What does the script for virtually all diets say:

> You are going to lose (X) amount of weight, over (Y) number of weeks!
>
> And how often does someone then approach the diet with the expectations that they will be able to lose (X) weight over (Y) weeks; and then be able to keep the weight loss going until they achieve their target?
>
> This approach causes you to have the expectations that your weight problem can be fixed by this simple approach. All the evidence say's otherwise!
>
> So a typical diet class treats the Symptom – Being overweight.
>
> This is bad Hi.

And what other Expectations are they bringing into the dieting process?

A lot more!

For example:

The expectation is: That once I have lost that weight I will be able to...

This produces the expectation that somehow or other you are going to be Motivated or Inspired to do other things that you are having trouble doing or that you can't do. Have you ever thought this?

As another example: How often do you see a diet being marketed with slim and attractive people in the advert or promotion?

How often are these people shown as being Confident, Happy, Self-Assured and Desirable; and living a lifestyle that you really want?

All the time!

This is because this is what we really want to see and this is what we really want to achieve from the dieting process; even if we don't admit it to ourselves.

> We want to have, and live, a Better Quality of Life!

So "Implicitly" they show you that you can achieve this by using their products and services. And a part of you buys into this. This is poor **Hi**.

Whereas; if they showed you their real success rates from their dieting solutions, over a period of years, you probably would not buy it. And they would go out of business.

However; having this real information would be good **Hi**.

In reality; Diet classes run with very high failure rates and they always welcome you back.

And you find that once a diet approach has run its course and numbers are falling off; they revamp it and begin marketing it again using words like:

- New!
- More effective.
- New formula.
- Eat more of what you like.
- Easier.
- And they often include Scientific Sounding claims and words.

How many of the people who are providing diets have taken the time to understand the "True Nature" of a real weight control problem?

> Don't confuse the ability to sell diets with understanding a weight problem. They are not the same thing.

Failing to understand the real nature and structure of the problem that you are dealing with; and instead treating the consequences, is doing the following:

> It can make you feel temporarily better; and this can be like a Placebo Effect.
>
> *With a Placebo; it doesn't do you any real good, unless you think that it does; but the Placebo is also meant to do you no real or lasting harm.*

We could look at the practices of most of the diet industry in this way; but I don't think that it is as benign as the placebo effect.

In reality I think that there are hidden consequences and costs that we do need to understand.

> The failure to achieve with a diet not only shows in someone's weight; it is also experienced through other areas of their life. It has knock-on effects!

My view is that people are harmed by the Consequential Effects of repeated dieting; which fails to deliver on the promises made through their advertising and promotions for the different brands that exist.

The truth is that Weight Problems require a good dose of reality; and they need to be grounded in reality; for solution to be effective long term.

Reality is however; both sweet and sour and it is more difficult to market.

Marketing people want to focus on what you are most likely to buy. And if you offer people a choice of having sweet things or having sour things; then most people will go for the sweet option.

> In order to keep selling the products they will keep offering you sweet sounding solutions; when in reality you need some sour medicine.

> And this then sets-up the cycle for Symptom Solutioning to continue and grow as you pursue the sweet sounding solutions in preference to the ones that are both sweet and sour.

> This is bad **Hi**.

The truth is that lots of people can help you to lose weight in the short term. It is fairly easy to do this.

What everyone struggles with is making it past the short term and turning it into a longer term sustainable result.

So because everyone can achieve something short term; everyone focuses on the short term. This includes:

- The seller and provider of the diet.
- The use of the diet.
- The seller of consumable products.
- The user of the consumable products.

This bias towards short term thinking, short term results and small amounts of effort; just pushes people more towards "Symptom Solutioning" and away from the more difficult but more successful long term solution that they really want and need.

If the solution you are applying to the problem cannot resolve that problem; then there is no way that it can work; other than through luck!

Why rely on luck when you can rely on solutions that have been developed to deal with weight problems in the right ways. However; they will be both sweet and sour.

"Symptom Solutioning"

I may also have coined the phrase; Symptom Solutioning.

Symptom Solutioning is a process of dealing with the consequences of problems; in isolation, or without proper regard to the things which are actually causing the problems.

And then repeating this process with new and ongoing problems.

Over time, as a result of doing this, you lose touch with the real problems and you become more focused on dealing with the consequences that the problems produce.

You ignore Causes and you focus on Symptoms. This is bad **Hi**.

Symptom Solutioning also involves distracting people away from their life problems and dissatisfactions; by claiming that you can provide them with something which helps them achieve the good things that they desire, in a simple and easy way.

This distraction process often involves fantasy thinking and unrealistic expectations. And if you look at Television any day of the week you will see hundreds of examples of this in commercials for all sorts of products and services.

Weight problems are a classical example of Symptom Solutioning at work and the consequences of Symptom Solutioning.

Life Improvement Programmes Focused On Weight

With my Life Improvement Programmes and the other work that I do; we work with reality from the start.

We have too; or we just end up going in the wrong direction and wasting time.

When things are done in the right way and with the right expectations, I find that people with weight problems can and do handle it well. They can accept that we need to have sweet and sour and they can cope with this; when they understand it.

The structure of the Programmes means that we are in a better position to deal with the difficult life issues that are part of the weight problem.

Our structure also helps those who are on the programmes to learn and develop new skills and new ways of dealing with difficult and complicated issues.

In my view: Weight problems are really Lifestyle Management Problems that are currently majoring on weight.

This is what we work with as part of a Life Improvement Programme – How to manage our Lifestyles better so that we can achieve the Life that we want; and become free of the tyranny and pressures of dieting and weight control.

Understanding this is good Hi.

So what do I want you to take away from this chapter?

All problems have a structure and that structure can be understood. All solutions have a structure and that structure can be understood.

The better the fit between the structure of the problem and the structure of the solution; the higher the probability of a successful outcome.

The worse the fit, the more reliant we become on luck.

Perhaps more diets should be called: The Lucky Diet.

As you move into different Zones on The Dieters Scale, problems will increase in size and complexity.

Understanding this is good Hi.

Chapter 20

The Role Of Food In Your Problem

Have you ever heard someone with a weight problem say:

"An alcoholic can stop drinking but I can't stop eating or I will die!"

If you haven't heard this particular saying then you may have heard of other sayings that justify someone's eating behaviour.

Part of the problem which we have, as Imperfect People, is that we want things to be simple and easy; even when it's not possible for them to be simple and easy.

So, if we can Easily and Simply avoid the Responsibility for the Consequences of our Dietary Practices and for the things that we have Consumed; then we will happily do so.

"I'm not taking the responsibility for eating that Food; it's the Foods fault!

Yep! That's food for you; it jumped straight off that plate and into your mouth.

Then it forced your mouth to chew on it, and then you were forced to swallow it and repeat this until all the food was gone.

We have just made a fantastic discovery to explain weight problems:

"Ninja Food"

The reality is that "Ninja Food" just does not exist.

The reality is that Food serves many different purposes other than the basic requirements for nourishment.

Food can be a powerful and seductive force; and it would help us if we can acknowledge the other roles that food has within our lives and within our social habits.

In different cultures the preparation, serving and eating of food has cultural and social implications.

We can respect all of these different things and we can still take responsibility for what we consume.

"I'm Powerless in the face of Food"

There are some who say that they are Powerless when they see or have to look at food.

The reality is that at some point, if you want to be treated as an Adult, then you have to behave like an Adult and show some Restraint and Control.

If you are never going to show Restraint and Control but you want to continue to be treated as a Responsible Adult; then you create a Paradox.

The Paradox you create is the:

> I'm an Adult and I want to be treated as an Adult.
>
> BUT:
>
> When it comes to my behaviour with Food and the consequences of my behaviour with Food; I can't be held to be a Responsible Adult and I don't want to be treated as if I am a Responsible Adult – Paradox.

Now if you don't want to be a Responsible Adult with Food then other things can happen.

Many years ago FAT PEOPLE who could not help themselves and who developed health problems because of their weight were offered a great solution.

They could have their jaws WIRED SHUT!

All their teeth would be wired and then their teeth would be wired shut so that they could not eat anything because they could not open their mouths.

However; these Adults "who could not help themselves" would do things like:

- Use pliers and cut away the wire when they wanted to eat.
- Liquidise high calorie food, such as chocolate, so that they could pour it through the wire.

And what of those who left the jaw wiring in place and who lost weight; do you think that they continued at that weight when the wiring was finally removed?

Our modern equivalent of this is the Stomach Balloon, the Gastric Band, the Stomach Reduction and other things which are all trying to do the same thing:

> They try to save people from themselves: By giving the Adult who Can't be Responsible for their own behaviours, an easy way to deal with the consequences of their own behaviours.

And those who are having these procedures are demonstrating the same outcomes as those who had their jaws wired shut.

Questions that we should be asking ourselves are:

> Given the increase in the number of people who are having problems with their weight; will we reach a point where they begin to be treated as Disabled People?
>
> Will we reach a point where doctors can determine that the person is "Incapable" and therefore they need to be treated without their consent; for the common good and for their own protection?

Not pleasant thoughts but with about 33% of adults in North America being classified as obese; where do you think this thing is going?

The power to change this is in the hands of the people with the problem; and it is only the people with the weight problems who can change this. Politicians can't!

> The problem isn't only the food. The problem is the choices that we make and the actions that we take. Understanding this is good **Hi**.

One of the problems with food today is that it is so easily and readily available and so easily and readily stored and moved around.

As a result of this, food has moved into new areas of life and new types of food have been created.

> Portable food has never previously been as readily available as it is today.
>
> And this contributes to the problem for someone with a food problem.
>
> All they have to do is reach out and they can have some food.

When you have reached a point in your life where you are using food in the wrong ways, and you are not exercising the right choices. Then quick and easy access to the thing which you are misusing just makes life more difficult.

And it makes managing the problem more difficult.

However; the reality is that all it takes to being making long term effective change is:

One Positive Action at a time!

The truth is that I don't see many people being held down and being forced fed food. In fact; I don't see it ever!

However; you will see people holding themselves down and force feeding themselves! *You will actually see this a lot if you look at the problem with the right focus.*

In reality; most of us, most of the time, have a choice about what we consume, ingest or allow into our bodies.

You can exercise a Pro-Active choice that will benefit you long term; or a Negative choice that will hurt you.

Which do you want to do?

Are You in charge or is the Food in charge of You?

A number of simple questions show that you are actually acting in ways that puts you in front of the food that contributes to a weight problem.

- When you go shopping; who actually agrees to pick up the food and who actually puts the food in the trolley?
- Who pays for the food?
- Who takes the food home?
- Who cares for and looks after the food?
- Who prepares the food?
- Who puts the food on the plate?
- Who eat the food?

You see:

- Food has no Will.

- Food has no Speech.

- Food doesn't follow us home from the store.

- Food doesn't go out and buy People; People go out and buy food.

- Food doesn't grow people; People grow food.

- Food doesn't abuse People; People abuse food.

Food is Passive and we can put food to any purpose that we want. Good or Bad.

What choices do you want to make today?

Let's imagine that we were to apply The Dieters Scale to all the food and other items that you buy and consume.

And if all the items that You were OK with, were put into the Green Zone; what would go into the Green Zone?

If all the items that you had a medium level problem with were put into the Amber Zone; what would go into the Amber Zone?

And then if we put all the items that you had a high level problem with in the Red Zone; what would go into the Red Zone?

This simple process would show you the Zones that you think your food falls into and also the difficulties that you have with the foods that you are buying and eating.

It will also show you which Zones your eating habits are occupying and give you an idea of how much time you're spending in each Zone.

> To do this properly you need to think in terms of your Normal Consumption. Not your consumption during a good period but during a Normal Period of time.

People with weight problems are going to be spending a lot of their time in the Amber and Red Zones.

The problem isn't **just** the food. The problem is the choices that we make and the actions that we take. Should you be making more Green Zone and Amber Zone choices?

Understanding this is good **Hi**.

So what do I want you to take away from this chapter?

People's bodies are not Consequential Vessels; and they Don't have to behave as if they are.

What this means is that you are not a bystander waiting for people and events to happen to you.

You are not the arena where bad things happen.

You can become the victim of your own long term behaviour if you want too; or you can Choose Not to be a victim.

The reality for everyone with a Weight problem is:

> That you have more control over this thing than you may care to admit to yourself or than you know.

In fact what is happening to you, that you don't like, is being driven, controlled and managed; largely or wholly by you!

This is the real level of control that you have; even if you do not realise that this is the case.

What I am interested in is helping you to exercise that control in another way.

Let's turn this thing into a Positive rather than a Negative.

If you don't believe this then let me ask you another question:

> Could this problem have occurred without you?

Food offers all of us a lot of Positives. So use and enjoy the Positives.

- Food is there to be enjoyed; so enjoy it.
- Food is there to nourish us; so nourish yourself with it.
- Food is there to celebrate with; so celebrate.
- Food is there to be appreciated; so appreciate it.

Chapter 21

The Role Of "Processed" Foods In Your Problem

I have talked about the Role of Food generally in relation to a Weight Problem.

Now I want to introduce some other aspects that are not normally talked about when we talk about weight problems or the consumption of food generally.

I thought that it was worthwhile including a chapter on Processed Foods because more and more food is being processed; and people with weight problems are eating more and more processed food. So this is important.

I want to take a different view of this area so:

What do I mean when I talk about Processed Foods?

I am going to break Processed Foods down into two distinct areas:

1. Processing to Produce and Create Foods.

2. Processing Out the bodies Normal Management of and Processing of Foods.

What we need to understand is: That unless a Food has a component in it; which is toxic or in some way immediately harmful to us:

- That Food related problems can take a long time to materialise.
- Then a long time to become recognised.
- Then a long time to become properly understood.
- And then finally, a long time to get dealt with.

When it comes to food, weight problems and Human Health; the type of question that I ask myself is:

Are we able to see the problem with the broader and larger scale view required to properly understand it?

My answer is that I think that in reality; the questions related to these issues are beyond the normal person. And this is what contributes to the problem itself; we assume someone else is protecting us and protecting us from harm.

I personally would say that these questions are also beyond our current Governments and the various organisations and groups who control, influence and regulate the food industry.

What I see happening are Responses to obvious problems in the Food Industry, in as simple and as easy a manner as it is possible to do.

In effect; the global food industry and those who Police it on our behalf; are caught up in the process of Symptom Solutioning.

They are working with the simple and easy problems and the consequences of other problems; but they are not dealing with the fundamental problems and issues which would make a long term difference.

To change this would require longer term thinking and actions of a type that people who are focused on short term results are not prepared or able to do.

So I think that we are stuck with what we have and that these various Governments and Organisations who control and Police Global Food; will respond from crisis to crisis.

So how does this affect the common man?

And what can we do to reduce the likelihood that we will suffer longer term consequences from the foods and other items that we consume and are exposed too?

What we can do is to try and be more informed and be more pro-active in the actions that we take which involves food.

So let's focus on my two points.

1. Processing to Produce and Create Foods.

2. Processing Out the bodies Normal Management of and Processing of Foods.

And let's deal with the first one.

Processing to Produce and Create Foods.

We have a lot more people on the planet than we had 200 years ago.

During the last 200 years many things have changed.

- New food production practices have been introduced and old ones phased out.
- A faster and easier to service global food market has developed.
- The preservation of foods through the introduction of naturally derived and man-made chemicals has dramatically increased.
- Out of season produce is readily available.
- Preserved, Tinned, bottled, vacuum packed, eradiated, disguised and counterfeit food stuffs have increased and become Normal.
- There has been the development of new classes of Foods that are labelled as "Healthy".
- As Weight problems have grown, so has the number and types of products produced by the Food Industry to deal with this problem.
- Product labelling systems have increased and so has the confusion on the part of the consumer.

In amongst all of this is the reality that:

People need to be fed.

And to keep them healthy, they need nourishing and nutritious foods at an affordable price.

This simple process creates Global Dynamics and Tensions which involves Governments, Businesses, Speculators, Banks, Financial Institutions, Food Producers, Food Processors and Major Supermarkets.

Because of the supply chain, the manufacturing base and the Consumption base; we are all part of this process one way or another and we are all effected by it one way or another.

At the Grass Roots Level we Effect this process through our Consumption, Purchasing and Use.

Most of us think we are Passive Consumers and that we cannot influence things long term. But the truth is:

Stores don't stock items for long that do not sell!

Ultimately the Global Food and Produce Markets are about suppliers needing to find Customers for their goods.

In this search they will look for different ways to replace expensive ingredients with cheaper ingredients.

Formulas for Foods and Produce will be changed, improved and Adulterated.

New chemicals, additives, mixtures, recipes and ingredients will be used.

And they will search out new markets and new applications for the Food and Food related items that they have to sell.

Much of this will be done on the basis of Trust and the Belief that our Governments; and the many different organisations involved in the production and distribution of foods; have our best interest at the heart of what they do.

> In reality some will and some won't.

I think the global problems that we are experiencing with increasing Obesity are partly as a result of Governments, and the Institutions of Governments, failing to understand what they are dealing with in the global food industries.

And if they do understand; they are incapable of coming up with an alternative.

It is also a failure on their part to sufficiently protect their populations; that it is their duty to protect.

There are many current practices; such as pumping water and additives into food, which should be curtailed and stopped.

Why should people be paying for water which has been forced into meat and what is the effect long term upon the meat and those who consume that meat?

> This is the background which takes me on to my next point and the point that is of most relevance to those with weight problems.

Processing Out; the bodies Normal Management of and Processing of Foods.

I think that hidden within some of the food manufacturing and production that occurs:

We have Consequential Processes which adversely affects the body.

In effect; what these processes of manufacturing and production are doing is:

Removing and By-Passing many of the Normal Inhibitors to Excess Weight Gain which Nature has given us.

And when you do this; you get Unintended Consequences!

We know about the increase in Weight Problems but what about all the other problems that are increasing in numbers; Like Diabetes?

When we By-Pass and Remove the bodies natural inhibitors, we can begin to change the speed at which things happen, and we can begin to change the scale at which things can happen.

Just like I mentioned before: We can change how the body manages and processes food; from one way to another way.

When we do this we change it from one Normal State to a different Normal State. We move it from being in the Green Zone to being in the Amber or Red Zones.

So what are the types of processes which are causing these Consequential Effects on people?

If someone gave you 2 lb's (1 kilo) of sugar in a bag and told you to eat that over the next 7 days: Would you do so?

If someone gave you 5 apples a day and told you that you have to eat them all; because tomorrow and every other day after that, you will have 5 more pieces of fruit to eat: would you do so?

If someone gave you 2 pints (l litre) of vegetable oil and told you to drink that over the following couple of weeks: Would you do so?

If someone gave you 2 lb's (1 kilo) of hard white, neutral fat and told you to eat that over the coming couple of weeks: Would you do so?

If someone gave you 2 lb's (1 kilo) of different fillers and bulking agents and told you to eat that over the next couple of weeks: Would you do so?

For most people the answers would be NO!

The Food Industry has become better at the use of Flavourings and Colourings. And as a result they can make more Foods appear to be better than they are or to be something that they are not.

> What they have been able to do with foods, through the manufacturing process; is to present foods to you in new ways; so that you are unaware of what you are actually consuming within those foods.

> Even when they label the ingredients we are still not informed because they can use lots of different names for a single ingredient.

Let's take something simple and see how this is being treated.

Let's take: Fruit.

Most of us would agree that Fruit is a healthy food and that consuming fruit must be a healthy activity.

By the normal way of things we consume fruit as a whole item. We eat an apple, a pear or a banana.

Because of our physiology there are Natural Limits on our ability to consume and digest fruit quickly.

So if I was to give you five items of fruit a day (apple, pears, bananas) and I was to ask you to eat them while you ate your normal meals; would you be able to do so?

For most people the answer would be No.

Our physiology gets in the way and you would get put off by the time and effort required for eating the fruit.

However; if I said to you that I was going to turn the fruit into a healthy fruit drink, which would give you your nutrients and vitamins for the day:

> Would you then be able to consume five items of fruit turned into a tasty healthy drink that was good for you?

For most people the answer would be yes! And to make it even better I have been able to use the phrase: A healthy tasty drink that will be good for you.

And this process of consuming fruit in this way would be By-Passing your Natural physiological processes and the limits this imposes.

Because by this process you can simply consume more fruit, faster, more broken down, with faster and easier access to the sugars in the fruit.

Of course you may not like fruit. But when it is converted into a tasty healthy drink; you can be convinced that it is good for you and drink it.

And now that we have broken the fruit down into a drink; we can add flavourings and other ingredients to the fruit drink which was harder to do when it was whole. For example; more sugars and flavour enhancers can be added.

The point I am making is that if you have to sit down and physically eat five items of fruit a day; this has an effect upon your digestive system and it takes time and effort.

You can't access the sugars until you have physically digested the fruit; and this would take time; and the process of accessing the sugars would be slowed down.

You would also have had to use Energy in consuming and processing the foods; which has now been reduced.

So when we put the fruit into a drink and tell someone that it is healthy: What we have actually done is:

Your body no longer needs to process the solid fruit to get to the sugars. So it's faster.

You no longer have to process the roughage in the same way through your digestive system. So you lose that benefit and your body isn't doing that work.

You no longer have to chew through five items of fruit; so that inhibition to consumption and over consumption has been removed.

So the processed fruit has Removed and By-Passed many of the Normal Inhibitors to Excess Weight Gain, that Nature has given us for eating fruit.

You see not many people would naturally sit down with any real frequency and consume large quantities of fruit along with other foods.

But put them into a drink and you can begin to do this easily and regularly!

And this is the type of thing which has been done to many items of Food.

Things have been added to them which you would not normally consume in that way, in that quantity, in that frequency or in that format.

We have also had things added to foods that you would never, ever want to eat.

And the more that our food is adulterated in this way; the more normal it becomes for us to eat and consume Foods which are adulterated.

Over time our New Normal becomes the Consumption of adulterated Foods, because we now have developed a taste for them; and our bodies have become used to processing them.

And in our Life Profiles we have written new chapters which include eating and developing a taste, habits and behaviours for adulterated and processed Foods.

So now you can begin to see how this all fits together!

> In many instances; if you knew and saw what went into the production of many popular foods; you would want to know more and you would not want to consume many of the items that you found out more about.
>
> And in a world where we are supposed to have greater access to Information; we are actually becoming more ignorant and uninformed about the Foods that we are consuming.

I think that to begin to effectively deal with the issues created by long term weight problems. That you need to take an approach that is not necessarily that of everyone else.

In reality you have to take a stand for you!

Normal thinking in so many areas of life is around:

> What do we need to do to alleviate the problem?
>
> It is Not:
>
> How do we alleviate the problem AND stop it from happening again?

If you wait and rely upon the various Governments, Institutions and those who control the Global Food and Produce markets to make you healthy. Well you are going to be waiting for quite some time!

So let me tell you what I personally do with foods.

I am one of those people who reads the labels on many of the items that I purchase.

In my view: The food industry doesn't actually want us to be informed enough; so that we can EASILY discriminate between the foods that we purchase and consume.

In order to be able to understand the different names and numbers which are applied to many of the ingredients which are in much of the food; I would have to do a lot of research, and I find this difficult. I also don't really want to have to do it.

So this is how I personally handle things.

For a few items I accept that this thing has ingredients in it, that I am being told about. But I am being told about them in such a way that I really don't know and understand what is in them.

Then I decide if I actually want it under those terms at that time.

Sometimes I buy and other times I don't. If the list of ingredients for the product is too long I will often put it back on the shelve and not buy it.

This would be things like sweets, cakes and sauces; such as pasta sauce.

I don't buy a lot of this type of thing or consume these items on a daily or regular basis. So my consumption of these types of items is low.

> In the second part of this book I will show you how to use The Dieters Scale to manage your food better.

With a lot of food items that I buy I try to get them as near to the natural state that they were created in as I can.

This would be things like fruit and vegetables, flour, sugar, breakfast cereals, lard, butter, milk, etc.

I have found that I do need to check the labels on some of these items because it is surprising what can be added without you realising it.

For example fruit can be coated in something to help preserve it and make it look better. Ingredients in breakfast cereals can be covered in other things.

I make a lot of what I eat, so I make my own bread, cakes, fruit pies, quiches, etc.

By doing this I find that I use a lot less sugar, salt and yeast. And I eliminate all the ingredients that have to be put into the foods by the manufacturers and processors because of legislation; to preserve the items for sale; and to make them taste and look better.

I also find that the food I make myself is normally better tasting, more satisfying; and it last longer most of the time. Bread and Pizza's for example.

I do still buy the occasional shop made donut or home-made cake.

I am not a fan of the over consumption of soft drinks and fizzy drinks and so I don't have these very often; in fact rarely. I am also not a fan of the performance drinks for athletes (a waste of time for most people). I am also not a fan of these so called high energy drinks that contain caffeine and sugars (which may be all of them) as they don't seem to take account of the potential long term effects of the over consumption of high amounts of caffeine.

I usually prefer to drink water, tea, coffee or pure orange juice. No I don't like caffeine free tea or coffee.

I personally do not drink much alcohol and I will have a drink of alcohol every now and again.

Personally I do not eat Beef. This is a decision that I made over 20-years ago and I have stuck with it. I do eat other meats.

I will try to avoid processed meats but I will have them occasionally. This will be things like sausages but I try to go for ones that my butcher makes in the shop rather than mass market ones.

I don't eat much in the way of prepared sliced meats as more other ingredients are being added to them and I can't see the point of adding them.

I like cheeses and I am happy to eat them but I try to avoid any where things like colouring have been added. Though this is getting more difficult and some colourings are acceptable.

I like different types of bread and I love home-made pizza's (the base has to be home-made). I make most of the bread that I eat.

I like fish and I probably eat more fish than meat.

I try to avoid most foods where colourings have been added to improve the appearance of the food; such as can happen with cheese and fish.

I avoid too much in the way of sauces and coatings which have been added to foods. I prefer to taste the food and not the sauces. Put the sauce on the side.

I do eat out. I do have a Take-Away meal from time to time. And I generally prefer simple but well cooked food.

So my diet is not too restrictive and I eat a broad range of foods.

If I am not happy with something about a food or a retailer; then I will change my choice and the retailer.

I try to have a rule that I follow: If I wouldn't buy and eat that food at home; why am I going to do so outside.

I don't have a weight problem but I know that when I eat certain foods too often, that I can begin to gain weight. When I do begin to gain weight, I then cut these foods out or reduce them in my diet until my weight gets back to the range that I am happy with.

All of this is part of my Lifestyle Management.

> I take an active part in the selection of the foods that I consume.
>
> I take responsibility when I consume something that may not be great but that I feel like eating at that time.
>
> If I see that I am gaining weight, then I take an active part in dealing with that problem. I take the step of altering my diet and my lifestyle.

We can't be 100% in control of all the Foods that we consume. But we can be in control of enough of it to make a long term difference to the quality of our lives and our health.

Understanding this is good **Hi**.

So what do I want you to take away from this chapter?

Ask yourself the question:

> Is any part of your weight problem being caused by behaviour or the consumption of foods which assist in:
>
> The By-Passing of the Normal Inhibitors to Excess Weight Gain that Nature has given us?

If you are; then you may experience Unintended Consequences.

We know about Weight Problems but what about all the other problems that are increasing in numbers; Like Diabetes?

> When we By-Pass and Remove the bodies natural inhibitors, we can begin to change the speed at which things happen and we can begin to change the scale at which things can happen.

Type 2 Diabetes can often be brought under control and resolved by good dietary practices, exercise and better Lifestyle Management. As can a weight problem!

Note
Many of the new fast fixes such as pills that help you to stop absorbing all the fat from the foods that you eat are, it would seem, simply attempting to put back some of the natural inhibitors that food processing has removed. This is just more Symptom Solutioning and it doesn't fix the problem.

Chapter 22

The Role Of Exercise In Your Weight Problem

Like many other things; Exercise has also been presented as a Quick Fix solution to weight problems.

How often have you heard things like:

- Burn that excess fat off through doing...

- Increase your metabolic rate and target those fat cells.

I can see the attraction of this approach to people who want to lose weight and look better quickly.

However there is a flaw with this approach.

It introduces the belief that you can somehow quickly affect your weight by doing exercise; and that this can burn off fat quickly and easily.

The reality of how the body works suggest that this is not going to happen the way that you may be being sold it.

According to my current understanding of Human Physiology these attempts at targeting the "Unwanted" and "Overweight Fat" and the "Bloated Fat Cells" through exercise are unproven **and unlikely**.

And the simple truth is; that if all this stuff was that simple and easy, then it would be really simple for the people who market these things to prove it; again and again.

> It would be as simple as 10 overweight people in at one end of the process and 8 slim people out at the other!
>
> And if it was that simple and easy then would we really have so many overweight people?
>
> Because I am sure that many of them would use this simple easy way if it was real.

In reality it takes time and concentrated effort for the physical accumulation of muscle and for the reduction in bloated fat cells. This is not a quick or easy process.

I am an advocate of keeping fit and being healthy without going to extremes.

I know and understand the benefits of working out and keeping fit, as I have done so all of my life.

There are obvious benefits to keeping fit and there are less obvious benefits.

Let's see how these benefits may Effect and Affect us; and benefit someone with a weight problem.

First let's clarify why I am using Effect and Affect.

> **Effect** is a Result or Consequence. Something which we bring about, accomplish, cause to exist or occur.
>
> Normally we need to Do something or Not Do something for this to happen.
>
> So doing exercise allows us to create a Result or produce a Consequence.
>
> For example; getting and maintaining a level of fitness would be an Effect as a result of doing more physical things with our body.
>
> **Affect** is a Feeling or Emotion; something which we can experience within our mind and our body as a consequence or result of other actions. For example; we accomplish something and we feel good about it.
>
> So when we get fitter than we are, we can experience the Affect of Feeling Better about ourselves. This then produces the Affect of Feeling more confident and positive.

Basically: What all this means is that Actions can lead to Feelings and Emotions; and Feelings and Emotions can lead to Actions.

So this process is a fundamental part of what makes us tick and it gives us a Formula to use that can help us!

> Emotions & Feelings can produce Actions.
>
> Actions can produce Emotions & Feelings.

Understanding this is good **Hi**.

I think that most people tend to think of exercise as:

> "Getting or Keeping Fit"

The reality is that Getting and Keeping Fit is just one purpose for exercise; there are others. These include the following.

> The mental discipline that it helps to create can be very beneficial to those with weight problems.
>
> The good feelings that you experience when you have completed a workout make it worthwhile.
>
> The satisfaction you feel when you have worked out; even though you may not really have felt like doing it when you started the workout; is positive.
>
> It can be very useful when you are stressed as it helps to release tension and use up the different hormones and things that are released by the body, as a result of stress and tension.
>
> Keeping fit when you are stressed helps to avoid and reduce stress related problems.
>
> And it can help to better manage longer terms problems that can effect our physiology; such as tension and the over release of hormones such as Adrenalin.

So in reality there are Mental, Physical and Emotional benefits to be had from appropriate exercise. Let's call these "Your Inner World Benefits".

And there are Lifestyle Benefits to be had from appropriate exercise. Let's call these "Your Outer World Benefits".

Regardless of your current views on exercise:

> Some form of physical activity which challenges your body in appropriate ways is essential for physical, mental and emotional health.

So why should someone with a Weight Problem; have any interest in this at all?

- After all: Exercise is just so much hot air, sweat, hard work, inconvenience, etc.

Maybe so: But let's take another look at the Formula that I said can help us to Influence and Change things.

- Emotions & Feelings can produce Actions.
- Actions can produce Emotions & Feelings.

If you can; now relate this to your Habits with Food?

- Do you ever respond differently to food as a result of how you feel?

- Do you ever feel better as a result of preparing, getting or eating food?

The answer should be Yes; of course you do!

In all the Actions and Re-Actions that we have to different things; the body is involved one way or another.

So Nature has given us all this wonderful free gift of a body.

It has given us the Free Will to use it as we want.

The question that you face is:

How do you want to use yours today?

Do you want to use it in a Pro-Active way and Positively Influence your life?

Do you want to use it in a Re-Active way and be influenced and controlled by whatever you come into contact with?

Either way your body is going to be involved; and as you live in your body, you will also be involved.

- Being Pro-Active gives you More Opportunity to Influence things in a Positive and Beneficial way. You have more control.

- Being Re-Active gives you Less Opportunity to Influence things in a Positive and Beneficial way. You have less control.

If you want More Opportunity to have the Life that you really want; then you are More Likely to Achieve this by Being Pro-Active.

And this is the simple prize that exists behind the Door of Opportunity called Exercise:

> Exercise lets you begin to be Pro-Active in a simple and easy way that is personal to you.
>
> As a result of the exercise, you begin to influence your emotions and feelings.
>
> And when you are someone with a weight problem; this is important.
>
> Understanding this is good Hi.

So what do people do wrong with exercise that screws things up?

The Wrong Timing!

Ok; so you have gone on a diet. And to burn that fat off quicker you have signed up at the local gym.

You're ticking all the boxes on the Go On A Diet and Get Fit campaign.

And within a short period of time; you're struggling.

Earlier in this book I talked about the stress of changing too many things in your life at the same time.

For many people; going on a diet and beginning a Get Fit campaign is too much.

All the stuff you are doing is too new. You haven't adjusted. Your body hasn't adjusted and you don't know how to handle it.

So what do I suggest to people when it comes to exercise?

Simple:

> You don't have to wait until you are on a diet to begin exercising.

Why not begin "Practicing" doing a little bit of exercise before you actually plan to go on a diet or undertake an exercise programme?

> Practice, Practice, Practice; and when you are ready: Do it!

Take a few weeks, or better still take a few months, and begin a gradual process of getting and maintaining Being and Feeling fitter.

Too Much, Too Soon!

Getting and Being Fitter does not mean that I want to become an athlete.

And If I play golf, it doesn't mean that I want to become a professional golfer.

It just means that I want to try and enjoy these activities, get some fun out of them, enjoy a degree of challenge and get the benefits of exercise from them.

And yet so many people who go on a diet and exercise programme; throw themselves into the process to such a degree that they cannot sustain it. They do too much, too soon!

On my Life Improvement Programmes I do not encourage people to begin exercising.

In fact I often discourage it.

The reason why I do this is that the person has enough to deal with at that time, without adding anything unnecessary; at that time.

You see what so many don't understand about Weight Control and making your body healthier is:
> That in all of this "Timing" is important.

There will be a time when exercise is appropriate and it can Add To and Compliment what we are doing.

However; there are times when it is Inappropriate and it can Detract From and Complicate what we are doing.

I find that as we move through the process of the Life Improvement Programme; that there is a point at which exercise and addressing the issue of exercise becomes appropriate.

And what I always suggest to someone as a way to begin getting fitter; is walking; just plain old simple walking.

Walking is often the easiest form of exercise for someone to do.

They can go as slow as they like, as long as they keep going.

It is easy to gradually increase the pace at which you walk and to vary the pace at which you walk.

It is easy to increase the distance that you walk and you have lots of choice about where and when you walk.

Walking can also be easily introduced into your lifestyle.

Try using the stairs rather than the lift. Try walking to the shops for small items rather than using the car. Try parking at the other end of the car park rather than close to the store.

Walking is a simple process that can produce great results that you cannot see but which you benefit from.

The Wrong Type!

I have exercised and chosen to keep fit and active for most of my life.

During this time I have tried many different activities. Some were very strenuous and some were very placid.

I now have a selection of activities which I do regularly.

I swim, I go for walks, I exercise in my gym at home where I cycle and run on the equipment that I have. I also like Skiing, ice skating and other activities.

So why do I cycle and run on equipment at home rather than go outside?

Simple: I have an injury to my knee which is permanent. If I run and cycle on the roads, the impact causes problems with the injury. If I do this at home I get the exercise, which benefits me, but without the injury problems.

Another reason why I work out at home is convenience. I don't have to travel to a gym, so I save myself all that time and inconvenience.

I can also work out at a time that suits me. It's more convenient and I can fit it into my lifestyle without much difficulty.

What we need to understand and accept is that as we move through life our bodies change. They become less subtle, less resilient and we pick up injuries and restrictions due to living life.

So it stands to reason that with all the different types of exercise that are available for us to do; that some Will Suit Us and Be Appropriate and some Will Not Suit Us and Be Inappropriate.

Also our exercise needs will change as the weight problem changes.

What we really need to do is to apply The Dieters Scale to the exercises that we are considering doing, so that we can get a proper measurement of them and make sure that we can do them and benefit from them.

In The Dieters Scale; we have the Green, Amber and Red Zones.

We know that the Green Zone is the easiest and most straightforward of all the Zones.

For the purpose of putting exercise in The Dieters Scale we will use the following guidelines.

- Green Zone would be easy to moderate exercise.
- Amber Zone would be moderate to difficult exercise.
- Red Zone would be difficult to impossible exercise.

Now The Dieters Scale is personal for you and it is not intended to be used by your local gym.

They would see things in a different way to you and it is you that we are interested in and not your local gym.

So how would we use this?

Let's use walking as a way to understand the process of using The Dieters Scale for Exercise.

Let's begin with someone who has a weight problem and they are going on a diet.

They want to get fit and we want to see whether they will be able to sustain the exercises that they are planning to do. And we will assume that when they plan to begin exercising that they are not fit at all.

Green Zone Exercise's

So if someone was to begin exercising using the Green Zone level, what would that look like?

Any form of walking, slow or moderate pace, for up to 1 hour; or 3 miles in distance.

This would be the target that you would aim to be able to maintain your walking at.

You would look to achieve this over a period of say 1-2 months.

This is over and above any walking that you would normally do in your day-to-day life.

You would be Doing this twice a week, with a gap of 2-3 days between each walk and this would become part of your lifestyle.

This level would begin to get you fit, if you were unfit to begin with.

Amber Zone Exercise's

So if someone was to begin exercising using the Amber Zone level, what would that look like?

Any form of walking, from moderate to fast pace, for up to 2.5 hours; or 5-6 miles in distance.

This is over and above any walking that you would normally do in your day-to-day life.

Doing this two or three times a week with 1 – 3 days between each walk.

This level would get you fit and keep you fit; but you would struggle to do it and keep it going if you were not fit to begin with.

You would be Doing this 2-3 times a week and this would become part of your lifestyle.

So we can see that if you hadn't gone through the Green Zone process of Getting Fit to begin with. And you tried to do this as your fitness programme; that you would probably struggle and fail.

> I would NOT suggest that you try this level until you could easily do the Green Zone Level and had done that for several months.

Now let's look at the Red Zone level.

Red Zone Exercise's

If someone was to begin exercising using the Red Zone level, what would that look like?

Any form of walking, moderate to fast pace, for up to 4 hours; covering 10 miles or more in distance.

This is over and above any walking that you would normally do in your day-to-day life.

Doing this 4-5 times a week or more; and this would become part of your lifestyle.

This level would get you fit and keep you fit but you would struggle to do it and keep it going if you were Amber Level fit to begin with.

So we can see that if you were at the Green Zone Level of fitness to begin with; then you would almost certainly fail if you did a Red Zone level fitness programme.

Let's look at what is going on with the process of getting fit in the different Zones of The Dieters Scale.

As you go up the Dieters Scale, from the Green Zone to the Amber and Red Zones, the level of commitment required to achieve the results increases.

The time required to achieve the results increases.

The energy and level of fitness required to produce the results increases.

Your body has to have the ability to recover from the exercise quickly.

Your muscles need to be use to the exercise that they are undertaking to do this.

The amount of your life that is "Occupied" by the activities required to achieve the results increases.

So if we have someone who would struggle to exercise in the Green Zone when they begin a diet and exercise programme; and we put them into the Amber or Red Zone; what outcome would we expect?

- They would struggle.
- Increasing stress.
- Very uncomfortable.
- Injury.
- Hungry.
- Self conscious.
- Failure!

And often the more that the person needs the benefits of exercise, the less able they are to engage with exercise that falls outside of the Green Zone level.

Even when we take our Unfit person and we apply the Green Zone level of exercise to them; they can experience everything in the list above.

The big difference is that just about everyone can achieve the Green Zone level of fitness with a little effort.

Some degree of discomfort is just part of the process that people go through when they are unfit and they want to get fitter.

So; what often happens in the real world?

People who would be appropriate for the Green Zone level, go and try and do the Amber and Red Zone exercise level; with the inevitable result:

> They fail!

And this keeps the dieting cycle going and the weight problem going.

> What this book and my Life Improvement Programmes are about; is breaking and changing the cycle of events, actions, re-actions and outcomes.
>
> By doing this we help the person live a better life and become a more successful person.
>
> Every person has the ability within themselves to achieve this; what they usually need help with is finding, applying and managing that ability.
>
> This is good **Hi**.

Let's look at another myth.

I'm Not Sweating!

One of the Myths of exercise is that you need to sweat. And the more that you sweat; the better the exercise is for you.

In reality; we all need to challenge our bodies and this means working them harder.

If we work our bodies hard enough then we sweat.

As well as sweating when we exercise, we also sweat for other reasons.

- We are hot and we need to cool down.
- We are stressed, nervous, etc.

If you are very unfit, then you may sweat whenever you do anything physical.

What you need to understand about sweating is this:

> Sweating does not mean that you are exercising correctly or sufficiently.

When I work out I sweat. This is because I am doing a lot of hard work over a short time. I need to sweat to keep my body from getting too hot.

If I go out walking, then for most of the walk I am not sweating. This is because I am exercising but not getting too hot.

If I start walking faster or walking up hills then I am likely to sweat.

So if I do not walk too fast or up hills, then I can have a long walk without sweating.

So I can have what is called a Low Impact Workout.

Low impact workouts give you the benefits of exercise in a low key way.

This level of exercise would be in the Green Zone; and this is something that just about everyone can do.

Walking can provide a good low impact workout and this is why I will suggest walking as an exercise.

Don't worry if you are not sweating when you exercise; especially in the beginning. Sweating isn't the objective; getting a bit fitter is.

Sooner or later you will move to a position where you will sweat because you are getting fitter; and you can challenge your body in a more profitable way.

If you have exercised over a long time (months or years) and you don't sweat when you exercise. Then you may be failing to understand what exercise is; or you may need to increase or vary what you do.

> Sweating isn't good or bad; it is just an indicator.

So what do I want you to take away from this chapter?

Physical activity is a requirement for a healthy body, a healthy mind and a healthy lifestyle.

However: The level of physical activity, the type of physical activity and the longevity of physical activity varies from person to person and situation to situation.

It also varies according to what your long term goals are for undertaking the exercise in the first place:

- Are you getting and keeping fit?
- Are you training to be an athlete?

Very few people will get into difficulty with exercise, if they are exercising within the Green Zone level on The Dieters Scale.

The Green Zone level will get you fit and allows you to maintain a fitness level without too much impact on your lifestyle.

This is good **Hi**.

You have to get the Timing right for when you introduce exercise or increase exercise.

If the timing is wrong it just puts someone under too much pressure that can then impact other things.

This is good **Hi**.

> Remember: Exercise is not a good way of losing weight!

My examples of walking are not recommendations; they are to illustrate a concept.

I would not have any problems with recommending the Green Zone level of exercise to any of my friends or family who were looking to get fit. In fact I do.

Exercise, especially before meals, can affect the way that our bodies manage and process the foods that we eat.

We are only just beginning to understand these effects but there are positive results showing that the body handles the food that you consume in a better way after exercise; and it does not have to be prolonged hard exercise.

> *As a rule of thumb; we should always avoid exercising too soon after we have eaten; and eating too soon after we exercise.*

Chapter 23

The Role Of "Influencing Factors" In Your Problem

In a previous chapter I looked at the role of relationships in your problem; and I talked about the "Tips of the Icebergs" of the different issues that can exist around a weight problem.

What I want to do now is move this closer to you, and look at the people and other things which you come into contact with; and see how they may be Influencing you and your weight problem.

A way to think of this is that some of these may be the lower parts of the icebergs.

Where we look at people, I am not getting into any form of judgement of the people or how they live their lives.

I just want you to begin to take a look at the different relationships that you have, in a way that can help you to put your efforts into the ones that help you, rather than the ones that hurt you.

In reality; the different types of relationships that we have, whether they are good, bad or indifferent; are able to influence us in positive and negative ways. They can influence how we feel, how we behave; and how we look at ourselves.

> Therefore; they are Influencing Factor that can shape our lives.

And that is what we are interested in – Influencing Factors that can shape our lives; whether we are aware of them or not.

Many people never actually look at the relationships that they have with their family, friends and work associates in this way. Often they think that they shouldn't but really they should.

Another very important Influencing Factor to consider is The Media; in the form of television, radio, printed items like magazines and the Internet. These provide material that you are exposed to and which can influence you in many different ways; and sometimes in ways that you tend not to notice.

Because people tend not to look at these Influencing Factors with a critical eye; they fail to see when things are going wrong or see that there are issues which need to be addressed.

This happens with both Positive and Negative influencing factors.

So if we never discriminate between Positive Influencing Factors which help us and make our lives better. And Negative Influencing Factors which can harm us and make our lives worse.

Then we end up with a range of Influencing Factors which we Respond Too, and over which, we are exercising little or no real Positive Control.

So it's no wonder that things can get messy!

Now I don't know how many people you know and what sort of relationships you have with them. So I am going to lay this out in a general way and you can adjust this for your own personal circumstances.

There are a number of things to think about with Influencing Factors; including:

- How many of them there are.
- Whether they are Positive or Negative.
- For how much of our time are we exposed to them.
- How impactful are they on us.
- How dependent are we upon them.
- Do we need to end that relationship/exposure.
- Do we want to keep that relationship and change something about it.
- Are there Passive Influencing Factors which are affecting us that we are not noticing.
- Do we need to find new ones.

When we consider the people that we spend time with and are influenced by; there is a simple question that we want to know:

How close are they to you?

Generally the closer the person is to you; the more difficult it can be to do something about the relationship, if there are problems with it. The following graphic shows the people who are closest to you as being in the centre of your Circle of Influence.

How Close are they to you?

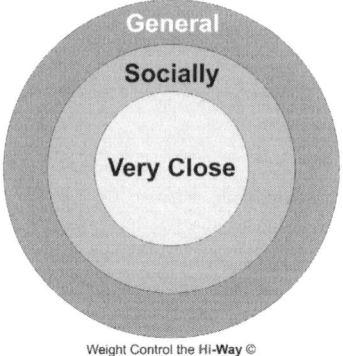

Weight Control the Hi-**Way** ©
The Human Intelligence (HI) Common Platform

Then the next layer shows those who you are not very close too; but who form part of your Social Network and who can influence you socially or indirectly.

This may be a friend, work associate, family member or just someone you occasionally run into.

The outside layer shows the rest of the contacts that you will have that can influence you. This layer includes general things like Television, Internet, Films and Games.

Now it may be that you don't have many very close people and that your life is very limited. It may be that you are spending most of your time watching the TV.

If so; then these become your closest influencing factors.

Where this is the case; the next thing would be to look at the types of programmes you are watching, the frequency and the amount of time that you spend watching them.

This helps us to understand the types of influences that watching TV brings into your life. Are they Positive; is it full of arguments and trauma; is it escapism, etc.

So it doesn't matter whether you have a very busy life with lots of people in your life or whether you have a very empty life with no people; but plenty of distractions.

What matters here is what you actually have and not what you want.

As you begin to allocate people and activities to the spaces that they occupy in Your Circles of Influence; you can also begin to consider whether they are a largely Positive or a largely Negative Influence.

> What you need to understand about Influencing Factors is that you don't need to be spending all your time or large amounts of time with them; for them to be having a big impact on you.
>
> Also the ones who are having the Biggest Impact on you; do not have to be the closest to you.
>
> Is there anyone or any activity that you feel affects your weight problem in a Positive or a Negative way?

The other reality with Influencing factors is that Legacy Issues can also be included. Legacy issues are those events which I mentioned earlier that happened in the past but which continue to ripple through your life and still affect you today.

In many instances people are still being heavily influenced by things from the past which remain at the centre of their Circle of Influence or close to it.

These things can also be dealt with and managed so as to reduce and alter the impact that they are having on someone's life. However; before it can begin to be changed you do need to be aware of it.

So what do I want you to take away from this chapter?

We all have a Circle of Influence which spreads out from ourselves.

Within that Circle of Influence there will be Influencing Factors. And there will be some Influencing Factors that we will control and some that we won't control.

These Influencing Factors can be people, their behaviour, their attitudes, their opinions, the way that they Do things and the Things that they want.

Other Influencing Factors can be the Media and other social pressures.

We can often be Influenced in a Positive or Negative way without realising that we are being so influenced.

Understanding this is good **Hi**.

We all have relationships which are Positive and relationships which are Negative.

Very few relationships are wholly Positive (Beneficial) or wholly Negative (Detrimental). Most relationships are made up of both of these.

However; most relationships will have an overall pattern to them which is such that; when we look at them honestly, will put them into the Positive or Negative Relationship categories.

As we become more aware of our Circle of Influence and our Influencing Factors, we can begin to Evaluate them and Move them in Directions which are More Beneficial for us.

Understanding this is good **Hi**.

Chapter 24

Confusing Problems

There are lots and lots of human related problems. The variations and variety of them is staggering.

So it should come as no surprise that Weight Problems also have lots of variations and varieties.

To help us understand the range and types of Weight Problem we can use the Spectrum of Weight Problems.

When we look at the Spectrum of Weight Problems virtually all of the Weight Problems which exist can be placed on the Spectrum.

However; from time to time we can come across a Weight Problem which is Confusing and difficult to place. It doesn't quite seem to fit neatly anywhere.

These confusing problems seem to defy easy labelling. So let's call these:

> Irregular or Episodic Problems.

What can be confusing about Irregular or Episodic Problems is that they may occur for a short period of time, occur every few months or even occur every few years. Sometimes there is a pattern; and sometimes their isn't.

Episodic Problems can also seem to "Just Appear" with no apparent justification.

The Impact of these problems can be very Intense and High; but may only lasts for a short period of time.

> We can also find that someone may have a weight problem but they normally manage it to some degree. They every now and again, for some unexplained reason, they have an escalation of their problem for a period of time and then they go back to how they were.
>
> If you ask them what caused them to increase their consumption or to change it; they often can't seem to give you an answer.

Episodic Problems can also be Covered Up quite easily and they can build up a history that becomes "The Elephant in the Room".

The problem becomes something that people are aware of; but because no-one is able to deal with the Problem effectively; it is allowed to Just Exist; often without being talked about or referred too.

What can happen with this dynamic is that the size of the Elephant can then begin to vary. Sometimes it gets bigger and other times it gets smaller.

Another thing that can happen is that this type of problem can continue for many years, and even decades, without being properly addressed.

When this happens, it can become "Normalised" as being a part of the Lifestyle of the person and of the family as well. It becomes part of the wallpaper of all of their lives.

It can then move to a point where it is considered to be a Normal Part of the Person and Who They Are.

As a result it can then move to the position of:

>It's just something I have to live with!

And once it reaches here, it can then become Disassociated from the lives and the other problems that may affect the person and their family.

So how do we begin to understand these problems so that we can begin to work with them?

Let's keep it simple!

Does the problem have a food component?

Is someone over eating, under eating or switching their diet?

What's the frequency?

What's the impact on their lifestyle?

And we can go on asking simple questions and building a picture of the problem and the impact of the problem. Often this will never have been done before.

Usually a good place to begin understanding and working with these types of problems is to start with the Impact on the person's Lifestyle; and the Lifestyle of others that they come into contact with; or are involved with.

Other techniques and tools can then help us to understand the problem in depth.

What can make these problems difficult is that Irregular or Episodic Problems may occur prior to, at the time of, or subsequent to annual events or anniversaries of events. These can Trigger the Reaction that produces the behaviour.

Also there can be a Disconnection in the persons mind between the Problem and the Casual Factors which leads to the Materialisation of the Problem itself. The actual Cause and Effect become disconnected from each other!

This type of problem is one that the Dieters Scale and the Human Intelligence (Hi) Common Platform helps us to understand, manage and resolve.

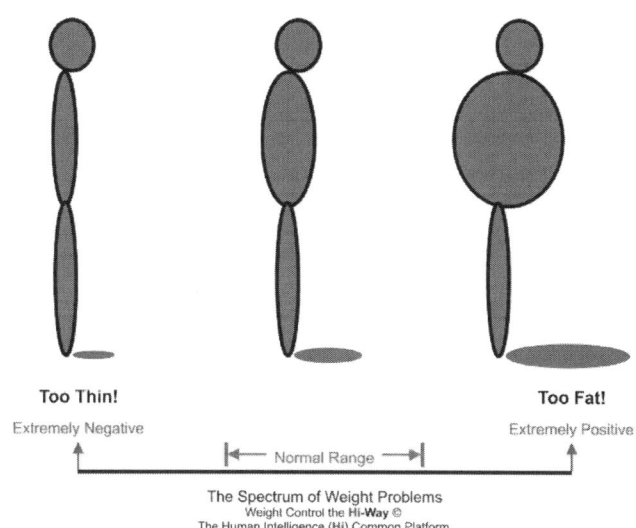

The Spectrum of Weight Problems
Weight Control the Hi-Way ©
The Human Intelligence (Hi) Common Platform

So what do I want you to take away from this chapter?

Irregular or Episodic problems can leave the people who have them, feeling as if they are isolated and not in control.

In reality Irregular or Episodic problems are just problems with an Episodic Structure; and Episodic Structures can be understood and worked with; just like any other problem can be. These will form a part of the spider's web and the icebergs that the person has.

Periodic Problems will fit into The Dieters Scale just like any other weight problem will.

What is extremely unlikely is that the Episodic Problem can be deal with without dealing with other directly and indirectly related behaviours and activities.

If you are suffering from an Episodic Problem there are people out there who can help. My advice would be to avoid the Quick Fixes which you will no doubt be offered.

Chapter 25

Body Dysmorphia And Social And General Dysmorphia

It is normal for people to have Distorted and Inaccurate perceptions in normal everyday life. We will all have experienced it.

When we are the person who is experiencing these distorted and inaccurate perceptions; they can be as real to us as any solid brick wall. And when we run into them, they can have the same Effect and Affect as running into a solid brick wall would have.

They can Affect us Emotionally: Causing problems with different aspects of how we perceive ourselves in different situations. And how we perceive ourselves as worthy and credible people; and they reflect upon how we perceive our place and position in the world.

They can Affect us in the Actions that we take and the behaviours that we employ with ourselves and with others.

Within the world of weight problems there is a condition called Dysmorphia.

Examples of this that are often used are that someone draws a picture of themselves; and certain parts of their bodies are either very large by comparison to the rest of their body or very small by comparison to the rest of the image they have drawn.

For example they may have an exaggerated and large head. Their hands or feet can be very large or their torso may be huge.

This process of distorting reality when it comes to our perceptions of our body is called Body Dysmorphia.

Like so many other human conditions Dysmorphia is something that has a number of different Components.

To my mind;

> Dysmorphia is a structured view of certain things that can be informed by particular insecurities, anxieties, stresses, beliefs, facts and circumstances that the person is experiencing at the time.

This real or perceived abnormality can also go along with an increased sensitivity and increased awareness of their own view of their physical form; and how others may be perceiving them. For example; a teenager in puberty; someone in their first relationship, someone having their first sexual encounter, etc.

The Dysmorphic Affect can then lead on to further problems in their attempts to manage and address their anxieties and concerns.

For example: If you are really slim but you believe that you are really fat and you go on a strict diet in order to change the mental image that you have of yourself; this can kill you.

Dysmorphia only really becomes a problem when it escalates and moves to another level. To help you understand this I am going to use a comparative example.

A comparative example would be:

> Someone with a small weight problem would be in the Green Zone on The Dieters Scale. This would be a Lower level problem.
>
> And someone with a large weight problem would be in the Red Zone on The Dieters Scale. This would be a Higher level problem.

So both have a weight problem but of different degrees.

> The person with the Green Zone weight problem would have fewer Consequences from their weight problem and would normally have fewer Associated Problems.
>
> The person with the Red Zone weight problem would have more Consequences from their weight problem and would normally have More Associated Problems.

So we are seeing and measuring the real difference between these two Zones by Scale and by the Impact on the person from the Consequences of the problem.

Now let's change this!

Imagine the person in the Green Zone believing that their weight problem was really in the Red Zone.

Imagine the person in the Red Zone believing that their weight problem is really in the Green Zone.

Because they now have Zone Dismorphia; fixing either of those weight problems is now going to be exceedingly difficult. And if their perceptions of their realities cannot be changed or shifted; then the person who has Red Zone Dismorphia will try to lose too much weight. And the person who has Green Zone Dismorphia will not do enough to lose weight.

This is because their perceptions will not permit them to undertake the necessary behaviours and actions required to fix the real problems associated with their real Zones.

And this goes against the good Hi we learnt earlier; which is:

> A diet can be thought of as a form of rehabilitation of habits. And if that rehabilitation does not go far enough, it will prove ineffective. And this tends to prove true for many people with weight control problems. The rehabilitation of their weight control does not go far enough.
>
> And to this we can now add: And the rehabilitation of habits does not go in the right direction; so it can never achieve its destination.

The truth is that I have come across many people, whose weight problems are in the Amber and Red Zones; who behave as if their weight problems are actually in the Green Zone.

In my view; Body Dismorphia can form a part of any Weight Problem that someone experiences. And when it does, it is simply a Component of the problem.

My view is that we can apply The Dieters Scale to Dysmorphia and use this to help us understand and work with it; in the same way that we would do so with any other problem component of a weight problem.

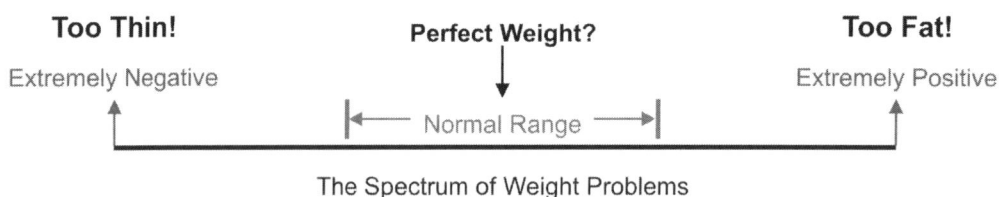

The Spectrum of Weight Problems
The Human Intelligence (Hi) Common Platform - The Dieters Scale ©

We do say that Reality is whatever we believe it to be. And sometimes that belief is accurate and at other times it is based on faulty and misleading information.

The more that I look at people and the Human Condition, the more that I am sure that Dysmorphia permeates what we do, and influences us more than we realise.

How much better would we be at understanding and dealing with situations; if we understood that it is our Perception of the Reality of those situations, and the Perception of our roles in those situations that may need some work?

> So a relevant question becomes: How often do we miss-frame, miss-understand, miss-perceive and miss-construct our Internal picture of the world in which we participate.

> When we do this not only does our Internal picture of the world become distorted; so does the way that we interact with the world; and so does our understanding of the impact of our involvement in the world.

For my own view of Dysmorphia, I think that it probably extends into all areas of human activity and behaviours.

For example:

Someone finds themselves in a situation where they are feeling vulnerable, lacking in confidence, experiencing low self-esteem and having a mental image of themselves that corresponds with the low self-esteem, low confidence and the feelings of vulnerability that they are experiencing.

> While they are experiencing this: Are they seeing a mental image of themselves doing something wrong and being embarrassed by the result?

> Are they sensitive to a blemish on their skin that they are sure that everyone must surely see?

> Are they in a situation where their lack of formal education or qualifications makes them sensitive and over aware of their surroundings and the people they are going to meet?

In a one-off situation we may accept anxiety as an answer and move on with life.

But what happens when it isn't a one-off and it happens more often?

When do we Cross the Threshold from an Acceptable Problem to an Unacceptable Problem?

So what do I want you to take away from this chapter?

Reality is Subjective. Many of the problems that we experience as people occur from that Subjective experiencing of Reality.

What we benefit from as people is learning that all of this is Normal and that we can influence, change and improve how we perceive the world and our place in it.

However; it will not necessarily be an easy thing to do!

Understanding this is good **Hi**.

Dysmorphia is something that we are still trying to understand.

Like all problems it has its own unique structures that move it one way or another way.

I am reminded of that saying:

> The Whole is greater than the Sum of its Parts.

Weight Problems can be just like that. They can produce something extra as a result of the different Components coming together and blending together.

> And like any problem; when we begin to work with the Structure and the Components which make up that problem:
>
> We can then begin to Change the Structure and Change what the structure Produces.

This then allows us to influence and change the nature of the problem.

It just takes time, effort and the Correct Application Of Actions to do so!

Understanding this is good **Hi**.

Chapter 26

Coping With Discomfort

Those of you who have a problem that falls into the Green Zone may not understand this related to dieting; but you may in relation to other problems.

Those of you who have a problem that falls into the Amber and Red Zones should have an idea of what I am talking about; and many of you will know it well.

So what is it?

When you deal with and want to change certain types of problems, you simply cannot avoid Discomfort.

By managing the different processes, you can reduce the levels of discomfort and take the edge off of it, but you cannot eliminate all of the discomfort.

To avoid the discomfort many people will do things like; seek medication, begin drinking more or have an increased impulse to eat and consume certain foods.

It is when people are seeking alternative ways of dealing with discomfort that they enter a Danger Period. This is because this is a time where one type of undesirable behaviour can be replaced by another type of undesirable behaviour.

In the drugs and alcohol field this is a time where people can: Switch Addictions.

When someone Switches Addictions it does not have to be from one substance to another; it can be that they use a behaviour to replace a substance.

For example; someone may use Exercise and throw themselves into it. Other people may choose to Cook, become more Religious, want more Intimacy and Sex, begin Cleaning more, throw themselves into family activities, and so on.

What I have seen is that this type of Replacement behaviour can appear to be doing the job; but because of how it is being used and what it is being expected to do:

> It cannot sustain itself and it crashes; and the person is back where they began or perhaps further back, and in more of a mess.

The reality is that none of us can avoid the discomfort of change; but we have the ability to manage it and understand what is happening while it occurs.

There are reasons why Change is often a difficult process to experience; even if it is Change which is wanted and desired.

A simple reason is:

> That you are going to change your Normal Unwanted behaviour to a New Wanted Behaviour; and to achieve this you are going to move from one place to another on The Dieters Scale.

So if you prepare for and accept that there are going to be times when you will have to:

> Go through The Shredder and feel uncomfortable!

Then when you do so; it becomes less difficult.

Why do I call it The Shredder?

I call it this simply because this is what it can feel like at the most difficult times.

The good news is that if you follow the right processes for dealing with the problem; that you can get through The Shredder and complete the transitions in an easier and more comfortable way.

What you also need to understand is this:

> You may hit The Shredder a number of different times and in different ways, as you encounter and deal with the different aspects and components of your individual weight problem.

> By following our 3 Steps Approach you will be able to minimise discomfort. Our approach of Preparation & Practice reduces stress and increases the chances of success. *You will be introduced to these in the next part of this book.*

So what do I want you to take away from this chapter?

Depending on where you are starting from and the degree of your problems; sooner or later, most of us will hit The Shedder!

A good way to think of it is like Turbulence being experienced by an airplane as it flies through the air.

Turbulence can make the journey unpleasant and scary but most people land safely and in one piece; if they stay in their seats and complete their journey.

Those who jump out of the plane when it gets unpleasant may avoid being bumped about; but now what?

> Understanding this is good **Hi**.

Chapter 27

Are You A Secret Eater, Boozer, In Denial...

Whenever we deal with difficult and complex problems, we always have to be aware of certain difficult realities that exist.

Many of these difficult realities relate to the behaviours that we have developed, fallen into, joined in with or are forced into adopting; but that we keep hidden.

For many people, using these hidden behaviours is what gets them through. It helps them to survive another day.

So when someone is looking at changing, improving and developing their lives in a better way; they reach a point where these hidden behaviours can begin to undermine the work that is being done to achieve the new life that they want.

In other words: We reach a point where we have to deal with parts of the spider's web that we haven't yet touched.

There are a myriad of ways that people can use problematic, complex and difficult behaviours. What I am interested in here are ones that will fall within the scope of this book.

These can be thought of as being the tips of the icebergs that I mentioned earlier.

For example; are you:

> A secret drinker.
> A secret eater.
> In denial.
> An automatic grazer of food and drinks (usually soft drinks).
> A binge eater.
> Someone who Purges.
> Someone who Fast.
> Someone who Self-harms.

These are just examples and there are many more of these types of behaviour out there.

Other behaviours that can have an effect upon outcomes are:

> Lies and Deceptions.
> Denial.
> A Fear of Engaging with Difficult Issues.
> Living On Auto-Pilot.
> Not being allowed to be Who or What you really are.

In reality: To achieve the life that we want; we all reach a point where we need to deal with the difficult behaviours that may be being kept secret or hidden.

Usually this is not as difficult as people think it is going to be; once they commit to actually dealing with them.

The reality is:

> Every day you get the Opportunity to write another chapter in Your Life Profile; and to develop a new style of future without the secret behaviour.
>
> And you get the Opportunity to stop having to live in the old chapters of Your Life Profile and to live in the new ones.

So what do I want you to take away from this chapter?

A reality of life is that we all hide things and we all have secrets.

This is normal.

The trick is to understand when a secret is healthy and when a secret is harmful for us.

Understanding this is good **Hi**.

If you have a weight problem then it is, in my experience, normal to have other problems and issues as well.

You may have already tried to deal with your weight problem and the other issues that cause you difficulties. And you may have had some temporary success.

What you need to avoid doing; is to continually try to use the same old solutions that keep on failing.

So you need to think in terms of a new type of solution.

This is why I developed the Life Improvement Programmes: To provide someone with a new way of successfully dealing with the complex problems that they have.

Understanding this is good **Hi**.

Chapter 28

How Long Does It Really Take?

Achieving Weight Control and Living a Better Life.

Let's have a look at what I think are likely to be Realistic Timescales to deal with weight problems that fall into the different Zones on The Dieters Scale.

To be realistic with this we need to qualify a few things.

For my answers I am considering the Whole Weight Problem Package that someone has to deal with. This means not only the Weight Problem that the person has; but also all the other directly and indirectly affected areas of life which contribute towards the development and maintenance of the Weight Problem.

We are looking at being truthful here and not giving people false expectations so that they will buy a product or service. We are going to deal with my old friend: Reality!

So I will tell you what I really think and what my experiences show me.

At this stage we know that those who fall into the Green Zone on The Dieters Scale will have a less complex problem than someone who falls into the Amber or Red Zones.

So the question is:

> How long would it take someone to "Turn the Corner" and Really begin taking their Life in a Different, Sustainable Direction. Allowing them to move out of Fat Land and begin taking up residence in Slim Land?

To answer the question I am going to use The Dieters Scale and a Life Map.

By now we should have established that our life is like a Jigsaw with different pieces which fit together.

Those different pieces can have different shapes, sizes and colours.

To make sense of this we have used Green, Amber and Red Zones.

So when we look at the Jigsaw of our own lives and we look at the different shapes, sizes and colours of the different problems, issues and challenges that we need to deal with; we will find that we have a coloured map.

The graphic below shows an example of a Life Map with the different Zones. The larger the Zone the more that is happening in that Zone.

Your Life Map may be more Green, more Amber or more Red than someone else's. There is no right or wrong; it just is what it is.

As someone begins to properly deal with their basket of problems, the size of the Zones can change; as can the mix of Zones.

Your Life Map!

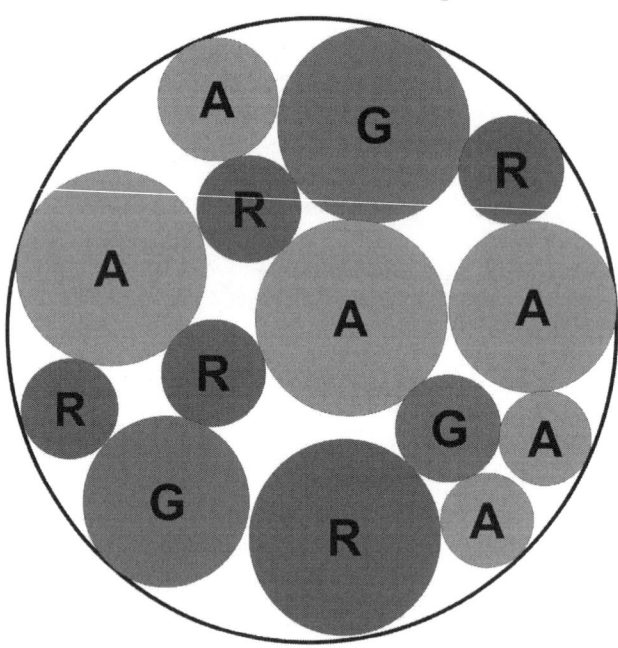

Weight Control the **Hi-Way** ©
The Human Intelligence (**Hi**) Common Platform

As a general guide; I would say that if your Map is genuinely all Green Zones that it can be dealt with in 1-year or less with the Correct Application of Actions. This assumes that you don't find any Icebergs along the way.

> No-one with an Amber or Red Zone weight problem is going to have an all Green Zone Map. If they do, then they are just getting things wrong.

As a general guide; I would say that if our Map is more Amber than anything else and some of those are going on Red; that it can be dealt with in 1- 2 years or less with the Correct Application of Actions.

As a general guide; I would say that if our Map has lots of bits that are Amber and Red; that it can be dealt with in 2-3 years or less with the Correct Application of Actions.

To put this into perspective you need to look at how much time, effort and money you have put into dieting so far in your life.

Ask yourself how much of your life has been adversely affected by having a weight problem. Then see if those timescales are really that far off the mark.

Understanding this is good Hi.

The timelines I am using would start from when you actually begin to properly begin to deal with these things. They are not timelines from you going on another diet.

You also need to take account of the following:

    Some problems may defy these guidelines and that is why these are only guidelines.

    Some problems may take years to deal with properly.

    Other problems may not be able to be dealt with and can only be better managed.

    Each case is different and each case has different dynamics attached to it.

    No case is impossible.

To get to the level of successfully dealing with long term problems; you may well need help.

This is because there are simply "a lot of things going on" and many of those things are going to be outside of your current awareness and your current ability to comprehend, to understand and to see the bigger picture.

You simply may not have the right level and type of Hi that you need to deal with this on your own. This is Normal and this is why I talk about Guided Experiential Learning, Preparation & Practice.

So what do I want you to take away from this chapter?

If you decide to use The Dieters Scale to grade the different problems, issues and challenges that you have; then be realistic.

Mislabelling your problem to make it look better is a waste of time and effort for you.

When you cheat yourself; you always lose!

Understanding this is good **Hi**.

Green Zone level problems are the simplest and easiest to deal with.

As you Unpack and begin to deal with a problem; you may find that the Nature of the problem actually changes; and that it is not actually a Green Zone problem but an Amber or Red Zone problem.

Amber and Red Zone problems are more complicated, more difficult and more complex to deal with; because of this they usually take longer.

With many problems an Annual Cycle is required so as to deal with things like Anniversaries of Events.

Things like Christmas, holidays and birthdays can trigger dynamics that are not there the whole year through.

More complicated problems may require more than one Annual Cycle.

To understand how problems connect with each other think of a spider sitting on a web. The spider feels the vibrations through the web and responds to those vibrations.

A weight control problem is the same.

You will respond to the vibrations that occur through your Life Map. You don't always see the things that you are connected too but you can feel them and be affected by them.

Understanding this is good **Hi**.

Chapter 29

Life Improvement Programmes; Why?

With many problems we try the quickest, simplest and easiest solutions first.

And for many problems these quick, simple and easy solutions work just fine.

So why should Life Problems be any different?

Well the reality is that for many Life Problems there are quick, simple and easy solutions that can be successfully applied.

The real problems begin when we reach the stage where we run out of quick, simple and easy solutions to apply.

Or:

When the nature of the problem that we need to deal with is such that quick, simple and easy solutions are no longer appropriate; and they don't work.

What do we do when we reach this stage?

For myself; as an innovator, developer and provider of solutions; I found that many of the solutions being offered to different problems were badly structured, inadequate, over sold and often unable to do the job they were being sold for.

This happens because people tend to prefer the sweet to the sour, the dream to the reality; and this makes it easier to sell sweet sounding solutions; even though that solution may not work properly or at all.

Sweet sounding dream solutions usually use words like; simple, easy, no effort, quick, solves all your problems, you get a high return for a small investment; you get the idea.

This type of marketing doesn't only happen with weight problems, it happens all through society.

- Businesses get sold and buy the wrong solutions.
- Governments get sold and buy the wrong solutions.
- People in all walks of life get sold and buy the wrong solutions.

This is Normal because of how people buy things and how people sell things.

However; just because it's normal, it doesn't make it right, desirable or beneficial.

Let me see if I can help you understand why this happens. Have you ever heard the saying:

> Just because something is good for someone; it doesn't mean that they will want it.

And this is how it is with Life Improvement Programmes for successful Weight Control.

They are great solutions but they have to deal with difficult issues that can be hard work, uncomfortable, not what people want to hear, and not always sweet and easy to deal with. But they do the real job that needs to be done!

So to get people using Life Improvement Programmes we have to go through a process of Education.

First we have to let them know that they are there, and then we have to help people see the benefits of a new weight control solution which does more than conventional dieting solutions; but which can also be sour at times.

For example:

Take a Life Improvement Programme focused on Successful Weight Control.

Life Improvement Programmes focused on Successful Weight Control have been created to work across the Spectrum of Weight Control Problems. This helps people to see and understand weight problems in a different way.

The Programmes are designed to work with The Dieters Scale and the mixture of Green, Amber and Red Zone problems that people actually have.

We use simple tools that have been specially developed to help someone understand and manage these problems in simple and easy to understand ways.

We will be guiding them on how to do things in a better and more efficient way; and showing them how to use things like failure in positive ways.

So this means that we will be considering and working with the person's life as a whole; and be helping them to increase their Human Intelligence (**Hi**) of their own Behaviours and Actions.

Through that increased Human Intelligence (**Hi**) they will be able to better understand, manage and resolve the different components that help to create their Weight Control Problem.

This process actually creates an easier way of being able to deal with their weight problem and to achieve long term weight control.

It teaches them how to manage and control themselves and the environments that they find themselves in.

They will then be able to go on and take the Human Intelligence (Hi) process into their other activities and continue to use it for the rest of their lives.

Working in this way involves working with the Management, Development and Structure of their life. Or as much of that as is relevant to what we are trying to achieve.

It is by working in this more holistic fashion that the more sustainable and more desirable long term results are achieved.

Simply put: These Programmes have a higher probability of being able to produce successful results that last a lifetime, than any diet that they will go on.

Achieving this requires more commitment from the person with the weight control problem than will be required to go to a diet class or to use dieting products.

However; the results that can be achieved from the different approaches are worlds apart.

And this is how we have to educate people about what we do.

Understanding this is good Hi.

So what do I want you to take away from this chapter?

Life Improvement Programmes which are properly structured and delivered can make significant differences to the Life problems that many people have.

If you are going to undertake a Life Improvement Programme you need to understand the commitment involved and NOT be looking for quick, simple, easy results.

Extraordinary results can be achieved but it is usually through a sweet and sour process that takes time and commitment.

The truth is that Problems are not all sweetness, sunshine and laughter. So why would you expect the solutions to be all sweetness, sunshine and laughter?

Understanding this is good Hi.

Weight Control The HI-**Way** is a Licensed process that is only available from Trained and Authorised companies.

Chapter 30

Balancing Lifestyle, Wealth, Health And Well-Being!

Continuing with our holistic approach; I want to cover something that would not normally be mentioned by anyone else dealing with Weight Control.

For a large part of my adult life I have been looking at and working with the structures that are required for achieving more successful lives; and for achieving more successful outcomes with different types of problems that involve people.

Over that time; I have found that there are many people who will tell you that they have the secrets to success of various types.

They will tell you that they can provide you with 100 easy ways to be successful with making money, with persuading people to do things, with losing weight, with being happier, etc.

In reality:
> Successful, Happy lives are about Balance.

> A balanced life is generally a happier life than one which is out of balance.

Over the years I have realised that we can break life down into four simple Areas which connect together. These are:

> Lifestyle, Wealth, Health and Well-Being.

If we can get these different areas of our lives to balance with what we want to achieve in life; then we tend to be successful.

If we neglect any of these four areas, then our lives go out of balance and we suffer the consequences of this.

> I can safely say that when people have problems, one or more of these areas is going to be out of balance. And that includes a weight problem.

So let's take a simple look at these four areas.

Lifestyle

Our Lifestyle is made up from the structures of our lives on a day-by-day basis.

It's the coming together of the little insignificant parts of our lives and the larger more significant parts of our lives.

When these combine, they help to define us as people and the type of Lifestyle that we have.

This also includes the Routines and Habits of our daily living.

Lifestyle includes such things as; shopping for groceries, cleaning the house, looking after the children, looking after our partner, our parents, etc.

All the things which we would normally take for granted in our lives; such as preparing food, watching TV, speaking to people on the phone are part of our Lifestyle.

It also includes things like hobbies, sports and our social lives.

The habits we have around work are also part of our lifestyle. Including getting out of bed in the morning, going to work and what we do after work.

Lifestyle includes the relationships that we have at home, at work and in the general communities which we inhabit.

It would also include On-Line relationships and communities that we use.

So Lifestyle covers a large part of our life and if there are things in our Lifestyles which are wrong; then they can affect this area and other areas. It's the spiders' web principle.

If you were to think about your Lifestyle and then you were to apply The Dieters Scale to the different areas of your Lifestyle:

>   Which parts of your Lifestyle would be in the Green, Amber or Red Zones?

Wealth

In all of our lives we have to pay some attention to wealth; either in getting it, spending it or both of these. This is simply because we all need money to live and we all have bills to pay.

Wealth covers:

>   Our Income.
>   Savings.
>   Investments.
>   Inheritance.
>   Other people's finances which effects us.
>   Our work and the means by which we earn money.
>   Taxes.

It also covers:

Our expenditure.
Our Liabilities.
Financial Commitments.
Unexpected Expenditure.

As we move through our life our wealth requirements change and we all eventually give up working.

In most households someone will have a job or be living with someone who has a job.

In the current economic climate many people are relying on assistance from other people or State organisations to survive.

Many people are defined by the Possessions that they have and that they enjoy.

If those Possessions are removed or lost; what then?

Many people are defined by what they do to make a living. Their Occupational Status defines who they are and their Occupational Status links to their ability to create wealth.

Where this is the case; what happens when someone loses their job or cannot work anymore?

When people manage their wealth poorly, they tend to suffer at some point.

Sometimes poor financial management leads to bankruptcy and other times it leads to permanent financial stress.

Virtually everyone is capable of paying sufficient attention to their finances; and they are capable of learning how to manage them well.

For anyone who has had the experience of not having the money that they need; then we know that:

The quality of our lives can be affected by not having enough money.

And another truth is:

That sometimes; someone's Lifestyle demands financing which outpaces their ability for wealth creation.

Another thing about wealth is:

> Successful people may become wealthy.
>
> However; being wealthy doesn't make you a successful person.

I have come to realise that very few people will really become fabulously wealthy. And; that although many people would like the advantages of being wealthy, this is not really what they truly want.

Most people that I talk to about being wealthy; actually just want to be better off than they are now and not have to worry about money.

If you were to think about your Wealth and then you were to apply The Dieters Scale to the different areas of your Wealth:

> Which parts of your Wealth would be in the Green, Amber or Red Zones?

Health

Under Health we would include:

> Physical Health – our bodies.
> Mental Health – our minds or psyche.
> Emotional Health – our ability to manage our emotions/feelings.
> Psychological Health – our ability to manage our mental processes.

We know that health concerns can drive us to take action through fear. Health concerns may well have made you read this book.

Good health does not exist in isolation to our Lifestyles or our Wealth. Our Lifestyles and our Wealth contribute towards our health and helps to shape it over the medium to long term.

I personally believe that we should do what we can to maintain our health and to address any health concerns that we have.

Good health is something that most of us tend to take for granted. It is only when we are not well that we have the contrast between Good Health and Poor Health.

Dealing with a weight problem is something that you have a choice about; the question is:
> Will you take it seriously this time?

Weight problems can affect all the areas shown at the beginning of this section.

This means that they can affect our Mental, Emotional, Psychological and Physical Health.

Because many health problems occur over time; we may not appreciate that we are helping to create a long term health problem through our current behaviour.

Very often it is only in the future that we will make these connections.

At that time we will be able to see that what we have done in the past has contributed to or caused the thing which is now dragging our lives down.

> A simple long term health problem can cause our quality of life to reduce and it can make us miserable. So if we can avoid this; why not?

If you were to think about your Health and then you were to apply The Dieters Scale to the different areas of your Health:

> Which parts of your Health would be in the Green, Amber or Red Zones?

Well-Being

Finally we come to Well-Being.

Really this can make more sense if we turn the phrase around the other way.

Being Well.

This part of our lives is an Overview of how all the parts of our lives are working together.

It is the Reality of our Lives and how well these are blending together:

> How well we are actually Living, the Quality of our Lives, the Happiness, the Contentment, our Dreams, our Achievements, etc.

Another way to think of it is: It's the Accounting House of Who, How and What we are Being and Doing.

Being Well is about how much Positivity and how much Negativity is in our lives and how this affects us.

Well-Being is often talked about as; A State of Mind.

What State is your mind in?

If you were to think about your Well-Being (or Being Well) and then you were to apply The Dieters Scale to the different areas of your Well-Being:

Which parts of your Well-Being would be in the Green, Amber or Red Zones?

So what do I want you to take away from this chapter?

None of us are completed works. We are all works in progress.

We are all able to make something else of ourselves; other than what we are now.

Any weight problem; anywhere on the Spectrum of Weight Problems can be Resolved, Improved or Managed in a better way.

What we need to Be Successful In Our Lives is:

> Purpose.
> Direction.
> A Path to Follow.
> Realistic Timescales.
> The Correct Application Of Actions.
> An Open Mind.

And if you can't really do it on your own; get appropriate help. This book will give you help, but it may not be able to give you all the help that you need. This is why we have the extra support from our Workshops and Programmes.

> Understanding this is good **Hi**.

Chapter 31

A Different View Of Diet, Weight Loss And Exercise Classes

In reality there are lots of diet and weight loss clubs; and lots of exercise classes.

So finding one will not be that difficult for most people.

The thing is; that once you have found one:

> How do you avoid doing the same old things once again; and avoid ending up back in the same old place once again?

I guess that the best thing to do is to start looking at this with the question:

> Why do you end up there in the first place?

We can't get away from the simple fact that diet, weight loss and exercise classes exist and that many of them are big businesses dealing with millions of people each year.

These businesses market themselves as being providers of successful weight loss and weight control solutions.

At a surface level this looks to be a fantastic thing and it's what you really want as well. So it must be a perfect fit; Right!

Well maybe not such a perfect fit as we first think it is. So let's have a better look at this thing.

They did it and so can you!

In reality; the Holy Grail for Diet, Weight Loss and Exercise providers, is to have someone go through their programmes and to lose lots and lots of weight.

This person is then held up as an example of what can be achieved.

In addition; they will often heavily market that person's success at weight loss as a validation for their system. Those with weight problems will be familiar with this type of marketing.

That simple marketing method of:

> They did it; so can you with brand (X) Diet!

And we will see a happy, confident, smiling person in all the adverts.

But what happens when we get behind the marketing image and into the everyday reality?

It might be useful if we look at these classes and meetings in another way.

Understanding the Marketing and Reality Gap

My way of viewing this would be:

> How many of those who start these Diet, Weight Loss and Exercise classes, actually achieve and maintain the results that they wanted to achieve, when they began these classes?

And the reality is that we will never know the answer to this question, because no-one will ever provide this information.

This is because it is easier to attract people to a big marketing promise; than it is to deliver on that big marketing promise. It's that sweet and sour thing again.

For example:

> You may attract 10,000,000 people by making big marketing promises.
>
> However; it is when it comes time to delivering on those big marketing promises to those 10,000,000 people that the game actually changes.
>
> So how do they make easy weight loss and feeling better a reality for those 10,000,000 people?

As the number of overweight people has continued to increase, it has become more difficult to deliver on marketing promises as more and more people want sweet and dreamy weight loss solutions.

So now we have the legends that have been added to the marketing material to provide an escape clause to those sweet and dreamy promises. Those legends are:
- Can work as part of a calorie controlled diet.
- Lifestyle changes may be required to achieve and maintain longer term results.

So when the diet doesn't work, it wasn't really the fault of the diet. The person didn't do enough to make it work.

And sometimes this will be correct and other times it will not be.

Either way this leaves the door open for you to return to the diet, weight control and exercise industry for another attempt at achieving the dream that they are selling you.

The simple reality is that so much of what makes a difference to the Success or the Failure of someone's weight control; is outside of the ability of the diet, weight control or exercise plan to influence.

So try to recognise the Reality Gap with marketing and avoid falling into it.

Can Diet, Weight Loss and Exercise classes really help you?

What you need to be honest about is; what you are hoping to really achieve. Is it:

- Weight loss.
- Weight control.
- Fast easy weight loss.
- Want to feel better.
- Want to look better.
- More control over your life.
- Deal with the other issues.
- Looking to improve your life.
- Being more successful in life.

The reality is that on a monthly basis, there are millions of people using diet and weight loss programmes and exercise classes.

And when you get to the foundation stone for all the different reasons why people are doing so; you find that all of these people have a simple goal in mind:

> They are looking to Improve their lives and be happier than they are. And they are hoping that this will help them do that.

So once again let's use The Dieters Scale to help us understand this. And let's see if we can use The Dieters Scale to improve success rates by matching things in a better way.

> What we do know is; that it is easier to deal with people with Green Zone weight problems; than it is to deal with people with Amber and Red Zone weight problems.

So those in the Green Zone can achieve success easier than those in the Amber and Red Zones: If they do the right things, in the right way, at the right time, for the right reasons.

The Life Map lets us visualise the different aspects of someone's life that forms a weight problem; or which are affected by their weight problem in one way or another.

Each circle in the Map represents an aspect of their life, how important it is and the Zone State that it would currently be in. So it can give us useful and helpful information that we can use and work with.

Your Life Map!

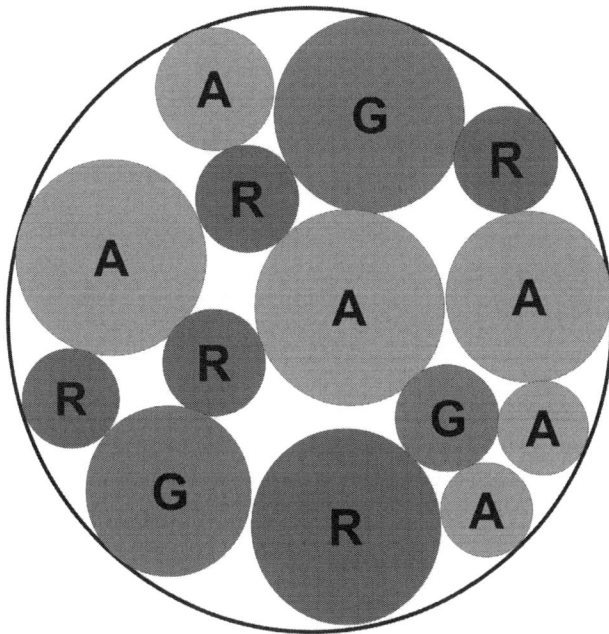

Weight Control the **Hi-Way** ©
The Human Intelligence (**Hi**) Common Platform

In this Life Map you can see that we have all the different Zones represented. This would include things like weight, fitness, relationships, self-esteem, confidence, etc. *They have not been written in because it would make the diagram look too busy. However; on a Life Improvement Programme we would do this.*

So the question to ask would probably be:

> If the class you are going to attend is only going to deal with one or two of the Zones that are Green; then how will the other Zones be dealt with?

So what do I want you to take away from this chapter?

> All problems have a structure that can be understood.
>
> All solutions have a structure that can be understood.
>
> The better the fit between the two; the higher the probability for a success outcome.
>
> Understanding this is good Human Intelligence (**Hi**).

Chapter 32

Putting It All Together

So how do you put all this information and new thinking together?

If there is a message that I have been trying to get across in this part of the book, it is that things happen a bit more slowly than people want and often in a different way than they think they do.

If I was in your place what would I do?

First I would read through the whole of this book without skipping bits. And I would allow thinking time while I read it.

Then if I thought I needed to: I would read it again and answer the various questions.

I would keep the book available so that I could refer to relevant chapters as this will help with increasing my Human Intelligence (**Hi**).

I would make sure that I understood The Dieters Scale and I would answer the simple questions in part one and part two of the book.

You will find that The Dieters Scale and the other tools like the Life Map will be useful for you in many different ways.

Before I did anything I would make sure that I understood whether I thought my weight problem was a Green Zone, Amber Zone or Red Zone weight problem. And I would be as accurate with this as I could.

I would accept that I don't have a weight problem that exists in isolation to other aspect of my life. So I would ask:

> What Components does my weight problem have and where do I think these are on The Dieters Scale?

This would be things like Confidence, Self-esteem, etc. *I will help you with this in the next part of the book.*

I would then look at the options that I am considering using to deal with my weight control problem.

- Am I considering another diet?
- What pressure am I putting myself under?

- How long am I allowing myself to deal with this problem?
- What am I going to be relying upon?
- Do I need to do something different?
- Why am I doing this now?

Then I would look at "When" I was going to start this and I would try to be clear about my Timing.

I would be asking the question: Is there something else which is driving this decision at this time?

I would be looking at how I am going to deal with the various issues which may have been raised throughout this book. Am I going to use the book or do something else?

I would accept that I might begin this and that I might follow my usual path and stop when things get difficult. If I did that, then I would read the section about Imperfect People again and the section about Failure.

At some point I would have to accept that:

> If I keep doing the same sort of thing and I keep getting the same sort of result; then at some point I will need to do something quite different in order to achieve something different.

And this may be what has brought you to this book:

> Could it be that you are Looking for something else that you can do to sort this weight control problem out?

And the next part of this book; with The Stepping Stones Approach, may have the answers that you seek.

Whatever you do just remember this simple truth:

> If you participate in the Solution to your problem in the right ways; then you can resolve, improve or manage your weight problem in a better way.

So what do I want you to take away from this chapter?

- Be realistic.
- Don't be over optimistic.
- Understand that virtually all weight related problems can be dealt with.

BOOK PART 2 INTRODUCTION

In this part of the book we are going to build on the Human Intelligence (**Hi**) that we introduced you to in the first part of the book. We will also continue to introduce you to new Human Intelligence (**Hi**).

When it comes to the Weight Control process we are going to take the Human Intelligence (**Hi**) Common Platform and combine this with a PALM Solutions Problem Management Platform to create Weight Control The **Hi-Way**.

Our objective with combining these two things is that we are going to take a complicated and difficult problem and we are going to simplify it.

To help with this I will be using the **Hi-Way** *lite* approach to simplify and understand the journey that someone with a Weight Control problem has to undertake.

We are going to do things differently from the normal dieting approaches and from what your dieting books and clubs will tell you.

In this approach Preparation and Practice are going to be things that you will hear a lot of. The reason for this is that Preparation and Practice increases the probability for successful outcomes and it makes the process easier.

With normal dieting approaches there is usually little or no preparation done and certainly no practice. So we are going to turn many of the normal dieting rules upside down and throw many of them away.

You have been introduced to The Dieters Scale and the different coloured Zones that we are using. We will continue to use this simple process and apply it to the different components of the Weight Control problem.

I will use The Dieters Scale to help you understand things like Nutrition, Calories, Food volume and Frequency; and the essential relationship that exist between these four things. Once you understand this relationship it will help you with the ongoing management of food; regardless of the type of food that you actually eat.

I will be using the concept of Fat Land and Slim Land to help you understand that you are moving from one distinct place to another distinct place. This is because these are different destinations and people want to go from one to the other.

We will be using the concept of your Slim Land identity and your Fat Land identity. We are doing this because when you live in Fat Land you develop a Fat Land identity that extends to your Lifestyle and how you live your life. It also extends to how others may be perceiving you in the life that you are living.

Your Fat Land identity will also contain all the different components of the weight problem that helps to keep you going back to Fat Land; and that keeps you living there.

So it makes sense that there needs to be changes with that identity. And this is why we want to develop the Slim Land identity.

The Slim Land identity is the real structure that you need to enable you to move to Slim Land and take up residence in Slim Land. This ties in with Your Life Profile and creating new Special Chapters in Your Life Profile.

When it comes to the actual Weight Control process and the dieting itself; we are going to take a different approach to a number of things.

We are going to avoid jumping into things as dieters often do. We have touched on the reasons for this in the first part of the book and I will be expanding on these in this part of the book.

What I am going to do is to introduce you to the concepts of Preparation and Practice. These are not normally used with Weight Control and other problems; but when they are used right they can make a very big difference to the final results that are achieved; and to the number of people who can achieve them.

We will also be using Preparation and Practice to avoid the sudden jumps off cliffs that many dieters take. They end up doing this because they just go straight into a diet or exercise programme with little or no preparation and big expectations.

Poor Preparation and Practice leads to poor Performance and a low Probability for Success. Personally; I think it is time that we changed this for people with weight problems.

When it comes to the Weight Control journey; you need to understand that you have always been on a Weight Control journey; and that you always will be on one.

This is because it is incumbent upon human beings to make decisions about what they consume, when they consume it, how much they consume and how often they consume.

This has been true in the past, it is true today and it will be true in the future.

The responsibility that you have as a human being is to consume what will keep you healthy and fit. It is this that makes a difference to your quality of life and how well you enjoy that quality of life.

Unusually for a diet book; this book can be used by people who are underweight as well as those who are overweight. This is because we are aiming for Weight Control rather than weight loss.

Whether someone needs to lose weight or gain weight, they are both looking to achieve the same result:

> Weight Control within a weight range.

The principles of Weight Control apply to both groups and both have the same question:

> How does someone get to a target weight
> and maintain that weight over the long term?

I am going to show you how to do this using our proprietary system and our proprietary tools; to begin to alter a Weight Control problem into a Weight Control Solution!

Weight Control
The **Hi**-**Way**

Mind - Body - Attitude
&
Human Intelligence (**Hi**)

In this part of the book I am going to introduce you to The Stepping Stones Approach. And in the Stepping Stones Approach it doesn't matter what your previous dieting history is like.

It doesn't matter whether you are a seasoned dieter or someone who is about to undertake your first diet; this approach can help you; if you work with it.

It also doesn't matter if you are a little overweight or a lot overweight; the **Hi-Way** Stepping Stones Approach will apply to you; and you can use it to achieve positive results that can be sustained.

With this approach it also doesn't matter what diet you want to use; whether you are going to an organised slimming club or doing it on your own. The principles of The **Hi-Way** Stepping Stones Approach apply in all cases.

This means that you can go to a slimming club and use The Stepping Stones approach; but you need to separate out what I am saying from what they are saying; and don't let yourself get confused or let yourself be taken in the wrong direction.

This means that you need to understand what good Human Intelligence (Hi) is when it comes to dieting information and expectations; and what poor Human Intelligence (Hi) is when it comes to what you really need to know to improve and resolve your Weight Control problem.

At the time when you are making the decision about your diet would be when you would use the Hi information from the first part of this book. This good Hi will help to keep you on track and help you avoid getting drawn into sweet promises and dream results.

Often the Dieting Industry may use information and facts that its claims to be true; but this does not make them good Human Intelligence (Hi) for someone with a Weight Control problem.

What you need to remember about slimming clubs and dieting organisations is that they have very high long term failure rates. As much as 84% of their members fail. This means that there is a lot of bad Human Intelligence (Hi) around and a lot of people are using and believing in that bad Hi.

With the Hi-**Way** Stepping Stones Approach; I want to speak to that 84% who normally fail. I want to help them to do a better job and achieve better results that can last them longer; hopefully for a lifetime.

So if you use a slimming club, weight watching club, or provider of packaged meals, you need to understand their limitations and their business focus.

Try to look at the results that they really do actually achieve over the long term for most of their members; and don't let yourself get distracted by the marketing hype that focuses on what only a few people really achieve.

If the truth is that you really need to go on one of our Life Improvement Programmes or Experiential Workshops, then you should do so.

In the Hi-**Way** Stepping Stones Approach it doesn't matter whether you can exercise or not. Exercise is not required as part of losing weight and keeping weight off. In this book I have already made my view clear about using exercise as a weight loss tool. I will expand on that in this part of the book.

You can think of the Hi-**Way** Stepping Stones Approach as being a Strategic

Journey that you will undertake to improve your life; and achieve a lifestyle that you are happy with.

We don't want you to be a super model, we want you to reach your "Happy Point" and to be happy with who and how you are.

When you are using this simple approach, you will know which Stepping Stone you are on at any time; and you will know what you need to do to establish a foothold, stay on it and continue to progress forwards towards Slim Land.

If you do have a problem and fall off, you will know which Stepping Stone you have fallen off or tried to skip over; to try and get into Slim Land faster. If this happens it doesn't matter because this is life and this is what happens in life.

Falling off a Stepping Stone is not a problem. Failure doesn't matter in this process, because failure is simply part of the journey to success that you need to undertake to get to where you want to be: Slim Land.

When you have had enough of failure you will then take the appropriate time, and put in the appropriate Preparation and Practice required to complete the **Hi-Way** Stepping Stones journey in the right way.

In the **Hi-Way** Stepping Stones Approach we believe that practice makes perfect; and that it's OK to make mistakes when you practice. It's what practice is for!

Remember that no-one is perfect; we are all Imperfect People!

The truth is that this is a personal challenge that you alone will undertake!

You will find that there are no real short cuts; there are just opportunities to waste time, effort and more of your life.

Instead of wasting these why not just do what really needs to be done.

Some people may use the **Hi-Way** Stepping Stones Approach a number of times.

Each time they will move closer and closer to being able to live in Slim Land.

It is also in the nature of journeys that sometimes we need to go backwards to enable us to progress further forwards.

Your journey from Fat Land to Slim Land can also follow this same path. And if it does; do not worry because this approach has been designed to deal with that.

Taking a bit longer to get to Slim Land usually produces better and more sustainable results than going at it too fast. Slow creates foundations, fast builds castles in the sky.

It is perfectly acceptable to use a baby steps approach where you are Practicing and Learning from each attempt; and you are progressing slowly forwards. This helps you to build solid foundations and it fits with our Preparation & Practice approach.

At some point you may come across someone who claims that they have short cuts for the **Hi-Way** Weight Control Approach and that they know simple and fast ways to cross the Stepping Stones. They don't!

In reality the people who keep looking for quick fixes and easy ways; often end up doing things the hard way, and not achieving what they really want as their life clicks past and they waste time and effort.

Why waste time and effort when you can use them in a positive way? If you get tempted by these claims go back to the section about Symptom Solutioning and read that again.

Try to think of this journey that you are about to undertake like a Quest.

Your destiny is in the Stepping Stones and you need to fulfil your destiny. To do this you need to undertake the journey of The Stepping Stones.

The Stepping Stones Approach is really about you. Not anyone else; just you!

You see I could work with 100 people and each one will need to do things at the pace that is right for them and in the way that is right for them.

It doesn't matter that I could push them to do things faster and to lose weight quicker. You see what I am after is successful long term results that you can build on and develop further.

I am not interested in the short term results that cannot be sustained and which fall away quickly; leaving you disappointed and worse off than before.

What you need to understand is that most dieters who use normal diets and diet products fall off and fail on the 2nd Stepping Stone.

Most dieters are never told about the 1st and the 3rd Stepping Stones.

As a result most dieters try to jump from Fat Land straight onto the 2nd Stepping Stone (Dieting); and from there they try to jump over the 3rd Stepping Stone and into Slim Land.

No wonder so many of them fail; because it just can't be done by most people; the distances are simply too great to do this.

Normal dieting becomes like one of those obstacle courses you see on television, where people keep getting knocked into the water despite their efforts.

Splash! Back to Fat Land.

The **Hi-Way** Stepping Stones Approach really isn't afraid of dieting failure; because for 84% of dieters, failure is a reality of their normal dieting experiences.

We need to embrace dieting failure and use it as a guide to achieving success.

> Failure is simply showing us that we are not doing the right things, in the right way, for the right reason; at the right time!

So if you want to be successful then you need to do something different from what you have done in the past.

With the **Hi-Way** Stepping Stones Approach we can make good use of any dieting failure that you experience and turn it into something useful; rather than something which makes us feel bad.

We can turn the negative dieting experiences into something positive:

Hi-Way Knowledge!

We can turn your dieting failure into **Hi-Way** Knowledge because we can use your "failure experiences" as an opportunity to learn and do something different in the future.

> Rather than throw our toys out of the pram, let's be adults and accept that what we are about to do is a tough thing to do; and that problems do occur when you do tough things.

So without further ado: Let's begin your journey from Fat Land to Slim Land in 3 Steps!

My suggestion is that you read through the whole of the book first and then begin working through it.

If you jump sections and ignore sections; then you will reduce your probability for being successful.

Keep the book available so that you can make sure that you are doing the right things and to avoid getting seduced by the marketing promises of the Dieting, Beauty and Health industries.

Remember: You want to develop and use good quality Human Intelligence (**Hi**) and avoid using poor quality Human Intelligence (**Hi**).

Many people may try to take you off the path that you are on and try to keep you in Fat Land; don't let them do it.

The only person that you really need to be on your side, so that you will succeed; is you!

Understanding this is good **Hi**.

As part of your Journey you need to establish a foothold on each Stepping Stone in turn. And then complete Your Quest to begin living in Slim Land.

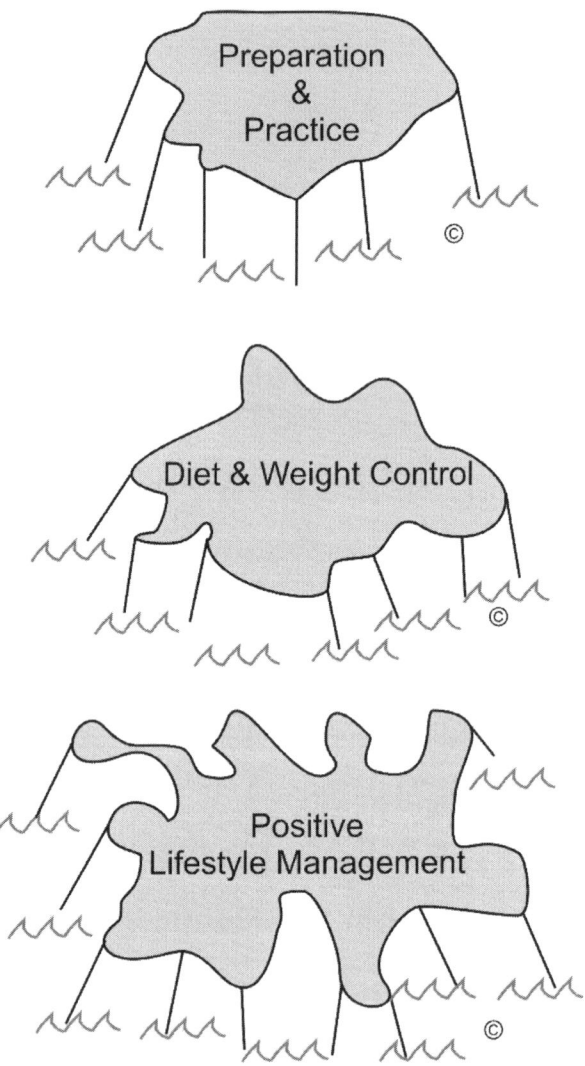

The Hi Common Platform - Weight Control The **Hi-Way**
The Journey from Fat Land to Slim Land across The Stepping Stones

Chapter 1

The Stepping Stones Quest

You are going to undertake a Quest. On that Quest you will journey from Fat Land to Slim Land.

And like all journeys of this type; it's the experiences that you have along the way that really count.

Before you can begin your journey; you first need to understand what part of Fat Land you are actually living in.

To help you to understand this I have divided Fat Land into different Zones.

The different Zones are Green, Amber and Red.

> A Green Zone (G) is easier to navigate than an Amber Zone.

> An Amber Zone (A) is easier to navigate than a Red Zone.

> A Red Zone (R) is the most difficult to navigate.

As a result of these different Zones (and the various obstacles in them) people need to travel by different routes; and overcome challenges to get out of Fat Land and into Slim Land.

> They can't all go by the same route because
> they are not all starting from the same place!

To help you understand where you are living in Fat Land; and to help you work out what route you need to take to get to Slim Land; we will use and apply The Dieters Scale.

The Dieters Scale is a simple process that is part of the Human Intelligence (Hi) Common Platform.

The Dieters Scale will help you to see how difficult your problem really is.

And we will use The Dieters Scale to see whereabouts in Fat Land you are actually living at the moment.

So are you ready to begin your quest?

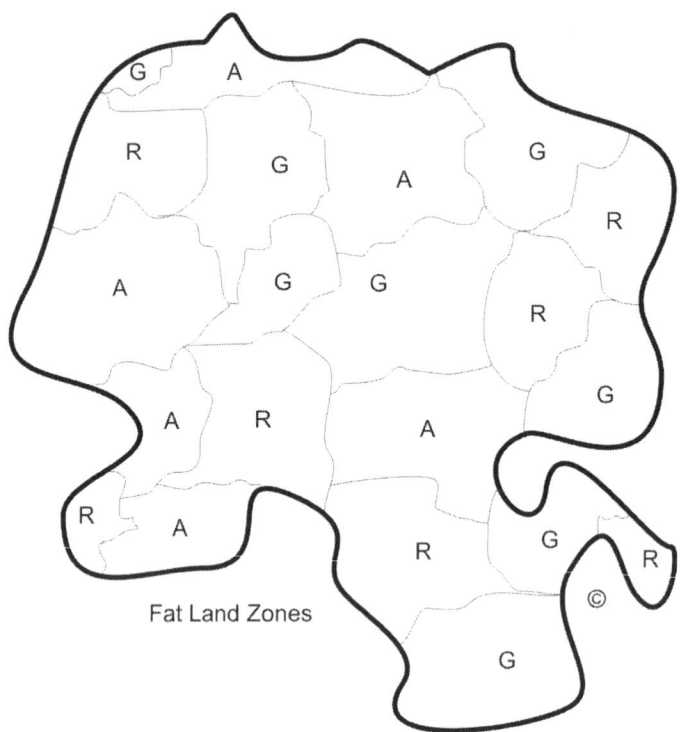

Part of the Human Intelligence (Hi) Common Platform
Weight Control the **Hi-Way**

Above we have a map of Fat Land. You are currently going to be living in one of the Zones; somewhere?

You might be living in an easy Zone or a more difficult Zone. We need to find that out first, as it affects the route you will need to take.

What we need to know is: Do you need to use one of the Green routes, one of the Amber routes or one of the Red routes?

On your Journey there are going to be challenges and victories. Some things you will find easy and some things will be harder; but if you keep going you will get to Slim Land and be able to take up residence there.

To get out of Fat Land and into Slim Land you need to reach and then cross The 3 Stepping Stones.

If you try to rush across The Stepping Stones to get into Slim Land quickly; then you will wake up one day and find yourself back in Fat Land.

If you try and cheat to get to Slim Land, then the same thing will happen; you just simply won't be able to stay there and you will find yourself back in Fat Land.

Cheating more often and harder will just work against you, and you will get very frustrated.

If you fall off any of The Stepping Stones while you are undertaking a challenge; then you will go back to Fat Land.

However; falling of a Stepping Stone is not a bad thing. We use this to learn about what went wrong or what didn't go right; and then we can get it more right the next time.

Not succeeding is often part of the DNA of a Weight Control problem. Our Approach works with this DNA and it gradually alters it so that Failure occurs less and less often. So we need to be prepared to try and fail and then try again; this is the nature of challenges.

To begin your quest you need to reach the 1st Stepping Stone and establish a foothold on that Stepping Stone.

The 1st Stepping Stone is called Preparation & Practice.

To help you get there we will repeatedly use The Dieters Scale. So you will become very familiar with this and begin using this simple tool in a variety of different ways.

Now let's explore the first Stepping Stone!

Establishing A Foothold On The 1st Stepping Stone

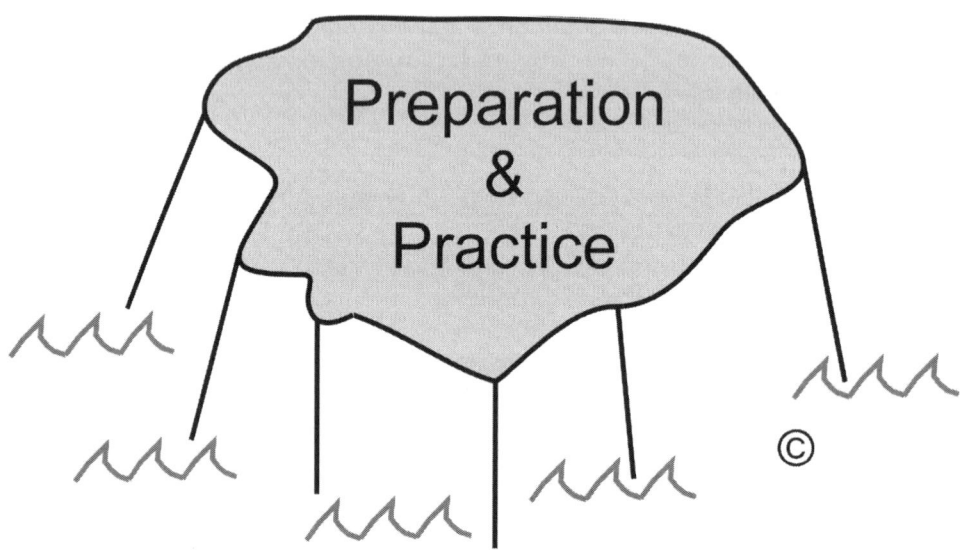

Weight Control The **Hi-Way** ©

Chapter 2

Preparation & Practice – The Real Key To Success!

The 1st Stepping Stone is critical and it is usually missed and ignored by most dieters and those seeking to control their weight.

And yet; this is the part that greatly increases their chances of being successful; and it creates the foundations for what they will do in the future. So it doesn't make sense not to do it.

What we do on this Stepping Stone is to prepare ourselves for the 2nd and 3rd Stepping Stones.

> Warning!
>
> If you haven't spent any time considering and answering the questions from the first part of this book; then you need to go back and do so. This will help you to begin to understand that weight problems are different and that they need to be dealt with in different ways.
>
> If you have answered the questions; you will now have an idea of the Zones that you are in on The Dieters Scale with your weight problem and associated issues.
>
> They are Green Zone – Amber Zone – Red Zone

In our Preparation and Practice we need to Prepare and Practice according to these Zones. So which Zones are relevant to you?

In reality; most people will have a mixture of different Zones for their weight problem and the issues that are associated with their weight problem. We will use the Life Map as an example.

Your Life Map!

Weight Control the **Hi-Way** ©
The Human Intelligence (Hi) Common Platform

To sort out what level of Preparation and Practice you need to do is simple.

If you have only Green Zones then do the Green Zone level of preparation.

However; even a Green Zone person would be better off preparing more than they think they need too.

So in reality; most people should do the Amber and Red Zones' level of preparation.

If you do choose to do the Green Zone level of preparation and it doesn't work; then simply move up to the next Zone.

> It doesn't hurt to work as if you are in a Zone above where you are; it <u>does</u> hurt to work a Zone below where you actually are.

This is what is great about this approach: We just have to focus on the right Zone and do the things that are right for that Zone.

Another great thing is that we only need to be able to understand the difference between Red, Amber and Green Zones; and everyone can understand this.

What you have to understand here is that no Zone or colour is bad. What the colour is telling us can be likened to someone needing to understand the weight of different objects that they are going to have to lift up and move around.

If we know that we are going to lift something light we would take one approach to it. And if we were to lift something large, bulky and heavy; we would take another.

It becomes simple common sense that we would apply to the task of lifting and moving things that could be heavy, bulky and awkward to move. Weight Control is just the same.

At this point I need to tell you something.

When we are doing the Preparation & Practice phase it does not matter if this is your first dieting experience or if you have dieted a hundred times before.

Everyone has to Prepare & Practice. And if you don't prepare and practice in the right way; then you will reduce your chances of being able to reach and stay on the 2nd Stepping Stone: The Diet and Weight Control Stepping Stone!

Here is a word of warning!

Don't put yourself under pressure to succeed and do everything right the first time.

Due to the nature of dieting and weight problems, you need to think of this like playing basketball.

In basketball you will take shots at the basketball hoop but they won't all go in.

If you miss one shot you don't stop playing; you keep playing and you get better at it with practice.

And this is what people will do with our Stepping Stones Approach; they will keep shooting at their goal and get better with practice.

For example:

> To begin with, a dieter may be deep in the Red Zone with their weight.
>
> Over time they will move closer to the Amber Zone, and then they will move into the Amber Zone.
>
> Once they are in the Amber Zone they will then work towards their goal, which will be in the Green Zone.

And in reality this is what this whole successful dieting and weight control process is about; getting closer and closer to your goals through a progressive process which can be sustained.

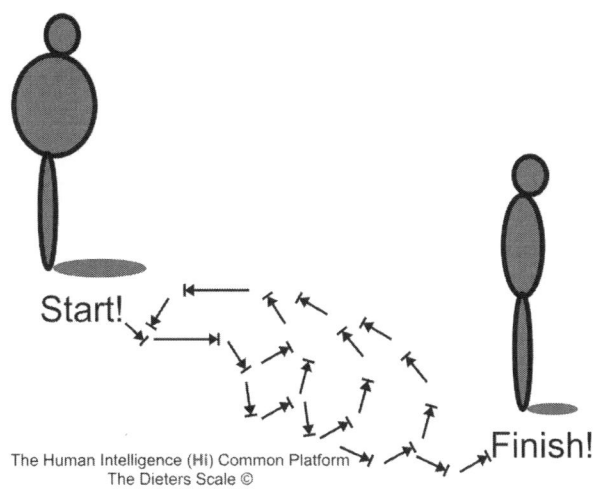

The Human Intelligence (Hi) Common Platform
The Dieters Scale ©

Another way to think of this is to imagine your weight problem as being like a train carrying freight. Each item on the train represents a part of your weight problem.

We can add carriages and freight or we can take carriages and freight away. When we do this it changes what the train does and how it looks.

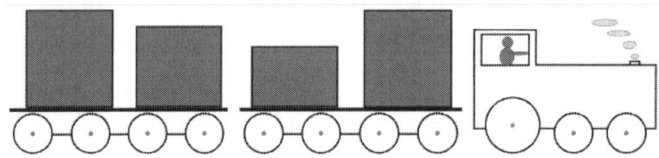

A Green Zone weight problem train.

The carriages (Zones) of your weight problem train are locked together into a structure with a certain size and shape. Your size, your shape, your habits, your lifestyle, your history, etc.

If you continue living your life as you are, those carriages on your weight problem train will stay as they are; and you will continue to move in the direction that you are going.

So if you are gradually putting on weight as each year passes; then you will continue to do this. And at some point your train will change from a Green Zone train into an Amber Zone train.

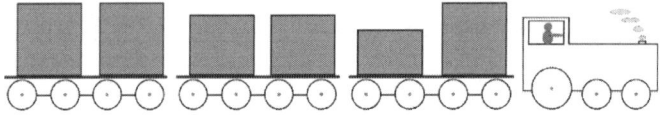

An Amber Zone weight problem train.

As your weight problem continues to change, you will add new items to your weight problem train. When you do this your weight problem can become bigger, larger and more difficult to deal with. It can then change to a Red Zone train.

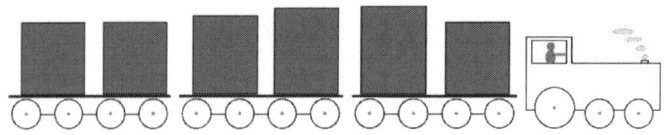

A Red Zone weight problem train.

And what we want to do with this approach is to stop you adding new carriages and new items to your weight problem train; and begin to change how your weight problem train looks.

So whether we are talking about a train, shooting hoops in basketball or your Life Map; what we are trying to be clear about is that there is going to be some work to do and we are going to have to keep at it.

So let's take the time we need to take to get the foundations for the Solution right!

So what is the Preparation & Practice that you need to do?

Let's begin with something that no-one has probably told you before. Those of you who are eager to get on with the diet won't like this but it really is something you need to know and understand.

Understand this makes a huge difference to your dieting experience and the results that you can achieve and maintain.

If you are a Green Zone person and you have had a good or reasonable diet but you have just put on a few extra pounds; then it is probable that your bodies processes are still in the normal functioning range; and your body will respond well to a diet programme.

If you are an Amber Zone or Red Zone person then it is probably the case that your bodies are <u>NOT</u> prepared for a diet programme.

This is a critical thing for you to understand as it has a big impact on your ability to successfully diet and to manage your weight long term.

> MOST PEOPLE WHO ARE IN THE AMBER AND RED ZONES, DIET BEFORE THEY AND THEIR BODIES ARE READY OR ABLE TO DO SO!

The result of ignoring this simple fact is that people who are in the Amber and Red Zones will find it the toughest to achieve the results that they want from conventional dieting.

This is because their bodies, their habits, their lifestyles and all the things which have helped them to live in Fat Land for so long; are still working to keep them in Fat Land.

To change this we need to change the preparedness of their bodies, so that they can use the dieting process in the best way; rather than just messing things up further.

And here's something else you are not going to like:

> Getting your body stable takes about 3 months or more!

But look at this time thing another way. You want to do something different to what you have done in the past; don't you?

By taking time to prepare for a diet we take away all the pressure that you would normally experience when you go on a diet. So we reduce your stress.

And by taking the time to prepare your body and get it working in a better way, we can increase your chances of getting the result that you want.

So it becomes a win-win process for you; rather than the lose-lose beat yourself up process that you are used too.

> The simple truth is; that the right type of Preparation and Practice increases the probability of a successful outcome. And that's what you want: Right?

So what is the right type of Preparation and Practice?

Weight problems that fall into the Amber and Red Zones are too complicated to deal with quickly.

They simply do not respond well to quick simple fixes because they are beyond that.

Yeah; you can go on a diet and lose a lot of weight quickly but it doesn't work and you have to deal with all that disappointment again as you put the weight back on.

We also know that a diet on its own is insufficient to deal with the real weight problem; because in reality there is more going on than a diet can fix.

> Yeah I know about all that stuff that you keep secret and that keeps getting in the way of the life that you want to live.

So how do we begin to sort this out?

Earlier I said that the different Zones were like carriages on a train that carried different items. Those different carriages helped to create the shape and size of your weight problem train.

So this means that each carriage and item on your weight problem train is a piece of your weight problem; and to sort out the weight problem train we need to work with the different pieces of it.

What most people try to do is that they try and change the train by working with the engine; rather than the carriages.

What we are going to do is to work with the train, the carriages, the items on the train and the route that the train normally takes.

Its common sense if you think about it.

Different dieters have different types of trains, with increasing numbers of carriages, with more items being carried, going along their different routes.

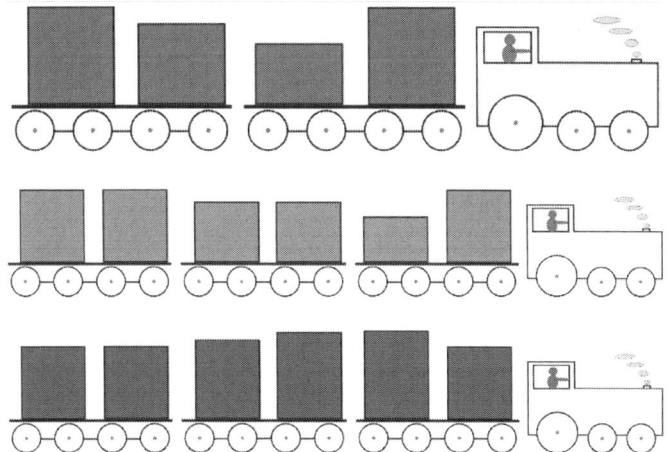

Chapter 3

Focus on the Right Things!

What undermines people's efforts and causes so many people who are in the Amber and Red Zones on The Dieters Scale to fail; is this.

> They focus on the diet itself and not on the "weight problem and the lifestyle management issues that helped to create and maintain their weight problem."
>
> You see; by the time they have moved into the Amber and Red Zones they have more complicated things going on in their lives.
>
> They don't realise that their lifestyle management helped to create and maintain their weight problem; and that they can't fix their lifestyle management issues by going on a diet.
>
> In reality; you have developed a Fat Land life and lifestyle; and you want to have a Slim Land life and lifestyle.
>
> To achieve a Slim Land life and lifestyle we need to resolve, improve and manage a number of things in a better way.
>
> So rather than set yourself up for failure; set yourself up for success!
>
> Success is achievable if you do the right things, in the right way, for the right reasons, at the right time.
>
> So let's start doing that.

First we are going to put a Plan together. It will be a Plan that you can keep to and which you can achieve; because it will fit into your lifestyle and it will fit your capabilities.

Are you up for that?

This Plan can be used by anyone, regardless of whether they are in the Green, Amber or Red Zones and regardless of whether they are male or female, and regardless of their age or any other factor. So let's call this:

MY PLAN TO GET FROM FAT LAND, ACROSS THE STEPPING STONES AND INTO SLIM LAND. Then you need a plan to stay there.

The following graphic shows Fat Land and some of the different routes out of Fat Land. Each route has its own challenges.

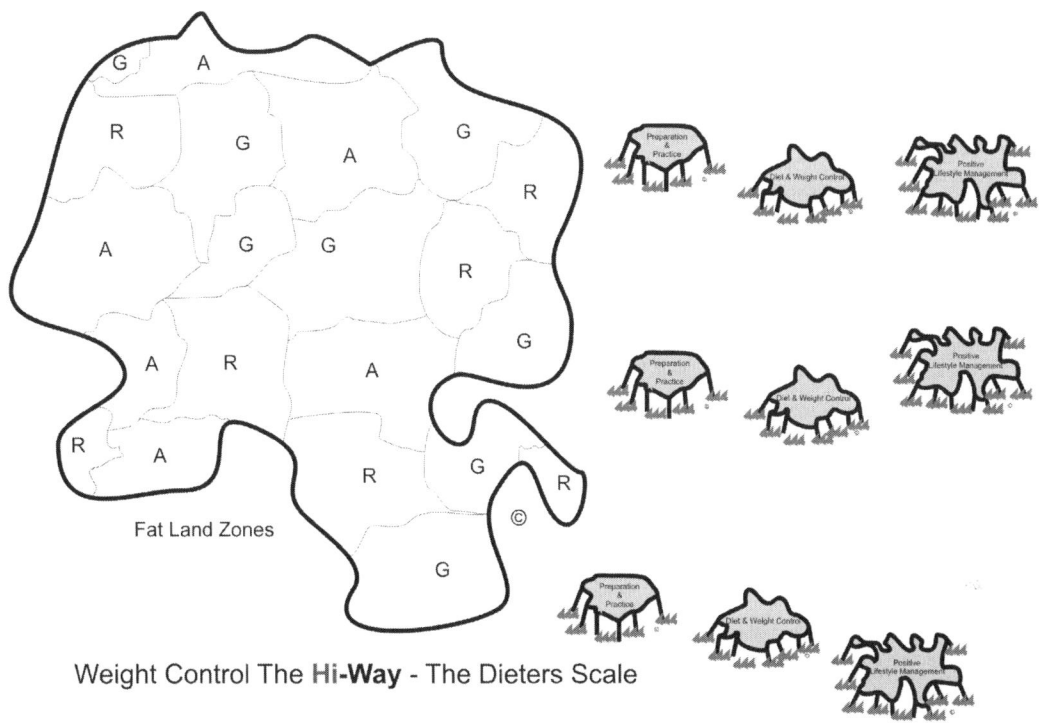

Weight Control The Hi-Way - The Dieters Scale

Before we begin there is something that you need to understand.

Every problem, issue and challenge that comes up in your life will be in either a Green Zone, an Amber Zone or a Red Zone. Or it will be moving from one Zone to another Zone (this is called Transiting Zones).

To deal with the different issues, problems and challenges that someone faces; we simply take them one at a time. We then progress them forwards to a point where they are stable.

And when one thing is stable enough; then we can work with something else.

We do this in a gradual evenly paced way. No rushing, no panic; make a plan and work with the plan. Make the plan small and focused on what can be done now; rather than make it a big plan with lots and lots of details that will constantly change.

We can work with any problem that is affected by your weight, and which affects your weight, by using the Stepping Stones Approach and following this structure.

- Identify the Problem. (In this case a Weight Control Problem)
1. Preparation & Practice.
2. Act and sort it out.
3. Consolidate and put it behind you.

Now what you need to understand is that difficult and complex problems are sorted out a bit at a time. This is the reality of working with complex problems.

So what we are going to do is to apply this simple 3 step structure to any part of any problem that we work with.

Rushing, putting yourself under pressure and having unrealistic time scales will tend to make you fall off a Stepping Stone because you will try to cut corners.

If you get it wrong and you fall off the Stepping Stone; simply begin the process again from the beginning. Don't waste time and effort beating yourself up; just be honest with yourself and avoid repeating the same mistakes again.

> Take the opportunity to Learn from your mistakes and increase your knowledge and wisdom of yourself and the problems, challenges or issues that you are facing. This is good Hi.

We have to recognise the limitations of this and any other book. I can begin to move you in the right directions and begin to help you look at things differently and behave differently.

What I can't do is give you the personal directions, information, support, guidance or other help that you may need to deal with your individual basket of problems and the spider's web that they create.

If things get difficult remember this: Keep it simple and don't over complicate it!

Life complicates things for us; the Zones help us to make sense of them

Everyone begins their life living in the Green Zone.

As things happen, different parts of our lives move into different Zones.

Over time this creates a complicated mix of different Zones with different levels of problem in each Zone. *Remember the Life Map and the Zones in that.*

As we deal with a problem that is in the Red Zone we don't tend to jump from the Red Zone to the Green Zone.

What we do is we work our way through the Red Zone towards the Amber Zone.

Then we move through the Amber Zone into the Green Zone. Then we move to the right place within the Green Zone.

As we make progress in the different Zones, different issues, problems and challenges come up.

To help someone manage this, they can use exactly the same process that we are using in this book; to help them understand and then deal with any problem, challenge or issue that they face.

This approach then provides them with a simple 1.2.3 formula that they can use to help them with their Lifestyle Management and Weight Control.

- Identify the Problem. (Self-Esteem for example)
1. Preparation & Practice.
2. Act and sort it out.
3. Consolidate and put it behind you.

Once you have used this process and found it useful; then you can continue to use it and apply it to new challenges, problems and issues.

The journey through the Zones

To understand the best way to progress from one Zone to another you simply follow this guide.

If you are in the Red Zone with something, then you want to work towards the Amber Zone.

If you are in the Amber Zone with something, then you want to work towards the Green Zone.

If you are in the Green Zone with something, then you want to work towards the right place in the Green Zone.

This will help you to progress in a steady way and get to the right place.

So now let's move on to the actual Preparation & Practice.

Green Zone Preparation

The Green Zone person has less of a job to do and so they will be able to begin a diet sooner. This is because their body should still be within Normal Ranges, be stable and be able to respond positively to a diet and weight control programme.

If you are a Green Zone person, then you probably want to lose the small extra bit of weight that you need to and then keep it off.

If you struggle with keeping the weight off, then my guess would be that the increased weight is as a result of Lifestyle Management issues that are not being properly understood and managed appropriately.

If this is the case then you really are an Amber or Red Zone person and you should do what they do.

If you are in any doubt about your body's stability then take the time to get your body stable and use that time to Prepare and Practice to go on the diet. If you don't then you are only setting yourself up for disappointment that could be avoided.

I suggest that you use that time to look at the other issues, problems and challenges that may be around for you.

Remember the 3 month rule for body preparation!

In any event it is usually better to over prepare rather than under prepare. If I was in your position I would prepare at the Amber Zone level as the extra preparation would not hurt.

You could use those 3 months for this!

Rather than do separate preparations for the different Zones (which would get quite complicated) I have separated the different levels of preparation by a simple method.

This is how someone will put their Green Zone plan together. The Green Zone person can look at the Amber and Red Zone preparations and take what they need from that. They can then put these into their Plan.

If you begin to find that quite a lot of the Amber and Red Zone preparation fits you; then move your preparation to the Amber and Red Zone levels because this is more likely to be where your problem really fits.

In the following graphic you will see The Dieters Scale represented in another way. I will use this form for most of what we need to do with The Dieters Scale in this part of this book.

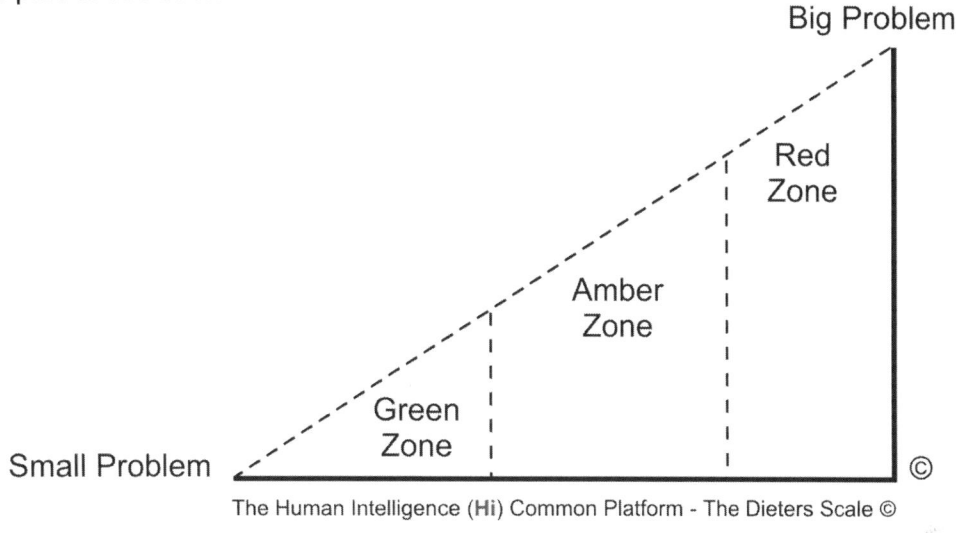

The Human Intelligence (Hi) Common Platform - The Dieters Scale ©

Amber Zone and Red Zone Preparation

Good preparation actually goes further than simply getting things together.

> The simple truth is that your body needs to be brought to a condition where it can actually use and benefit from the diet and weight management plan that you are going to use.

Good dieting and weight control preparation means that while we are preparing to go on our diet, over the next 3 months or so; that we begin to do things.

We begin to do the things that will make getting to and staying on the 2nd Stepping Stone (the diet) easier.

First there will be some lifestyle changes that you will need to make before you begin to diet proper. Don't even think about dieting before you have done these!

Some of these simple steps are:

The food that you keep around the house can be changed gradually; rather than quickly.

You don't need to tell anyone that you are planning to diet or tell then when you go on a diet, because you are not going to be doing it for their benefit; you are going to be doing it for your own benefit.

You don't need to buy any new clothes or anything like that, before you go on a diet. Who needs mementoes of failed diets or the pressure to fit into something that doesn't fit?

You can begin to move about a bit more. Nothing strenuous or over exerting; perhaps just simple walking to help your body work a bit better when you begin to diet.

Don't get mixed up with people who want to be competitive with dieting, weight loss or exercise. You don't need the grief and crap that goes with all that.

See if you can find something, other than food, that makes you feel good about yourself. It might simply be taking some time for yourself each day to walk around the garden or sitting quietly having a hot or cold drink.

Begin to allow yourself some time to consider your life and how you would like to change or improve it in the future. It doesn't have to be big things; often the small things are just as important.

Make a few notes for yourself and keep them somewhere private so that you can look at them from time to time.

Work out how you are going to handle the stress and anxiety from the unexpected problems, issues and challenges that are going to come up as you lose weight and begin to improve your life.

Rather that turn back to food or other behaviour that doesn't help you; how could you manage these things differently?

It is also worthwhile thinking about how you are going to handle things when someone you know wants to put you back in Fat Land; or they want to stop you getting out of Fat Land.

It often happens that people who live in Fat Land are easier to control. People who live in Slim Land tend to see the world in more positive ways and are less easy to control. Is this an issue for you?

In my experience quite a lot of people who live in Fat Land are unhappy with their lot in life; and when they finally move out of Fat Land and into Slim Land; they change their lives for the better; and they work to stay living in Slim Land.

Another thing you might want to consider is this: Who controls what you eat; the person selling you the food or you who gets and pays for the food?

Remember the good **Hi** that I pointed out in the first part of this book.

The reality is that you are probably going to have to change something about what you have been eating; and when and how much of it you have been eating;

but don't go on a diet to do this.

Before you do go on any diet proper, it can be a good thing to just practice changing a few things and see how it feels. This might change your view of the diet that you were thinking of using.

If you have got used to eating a lot of takeout foods and convenience foods; then your food taste will have been effected by eating this type of food. It influences your food preferences and it can change your taste towards foods that have higher fats, sugars, salt and other ingredients.

When you have got used to eating different types of foods it can take you some time to get used to the taste and textures of the new foods that you bring back into your eating portfolio. It can be a good idea to practice with this before you go on any type of diet.

Practice eating the new foods and gradually replace Red Zone foods with Amber Zone foods. We will go into replacing foods from one Zone, with foods from another Zone later in this part of the book. We will also look at how you can use The Dieters Scale to understand the relationship between Calories, Volume, Frequency and Nutrition.

I am taking a real world approach with this as many more people will be able to use this approach. It also has a higher probability of producing success.

> What I would suggest that you do, is you re-read the chapter on the Best Diet In The World when you are thinking about using your new diet.
>
> Ask yourself the question:
>
> If you have to change to fit the diet; can you really keep it up?
>
> It is better to take small steps and slowly change one thing at a time, than to try and change too much, too quickly. Understanding this is good Hi.

Another thing with food is volume. Large isn't always bad and small isn't always good. It's about having some form of balance with volume.

I will use The Dieters Scale and the Red, Amber and Green Zones to help you understand about suitable foods and balancing your diet for living in Slim Land.

Take the time to practice with all of this before you begin any diet proper. That way if things go wrong; well you are not on a diet anyway; you are just practicing!

Anyhow; all of this is just me trying to get you pointing in the right direction. So let's get back to sorting out your weight problem and putting your Plan in place.

Chapter 4

Preparation & Practice – Steps 1 to 5

I have created a list of 30 Steps for Preparation & Practice that will help you to establish a firm footing on the 1st Stepping Stone; and prepare you for moving on to the 2nd and the 3rd Stepping Stones.

These are a mixture of the Weight Control and the Lifestyle Management issues that affect people who have a problem with their weight.

What I am attempting to do here is this:

> With good Preparation & Practice there is often little or no difference between the Practice and actual Doing it. We want to keep that gap as small as we can.
>
> I want you to become so good at the Preparation & Practice that you hardly notice moving from one Stepping Stone to the next.
>
> Becoming good at the Preparation & Practice has the effect of automatically moving you forwards because you are ready and able to do so.
>
> So go through the Steps and add any that you think are relevant into your Plan.

The Steps that we are interested in at this stage are the following.

1. What are your dieting objectives?

Are you going to lose weight steadily over a period of time in order to get to your "Happy Point" or are you going to do it in stages with a little break in between? Either way is fine.

If you are going to do this in stages, then at the beginning of each stage you will go over the Stepping Stones from the beginning to the end. You will keep doing this until your final diet, when you will start living in Slim Land.

How much weight do you want to lose with this trip over the Stepping Stones?

> If you want to lose a lot of weight quickly then you will fall off the Stepping Stones and find yourself back in Fat Land. Be realistic!

Sustainable weight loss that lets you live in Slim Land does not happen fast for people who are in the Amber and Red Zones. Take your time and enjoy the journey.

2. Who are you relying on to make the trip across the Stepping Stones a success?

In reality; if you need a number of people to co-operate with you, so that you can lose weight; what happens if one or more of them doesn't do what you want?

> Your success should really be something that you take responsibility for and you should not make other people responsible for you achieving it.
>
> If you want to eat something don't make it someone else responsibility to stop you; accept that that responsibility is yours. Then you make the choices!

Reliance upon other people is one of the ways that your efforts can be easily undermined and this can cause you to fall off the Stepping Stones.

Don't give other people the power of Fat or Slim over your life; take it and keep it for yourself.

3. Are you really ready to leave Fat Land behind and start living in Slim Land?

Now this might seem like a daft question but the reality is that many people get scared when they really begin to lose weight and get control over their lives.

Part of the reason for this is that problems, challenges and issues that have been hidden in the background, and that have not been dealt with, can come back into focus as your weight recedes as a problem. *These are the icebergs I mentioned before.*

When this happens many people do not feel equipped or ready and able to start to sort these other things out. As a result they migrate back to Fat Land and the other problems go out of focus once again.

The result is that they return, unhappily, back to Fat Land, until the next time that they get fed up with living in Fat Land and want to do something about it.

Well the reality is that you don't have to do this!

You can do this journey in stages and take yourself a little bit further forwards each time. Then when you really are ready; then you can go over the Stepping Stones for the last time.

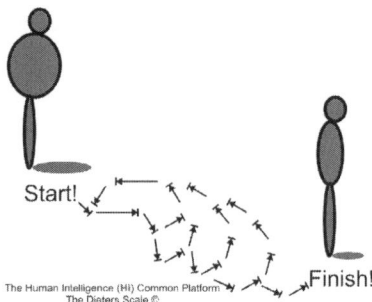

Success is usually a gradual process that involves small steps.

As well as going over the Stepping Stones with your weight, you are also going to go over the Stepping Stones with your other life problems; and your lifestyle management issues. These will also be in Zones as we saw in the Life Map.

A lot of dieters seem to take the view that they will deal with their weight problem and once that's all dealt with; then they will deal with the other issues.

The truth is that life isn't like that. When these issues come up and they are there; then they need to be looked at. A way to look at this is that this is life telling you that you can begin the process of improving, resolving or better managing them.

The way to begin to do this is to use the 3 Steps Approach and apply what you are doing with your diet to any other issue, problem or challenge.

You will also apply The Dieters Scale and use the Green, Amber and Red Zones to help you understand the size and complexity of any issue, problem or challenge.

I developed this approach to help you to focus on single issues or to combine issues and work with them together. However; it does take practice and you may well have things that you cannot deal with on your own.

If you find that you need outside help then use the information from this book to make sure that the help is real and that it can really help you in the proper ways.

It really is your choice. If you are not ready for something, you don't have to try and do it all in one go. Take baby steps and keep Practicing until you are successful.

I actually encourage people to take baby steps and to take their time with them. It is much easier to use small bits of effort to move a mountain than to try and move it all in one go.

Understanding this is good **Hi**.

4. The next Step is how are you going to handle the stresses of your life and keep on the Stepping Stones?

Stress is such an easy thing to ignore but it is such a critical piece of the weight problem puzzle.

Stress comes in many different shapes, sizes and forms.

Stress can be created by anything from work, to home life, to friends, to family, to shopping, to cooking, to sex, to health, to money, to lifestyle, to happiness, to driving, to looking after children, to being overweight, to your diet, to alcohol, to drugs, to not sleeping, to being at home all day, to not getting out and enjoying yourself; and being stuck as a fat person who wants to become slim but who is known for being fat.

The reality is that you have to take responsibility for your own stress and you need to find other ways of handling stress effectively.

This may involve you adding new Special Chapters into Your Life Profile that relate to managing stress.

The reason for doing this is that your eating habits and patterns of behaviour will tie into your stress and anxiety management processes.

> So when you go on a conventional diet, you will actually try to remove or greatly reduce the ways that you would normally use food and eating behaviours to manage your stress and anxiety on a daily basis.

As a result: When your stress and anxiety increases; it has no outlet.

It then bottles up and you increase the pressure on yourself.

As you increase the pressure on yourself, it increases your stress and anxiety until you reach the point where things revert to how they were before; and you once again use food and eating habits to manage your stress and anxiety.

The reason that this happens is that this is the only effective alternative that is in Your Life Profile and your operations manual will go to this when it has nowhere else to go.

So your stress and anxiety and your use of food and eating habits becomes a circular process which produces negative results for you; unless you change them.

Have a look at the following diagram.

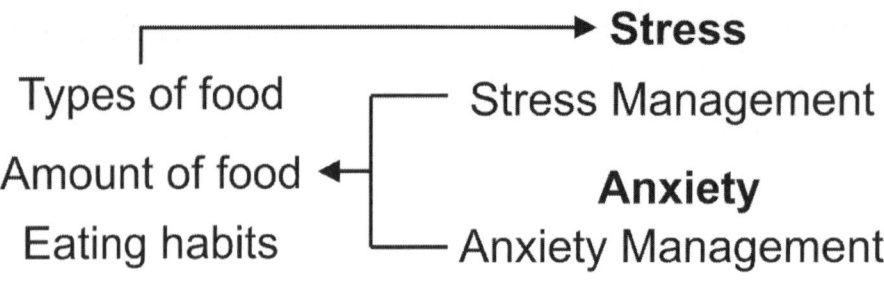

The Hi Common Platform - Weight Control The **Hi-Way** ©

What needs to happen is that we need to change this process and create another process to take its place.

Have a look at the next diagram.

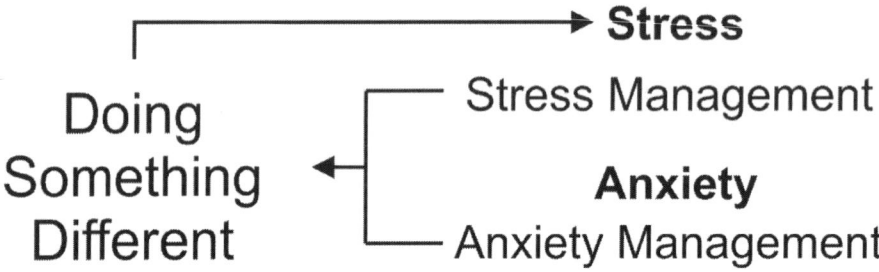

The Hi Common Platform - Weight Control The **Hi-Way** ©

By Preparing and Practicing new ways of dealing with Stress and Anxiety you can create a new chapter and new pages in Your Life Profile; that you can use when things become difficult.

This new process will help you to move away from compulsive and uncontrolled behaviour which affects your eating habits. It will help you to control those urges and to take more control over When you eat, Why you eat, What you eat and How you eat.

Now you don't have to have a single method to deal with everything stress related. The smart thing to do is to have a number of different things that you can do. It might be just taking a break and having a walk, having a coffee, watching a film or programme, having a chat with a friend, etc. Practice different things and see what works for you.

When it comes to stress and anxiety we have to recognise that sometimes it is just plain difficult. But you can make a plan and you can practice different things that can help with this before you go on a diet proper.

Imagine how much more difficult dealing with stress and anxiety is if you are trying to diet and lose weight; without having an alternative way to managing your stress and anxiety. Its nuts right?

So instead of being stupid; be smart. You are smarter than your weight problem any day of the week.

If you're not on a diet proper, then when you make mistakes and get things wrong it doesn't matter as much. You can't fail a diet if you are not on a diet. (Diet proper is officially being on a diet. I suggest that people never really go on a diet proper. I suggest that they Prepare and Practice and that gradually this moves to being how they actually do things)

5. What you need to consider now is the actual Weight Control Process that you will use.

You want to match the Weight Control Process to your lifestyle and what you are really willing and able to do at this time. The more you have to adjust your lifestyle to match the diet; the less likely you can sustain it.

What you have to understand about any diet where you want to lose weight is this:

> At some point you have to stop losing weight and move on to a process of weight management. This process of weight management needs to be something that you can easily do; so it needs to become an everyday part of your Positive Lifestyle Management.
>
> If you are trying to lose a lot of weight quickly, then you won't allow enough time for the Preparation & Practice; as you will want to quickly get to the second Stepping Stone – The diet & Weight Control Stepping Stone.
>
> If you do that; then it's only a matter of time before you fall off.

With Weight Control The **Hi-Way** it does not matter if you use a diet club, follow a diet plan or make up your own diet. However; there are things which you do need to remain aware of and take account off. So let me tell you what these are.

The **Hi-Way** Approach wants you to become independent of any diet or diet plan.

The reason for this is that you want to move to a point where Weight Control is automatic and an everyday part of your life. Weight Control should become a normal part of your Lifestyle Management and not something that is apart from it.

One of the problems that someone in the Amber and Red Zones has is that both their lifestyle management and their dietary practices are out of their previous normal ranges.

This results in them having chaos and chaotic behaviour in more than one area of their life at the same time.

And what happens when someone tries to adjust their chaotic lifestyle to a diet is that they get more chaos. More chaos means more stress and anxiety and then they are in trouble.

So let's take a step back and take another look at the dieting process and look at it Strategically.

There are just 4 things that you need to understand with food and dieting.

1. Nutrition
2. Calories
3. Volume
4. Food flow rate – Frequency of eating

Now you don't need to become an expert on nutrition or calorie counting or portion control. What you need to understand is the balance between these four components of food and healthier eating; and how you can use these to achieve control over any weight problem.

When we get to the 2nd Stepping Stone I will go into the balance between these four components of successful dieting and long term weight control in more detail.

We will be using The Dieters Scale and the Zones to help you understand dieting in a more user friendly way that you can use regardless of any diet that you follow.

In my view, diet clubs and weight watching organisations seem to want to sell a lot of other products to dieters.

I personally feel that this is something that you have to be careful about and watch out that you are not seduced by the sales pitches and sweet promises of what you can achieve by using these products.

Marketing promises are easy to make; higher than average results are harder to achieve and maintain.

And that is what we are after with the **Hi-Way** Approach; higher success rates which become higher long term success rates.

What you have to watch out for are the healthy diets and healthy foods which are not actually as healthy as you are being lead to believe. Just because a company is getting away with making big claims about their products does not make those claims true.

Use your previous experiences with the foods that you know you can and will eat; and use your knowledge of how you manage and control your own lifestyle.

Match what you will and can do now with the diet or weight management plan that you are going to use. As time goes on you can then change these.

Personally; I would never suggest that someone uses things like diet pills, meal replacements; and a variety of other low fat, low sugar, high energy drink foods.

Using these means that you are not learning the skills that you need for dietary management and you are still buying into the sweet promises and magical results that the diet industry promises.

Let your diet evolve as your lifestyle evolves.

Dave's Diet must have's!

In my view you need to:

        1. Eat regular meals.

        2. Of regular types.

        3. At regular times.

This helps your body to trust that it will have food at regular times, of a certain quality and at regular volumes.

If you lose that regular pattern then your body will adjust accordingly and you will feel the effects.

In my view you should always try to eat a good breakfast and not feel hungry. This helps to stop mid-morning snacking.

You should have a good lunch. If you have snacked and don't feel like eating lunch, then what will happen is that you will snack in the afternoon, and this will then effect your evening meal. The Knock on effect!

In the evening you should also have a good meal. This helps to stop snacking during the evening and avoids you then skipping breakfast the following morning because you have eaten a lot of undesirable things the night before.

Now you need to do this even if you don't really feel like it. This is because you need to establish a proper pattern of eating. If you don't then you are introducing chaos into the process; and we know what chaos produces.

Understanding this is good **Hi**.

Chapter 5

Preparation & Practice – Steps 6 to 10

6. Slowwww down the weight loss and create achievable goals.

If you do the right level of Preparation and Practice, in the right way; then you will move off the 1st Stepping Stone and you will move to the 2nd Stepping Stone – the Diet and Weight Control.

So many people fall of the 2nd Stepping Stone because they rush things. They want things to happen faster and in a linear fashion (they want to keep losing weight week after week in the same way until they reach their target weight).

The reality is that no-one's body works in that linear and regular fashion; unless they are ill.

Healthy bodies keep adjusting and making use of the resources that they have available to them. Factors like how active you are and the balance of Nutrition, Calories and Volume all come into play.

In my experience; People who want to lose a lot of weight over a short period of time are being seduced by their own desires; and ignoring the realities of the life within which they live.

It is much better to take a bit longer to lose that weight than to try and lose it quickly.

Fast weight loss is usually followed by fast weight gain and a quick trip back to Fat Land with potentially more problems to deal with.

7. Dealing with the PLATEAUS.

When you are a few weeks into a diet and you have lost weight what happens?

Your weight stabilises as you hit a plateau; and how do you respond? You cut out more food, increase the amount of exercise that you are doing; and then what happens?

You might begin losing a little more weight. And then what happens? The same thing again – you hit another plateau!

How often can you cut down on your food and increase your exercise before you give up?

Why put yourself through all of that if you don't have too?

What you need to understand is that Plateaus are your bodies' way of telling you that it needs time to adjust and it needs conditions to be stable.

So when you hit a plateau and you change your diet; you prevent your body from adjusting and doing the healthy thing it is trying to do; because you are not giving it the time that it needs; and you are not giving it the stability that it needs.

So what you are really doing is you are creating Chaos; and chaos lead to stress and anxiety which leads to...

Plateaus are a real part of being human. As you were putting on weight and moving to Fat Land, you went through different plateaus as you put on weight.

You just did not notice them.

I bet that when you put on weight it did not go on at the rate of 2lb (1kg) per week? I bet that you did not start off slim and then 14 weeks later you were 28lb's overweight?

Of course not!

You can't put weight on like this; and you can't take weight off like this either.

This is part of the diet industry nonsense that helps to keep you in Fat Land.

To be successful; you need to work with your body and not against it.

If you hit a plateau and you have the balance of Nutrition, Calories and Volume right; then keep doing what you are doing and wait.

It might take a few weeks or even a few months; but your body will adjust to the point where it can then begin to lose weight once again in a healthy and sustainable way.

While it is going through this process it will be gradually changing your body shape. You just probably won't notice this for a while but you will feel it in the way that you move and how things fit.

If you are weighing yourself and letting those scales control your life you will want things to happen too fast. This can cause stress and anxiety and quickly take you off the Stepping Stones and back to Fat Land.

When you hit a plateau you need to allow your body to stay there for a period of time while it adjusts from one Normal State to another Normal State. For example; it's beginning to move from the Red Zone towards the Amber Zone.

If you go at the weight loss too soon, then your body will not have made the step change that it needs to make. So it won't be able to move from the Red Zone.

This Plateau process is what we are trying to work with during the Preparation and Practice phase; while someone is still on the 1st Stepping Stone.

We are letting their body settle down and allowing it to prepare itself for their trip across the Stepping Stones.

Speed is often the enemy of achieving and maintaining good health.

8. Preparing your home and other people for your diet and lifestyle management changes.

We live how we are!

If you are someone who lives in Fat Land, then your home and work space will be that of a Fat Land person.

What we want to do is to prepare for leaving Fat Land behind and for our journey to Slim Land.

Now because we are going to take our time, we can make little changes here and there. As you are not on a diet proper these are not changes to your diet; they are just Preparation & Practice.

If you live on your own in Fat Land, things can be easier than if you have a family and other people in your household who also live in Fat Land.

Either way you have a job to do and the better you do it the easier you will find it to get on to the 2nd Stepping Stone and then on to the 3rd Stepping Stone.

So let's see what steps you may need to take with your home and work life.

- De-stress your home and work environment.

At home and at work, you can do simple things which gradually come together and make bigger things.

Simple steps like clearing up clutter, have other people clear up after themselves, clearing away after eating, having a schedule to get household chores done, sharing out the work required in the home, getting outstanding jobs completed, etc.

What you want to get fixed is all that stuff that you have to put up with that you really don't like and that adds to your stress and anxiety.

- Begin managing the food.

If you live on your own or in a household full of other people; you need to begin to manage your food. What this means is that you make simple and little changes by taking baby steps.

So what you need to manage are things like treats. Do you really need that emergency supply of comfort food that you keep? If it is easily accessible then it is easy to eat on impulse.

Look at your normal daily diet. How many take-outs are you having each week?

Look at any food the morning after and see if you would really eat that stuff cold?

Look at convenience foods. Are you buying prepared meals and then just heating them up?

Look at those drinks that you have through the week. How many fizzy drinks are you having? Are you drinking wine? Do you have sugar with your hot drinks?

As you look at these different things there will be things that you can easily change and improve. Now is the time to begin to do this because you are not on a diet proper and there is no pressure to get it right. You have the time to experiment with changing things.

- Prepare other people.

When I have worked with people to help them move from Fat Land to Slim Land, we often end up encountering a problem with other people.

These can be friends, family, work colleagues or just people that you know and come into contact with.

What you need to understand and appreciate is that all these people have got used to you living in Fat Land, having a Fat Land lifestyle and looking as if you belong in Fat Land.

Now you are going to change how they perceive you and how they have gotten used to thinking about you and treating you.

In effect: They will adjust with you as you move across the Stepping Stones from Fat Land to Slim Land and begin living in Slim Land.

And like all adjustments; they don't always go smoothly.

You need to prepare yourself that other people may let you down. They may put you under pressure to go back to Fat Land and behave like the person they are used too.

You need to be prepared for this and for those closest to you to do the unexpected; when you least expect it; and when you are least prepared for it.

I tell you this because this often happens and these can be very short and quick ways for you to end up back in Fat Land.

So start to make the little adjustments that you need to make. Drop little hints that you are going to make some small changes. Then begin making those small adjustments and changes; and stick with them.

As you are not yet on a diet proper you don't have to worry about your diet or explaining about your diet; as you are just preparing and practicing.

This way is less stressful and more easily achievable.

9. Allow time for your Fat Land Palate to change to a Slim Land Palate.

When we eat certain types of foods for long enough; our palate changes and those foods become Normal for us. So someone who lives in Fat Land is likely to have developed a palate for Fat Land foods.

So when the person from Fat Land wants to move to Slim Land, one of the things that needs to be allowed to happen is the adjustment to their palate.

People develop "the taste" for Fat Land foods because they often have extra fats, sugars, salt and other additives that our bodies can get used to quite quickly.

As a result it will take time to lose or adjust the taste for Fat Land foods. These are the foods that can have the extra hidden sugars, fats and other things that can get you in to trouble with controlling your weight.

Now something else that you need to understand is that the same food does exist in both Fat Land and in Slim Land. Let's use pasta as an example.

Slim Land pasta will be cooked in the same way as Fat Land pasta. It is what is added to it as it is cooked and after it is cooked that alters things.

Fat Land pasta may have a very tasty highly flavoured sauce mixed in with it. It needs to be highly flavoured because Fat Land pasta eaters have got used to highly flavoured foods. To achieve the high flavour, additives and other ingredients will have been added into the sauce. It won't be the pasta that is the problem; it's the sauce.

Slim Land pasta will also have a sauce added to it that is very tasty. But a Fat Land person has got used to a sauce that is full of other ingredients; and Slim Land sauce may not have the same punch. By comparison it can taste bland.

So you need to allow the time for your taste to change and be able to appreciate more subtle taste and flavours.

As you are not on a diet proper; this is a good time to experiment with that.

- Food Marketing

There is something that you need to understand about food marketing.

In Slim Land and in Fat Land people lie about and misrepresent their foods. In both places people will tell you that their food is healthy and good for you; even if it isn't that healthy.

In both places they will tell you that their food is low fat, low sugar, low salt and so on. What you will probably find when you actually look at these foods is things like this:

> Low fat food never actually contained any fat anyway; low sugar has been replaced by more fat to give it flavour; low fat has been replaced by more sugar to make it taste better; and so on!

The truth is that people and companies may comply with the Law in their marketing and in the promoting of the products that they sell. But being legally correct is not the same as being honest with people who are having problems with their weight.

So don't be seduced by someone who is telling you that they sell food to people in Slim Land and you should buy it.

Later on I will give you a guide to help you understanding the foods that you need and you can use this to help you.

10. Putting some of the changes in place before the diet proper.

It is a good idea to begin putting some of the changes in place before you consider starting your diet proper. It allows you and other people the opportunity to get used to those changes without any of the pressures of the real diet being there.

You will also need to begin practicing with your new ways of managing and dealing with the stress that you will experience; and the stressful and anxious situations that you will find yourself in.

Get used to the stress and anxiety management and begin using it. Then when it comes to the diet proper you will be familiar with your new ways of handling and managing stress and anxiety. This is because you will have begun to create new Special Chapters in Your Life Profile that you are using.

Chapter 6

Preparation & Practice – Steps 11 to 15

11. Getting used to the Stress Management before the diet proper.

Once you have your new stress and anxiety management strategies in place you can begin practicing them.

You know what types of situations make you nervous and anxious; and you know what you normally do during and after those situations. So why not take an easy one of these situations and see what happens in that situation when you apply your new ways of handling stress and anxiety.

Practice will help you when you do go on the diet proper. It will make you familiar with the feelings and emotions that you are going to experience during and after the stressful event.

With some things you may have to practice more than others. The reason for practicing is that in different situations you will have:

- Muscle memory
- Emotional memory
- Psychological memory
- Social memory

And each one of these will be trying to use your Fat Land responses; the ones that you have learned and been using all the time that you have been living in Fat Land.

You need the chance to introduce new responses that can help you move out of Fat Land; and this gives you the chance to practice with them before you begin the diet proper.

- Pressure Points! Like holidays and anniversaries.

A weight problem is part of someone's daily life. It lives with them as a companion and as part of their social life. What we are seeking to do is to help someone change those relationships, so that they are more of an asset to them than a burden.

Because of the way that your weight problem and you behave together, we need to consider some of the different situations and circumstances in which you will both find yourselves.

Times such as anniversaries, holidays and birthdays can become times of great stress and anxiety for someone with a weight problem.

What I hope that you do is that you plan for the holidays, anniversaries and birthdays and think about them beforehand.

As the tension builds leading up to the event your stress is going to increase. So the relevant question then becomes: How are you really going to deal with it?

Ignoring leads to problems.
Dealing with it leads to solutions!

When you begin to plan and prepare for difficult times, you begin to take a degree of control back to yourself. It is generally a lack of control that causes stress and anxiety; and we know where that leads.

In reality you need to think of your life as being on an annual cycle. Each year you will have a birthday and different anniversaries will come and go.

It is the same with holidays. Each year you will hope to have holidays.

If holidays have consisted of eating and drinking as much as you can and putting on lots of weight; then how is the next holiday going to be different?

By planning ahead and being realistic about what you are going to have to deal with; you can change and better manage the results.

12. Eating regularly and working with 3 meals a day to prepare your body.

Your body needs regular amounts of food, at regular times. This helps to produce a stability with your food intake that your mind and body can rely upon.

This simple process of eating regularly and predictably is what will help your body to stabilise and be ready to lose weight when you go on that diet. In effect; what you are trying to do is to create a natural plateau of balanced consumption.

By starting the process at this stage you can get used to it first and correct any problems before you go on any diet proper. If you wait to do this until you go on that diet proper, then you will increase your chances of falling off a Stepping Stone.

Remember; if you are an Amber or Red Zone dieter, then it can easily take 3 months or more before your body will achieve stability and be able to properly respond to a diet.

You can use that time to practice and get these things in place.

13. Getting your food stash out of harm's way.

If we were dealing with alcohol addiction, we would want to put distance between an alcoholic and alcohol. If we were dealing with a drug addict, we would want to put distance between the drug addict and their drugs of choice.

When the alcoholic or the drug addict is in a stressful, anxious or difficult situation, their proximity to their drug of choice determines how easy it is for them to get it; and then use it.

And in reality; comfort food, reward food, compensation food, stress food, anxiety food, and boredom food; are all the same type of thing.

What happens when you use those foods, at those times, is important because you are re-enforcing your old habits and making sure that you continue to live in Fat Land.

If that stash is easy to get to, then you will find it easy to eat it and easy to stay in Fat Land.

> Your proximity to the foods of your choice, when you are stressed or anxious determines how easy it will be for you to consume them.

How will you manage to change if it is too easy to get to your food stash?

14. Moving your body about before eating.

Over recent years there have been medical studies looking at how our bodies process and manage food.

Some of these have focused on the way that our bodies handle and manage food in situations where someone has been moving around prior to eating; and where the same person has not been moving around prior to eating.

These Studies have shown that our bodies handle food better and in healthier ways if some form of mobility has occurred before the consumption of the food.

What this means for the dieter is that a few minutes of simple exercise, such as a short walk, can help your body to better manage and process the food that you are about to eat.

This becomes a useful thing to know because at times you may find that you are going to go out for a meal, or going to eat with friends, and you don't want to miss the event. So being mobile shortly before you eat could help your body to manage and process the food better.

Like everything this needs to be done with moderation. If you try to use this as a means to overeat; then all that will happen is that you will stay in Fat Land.

15. Walking your way to Slim Land.

If you are an Amber or Red Zone dieter then you may not be as fit as you should be. Now being fit is often misunderstood by people with weight problems. Being fit doesn't mean that you need to become an athlete.

Being fit is about the level of health that you need to have, to enjoy and maintain the lifestyle and quality of life that you want to have and enjoy.

So if you want to be someone who lives in Fat Land and you don't mind that you can't walk anywhere; or that you can't run; or that you can't do activities that require you to do anything physical; or that you easily get out of breath and that you have no muscle tone; then fine.

If you do mind any of that and you want to improve and change your life; then what can you do?

Well I am an advocate of walking. Just plain old simple walking that does not require any fancy gear or products.

In reality; if you can walk, then you can begin the process of getting fit. Walking can also be a good way of dealing with stress, anxiety and boredom.

Why not give it a try before you go on the diet proper and see what happens?

Chapter 7

Preparation & Practice – Steps 16 to 20

16. Dealing with all the media pressures.

This might seem like an odd thing for me to say. You're unlikely to be a celebrity and have the press trying to take pictures of you. (If you are a celebrity and you are reading my book; why not give me an endorsement?).

Anyway: What I am talking about is all the background media pressure that most people come into contact with every day but may not notice; the magazines, the television, films, the Internet and the radio.

When you have a weight problem you tend to be constantly looking at other people and how they look, what they are wearing, and is there any fat showing.

The reality is that when we get over the age of 30 we don't have perfect bodies.

Life takes a toll of all of us and we have to do work to keep in shape and look good.

Any image that you will see in the media can and probably has been computer enhanced. This means that someone will have imperfections removed, their legs can be made to look longer, bodies can be made to look thinner, skin can be made to look perfect, hair can be made to look fantastic and so on.

When you see an image in the media and you try to conform to this; you may as well try to conform to a dolphin or a rhino. You see you are trying to conform to something that is not real, not sustainable and a fictitious creation of the media.

The reality is that just about everything that you will buy, want or need is going to be subject to marketing spin.

Marketing spin is used because they usually need to provide you with an aspiration to buy into, in order to sell to you.

Take back your life from the media and work out what you really want to be and then go for it. And remember: They need you more than you need them.

17. Don't buy any new clothes and things.

I have a Mother, 2 sisters, lots of Aunts and cousins. The number of times that I have heard people say that they have bought new clothes to get into when they lose weight.

My advice is: Don't do it!

For most people it becomes another pressure and if they fail on the diet it becomes a permanent reminder of that failure. Haven't you had enough crap in your life!

Why not treat yourself when you have achieved a stage of success.

If you are losing weight in stages, then when you hit a significant stage and your weight and lifestyle are stable; then treat yourself to something.

In the Preparation and Practice stage, which is where you are now, you can have a plan to treat yourself to something at a later stage in the process; but wait until you get there and you know that you are going to stay there before you celebrate.

Don't distract yourself by buying what you can't use now.

18. Tough choices and tough decisions.

We can't avoid them. We all have them and we all have to make them. At some point in time Tough choices and Tough decisions are going to have to be made and stuck too.

If you are going to move from Fat Land to Slim Land then it is likely that you are going to have to make these tough choices and tough decisions at some point along this journey.

In reality the best way to do these things is to see them coming and to prepare for them.

If you look at your life, you will have an idea of what you are not happy with and what you will need to deal with at "some point".

Well eventually "some point" arrives and you either back off from it and try to leave it; or you get in there and deal with it.

If there are major issues that you will need to deal with and you cannot deal with them on your own; try and get the right sort of help.

I find that sitting down and writing out the problem helps me. I also write out the preferred solution and then see what process I need to go through to get the result that I want.

At times that old saying: You can't make an omelette without breaking eggs comes to mind.

What this really means is that you can't leave everything as it is and change it at the same time. I have noticed that quite a lot of people try to do this and I have mentioned this process in this book.

Everything we are doing in this process is about; how you will get to Slim Land and how you will be able to continue to live in Slim Land and have a great life when you get there.

> The issues that cause problems in your life and which remain unaddressed are ones that can shorten your stay in Slim Land and carry you back to Fat Land.

What I am encouraging you to do is to develop ways of better managing and dealing with the problems, issues and challenges that you will face in life.

The reality is that these things can be challenging but if you adopt the Positive Lifestyle Management Approach that I advocate; then you can begin to live a positive life and seek to change your life in positive ways.

Living in a Positive Way doesn't avoid the tough choices and difficult decisions but it can put you in a better position to deal with them.

19. Snacks!

Snacks can be great but let's face it; there are a lot of rubbish things wrapped up to look nice that people want us to buy.

When it comes to snacks, and all the food and drink that you are going to consume, what you need to understand is this:

> Lots of people put water with crap and call it gravy!

> Just because it is for sale; it doesn't mean that it is good for you; or that it has had all sorts of test to make sure that it is safe to go on the market; or that it is safe for you to eat lots of them.

In reality if you are eating lots of snacks then there is something wrong with your diet. If you are eating 3 meals a day, then you have to look at why you are snacking.

Are you using snacks to manage stress, anxiety or boredom?

I am not saying don't snack but I am saying that it has to fit with your journey from Fat Land to Slim Land and your being able to live in Slim Land.

This means altering your Fat Land snacking habits and changing them to Slim Land snacking habits.

And now is a good time to Practice with them and find ones that you like.

20. Alcohol, drugs and medication.

In your life, with your diet and your lifestyle management, you have to look at what you are doing and why you are doing it.

If you are consuming a lot of alcohol then this will be having a number of different affects upon you.

These will be physical and psychological and it will also effect your weight and how your body processes and manages food.

In my view it is better if you consume no alcohol or very little alcohol on a daily basis. One of my reasons is that although alcohol can be fun and pleasant; it is in reality a poison for human tissue.

It is a poison that we can tolerate and use and achieve different results from; but it is still a poison and it will kill and harm people when used in large quantities.

Alcohol also alters our moods and perceptions. This is one reason why so many people use alcohol at times of stress and anxiety. They also use it to relax and let themselves go at parties.

From the point of view of someone living in Fat Land; alcohol also has lots of calories. Drinking too much alcohol makes you put on weight.

If we apply The Dieters Scale to alcohol, then no alcohol is the Green Zone.

As you consume alcohol you move out of the Green Zone and into the Amber Zone. As your consumption of alcohol increases above 20 units per week, you move out of the Amber Zone and into the Red Zone.

Using the Zones in this way is in relation to Weight Control, hidden calories and other effects; and has nothing to do with Government guideline for alcohol consumption. This illustrates risk like calories when consuming alcohol. Green is low risk and Red is high risk.

I have seen an increasing number of women whose alcohol consumption falls into the Red Zone on a regular basis. This can lead to someone regularly over consuming calories that they don't realise they are consuming.

When it comes to drugs and medication we need to segment these. Are they elective (you choose to take them) or are they are prescribed (you have a genuine medical reason to take them and you take them as prescribed)?

Now there are very valid reasons for people to take prescription medication. There are also people who abuse prescription medications.

With the elective use of prescribed and none prescribed drugs, you have to ask why you are doing so. Is it to make life more bearable?

Are you using it to help you cope with something?

What you need to consider is how the inappropriate use of alcohol, drugs and medication will fit into your new life in Slim Land and your desire to continue to live there.

Is it better to begin to address these issues before you go on a diet proper?

Only you can really answer this question.

Chapter 8

Preparation & Practice – Steps 21 to 30

21. Eating out - No-one likes to be a party pooper!

Enjoying a meal out is something that everyone can do. Doing it too often will present you with a challenge that you are going to have to deal with.

The challenge is that it is usual for restaurants to use more fats, sugars and other ingredients to increase the flavours and taste of their food than someone would at home. The result is that you lose control over what goes into the food that you eat.

While you are at this Preparation and Practice stage, it could be very useful for you to begin managing eating out in a positive and productive way. You could start by making a decision about how you are going to do it.

The question then becomes one of:

Are you going to eat out or are you going for a blow out?

Enjoying eating out is different from stuffing as much food into you as you can stand. One is fun and the other has a good chance of making you ill.

You know; I am not the fat police and in reality you don't need the fat police. If you think that consuming as much food as you possibly can, as often as you can is fun; who am I to get in the way of your fun.

All you need to do is take the responsibility for all that fun that you are having.

Simple!

I have also seen people who are overweight eating out at restaurants and they clearly want to have a decent meal. However; they order things like salad and they are clearly not enjoying eating the meal.

Why not just order a normal meal and eat that; if it is going to avoid you stopping at a take-away on the way home or stuffing yourself with things when you get home.

Remember: Go for a meal out; not for a blow out!

Understanding and practicing this is good Hi.

22. Holidays.

Holidays can be great fun and a real break from the difficulties and challenges of everyday life. They are also events where so many dieters get into trouble.

Real life continues all the time; even on holidays.

The body that you had before you went on holiday is the same one that you have on holiday and it will be the same one that you have after the holiday. So why would you treat it differently?

The truth is that going on holiday is about fun, relaxing and having a good time. So enjoy yourself!

What you do have to remember is that your body still has the same rules on holiday as it has the rest of the time. So if you are in the process of stabilising your weight and you go on holiday; then stick with the 3 meals a day process.

At any time you can really enjoy your food. You just have to watch the blow outs and the Fat Land diet.

You don't have to deprive yourself of anything but you will have to watch your volume of consumption.

Consume (eat and drink) too much and you can undo a lot of good work in the course of a couple of weeks; especially if you are trying to get your body stable.

If you do mess up your body's stability then you need to go back and start over again. The 3 month period will begin again.

Is it worth throwing everything away that you are working towards?

Will you do that every time that you go on holiday somewhere?

The reality is that if you do: Then you are really living in Fat Land and just visiting Slim Land from time to time.

23. Christmas and other festivals.

Every year there is going to be festive holidays and feast days. Fantastic!

Enjoy them and have fun.

Use the information from these different sections and work out a plan so that you can enjoy and get the most out of the festive break and feast days.

Remember that a feast is not a blow out. A feast is a celebration and celebrations are about enjoyment.

Feasts are not about being so stuffed that you cannot move.

Just remember what you are working towards and how easily you can throw away all that good work if you act like a Fat Land resident who has no self control and no self respect.

You are better than that and you are worth a whole lot more than some idiot who lets food rule them; rather than serve them.

Become the master of your own body; and what you want to do with it; and what you want to put in it. Remember that once it is in your mouth you lose control over it.

24. Treats.

Oh; don't you just love treats. I know that I do!

Does the treat need to be food?

In reality; as you begin to move out of Fat Land and develop your lifestyle management you will find that things, other than food, can be treats.

A nice day out at the beach. Watching a good film. Having a BBQ (yes it involves food but you can manage it right!). Going for a walk somewhere nice. Having some "Me" time. These are just some simple examples of what a treat can be.

Having a treat that involves food is OK. What you have to understand is that just because we call it a treat, it doesn't mean that the rules that govern our bodies don't apply.

If we eat a load of fast food until we are completely stuffed; it is still fast food that we have stuffed ourselves with.

If we eat lots of chocolate; it's still chocolate. If we drink lots of alcohol; it's still alcohol.

The real secret of a treat is that we enjoy the treat until we have had enough of it.

If we have the treat too often, then it stops being a treat and it becomes normal and every day. By its nature a treat is something that we do occasionally.

So enjoy the occasional treat that involves food but remember these simple guidelines.

25. Tough days!

As we all live real lives there are going to be tough days.

Very few people avoid having tough days. So if we know that they are going to happen; plan for them.

At the moment if there is a tough day what do you do?

Does it involve food?

In the future you don't want to revert to using food as a means of managing your stress and anxiety. You want to use other ways of doing this.

On bad days you will use these other ways to manage and handle the stress and anxiety. If these other ways prove to be insufficient then you will need to work on some more and learn some new things.

What you need to understand about stress and anxiety management is that you don't stop feeling and experiencing stress and anxiety; the purpose is that it helps you to manage and control how it affects you and how you respond to it.

It's like soldiers and fear. Soldiers do feel fear and they have to learn how to live with it and manage it. If they let the fear take over it creates problems and they can't do their jobs.

26. Catastrophes.

No-one likes it when something bad or something really bad happens.

The truth is that the really bad things in life don't tend to happen that often but they do happen.

When really bad things do happen it is important not to become self-destructive.

Hurting yourself does not help the situation.

In bad situations my view would be to do that which needs to be done.

It is usually better to assess the situation and understand what you are really dealing with; and then to work out a plan for how to manage and deal with things.

In all cases life goes on and those of us who survive have to continue to live. The best testament that survivors of catastrophes can make; is to survive and live their lives to the best of their abilities.

27. Booze.

Haven't we already done alcohol? Yes we have but now I am going to talk about booze and boozing.

Why boozing? In recent years more and more women have become big drinkers of wine and other alcoholic drinks.

Many women can easily drink a bottle of wine a day and certainly several bottles a week. Many will also drink lots of beer and spirits such as Vodka.

Why are we calling it boozing? It's because of volume, frequency, and why?

It's how much they are drinking, why they are doing so and how often they are doing so.

Boozing is using alcohol in the same way that someone uses food; in the wrong ways.

Boozing gives you the opportunity to take on thousands of calories, to hurt your body and mind; and to make yourself ill.

Boozing is another form of stress relief, anxiety management, making yourself feel better (temporarily) and being one of the lads or one of the girls.

Boozing is a blunt way of dealing with things by anesthetising yourself with lots of alcohol.

Boozing takes a toll of the body regardless of whether you are male or female.

Boozing may involve binge drinking or consistent and regular drinking.

Boozing helps you to take on lots of Calories quickly. Someone drinking in the Red Zone can easily take on several thousand booze related Calories each week or each month.

28. Food Addiction

In the first part of this book I looked at Food Addiction. If you think that you may have a problem with Food Addiction then you should read that again.

29. Weighing Yourself

How often are you weighing yourself and why are you doing so?

If something is going to help keep you in Fat Land; it is going to be the weighing scales.

Weighing and measuring yourself on a regular or frequent basis can mean that you end up feeling good or bad according to what weight the needle points at.

Weighing scales are more important if you are underweight; rather than overweight. This is because someone underweight has more risk to their health than someone who is overweight. This is because their bodies may simply not have enough nourishment and nutrition to keep them alive.

When people are overweight it is a different type of problem.

If you are overweight then weighting yourself something like once a month is best. And when you do weigh yourself the result needs to be considered along with a number of other factors.

Your body will vary by a couple of pounds according to what you have eaten and drank and when you did so.

Your body can also vary by a couple of pounds according to how well your digestive system is working and what is going through your digestive system.

Your body can also vary, especially in women, according to things like your menstrual cycle.

So with just these three things we could have 5-6lbs (3kg) of weight variation.

What we are really interested in is your journey from Fat Land to Slim Land.

And on that journey I <u>don't</u> need you to weight yourself because there can be many positive things which are happening which can make you seem as if you are getting heavier; when in reality it is your body working better.

Positive things that can happen, which can make it look like you are putting on weight include: putting on more muscle.

With Weight Control the **Hi-Way** we need to look at your weight when you begin; and we need to look at your weight when you are in Slim Land and comfortable with your weight.

It is when you are happy and comfortable with your weight that this creates your Happy Point. The point at which you are happy with your weight and what goes with it.

The diet industry normally wants you to keep looking at that scale and to continue being influenced by what it says.

Why listen to an industry with an 84% failure rate!

I don't need you to keep weighing and measuring yourself; as it gives you the wrong messages and it keeps you fixed on Fat Land behaviour.

I am more interested in where your real "Happy Point" is and in getting to it.

30. Prepare yourself and Practice things to get better at them

Now that you are seeing and understanding what proper Preparation & Practice consist off, the next thing is to prepare yourself for actually taking action.

Please don't be put off by Preparation & Practice. You don't have to do it all in one go. It is not a race so take your time.

Preparation & Practice is about bringing the things together that you need to do a job and making sure that those things can work for you. In this case it is the job of getting from Fat Land to Slim Land and then living in Slim Land.

Through the process of Preparation and Practicing you will be doing what is necessary to stay on the 1st Stepping Stone; and what is necessary to enable you to get on and stay on the 2nd Stepping Stone.

Time is a very important part of Preparation and Practice. You can't rush through the different processes and just tick boxes; it simply doesn't work.

You need to achieve the Experiential Learning that comes from actually Doing Things in the right way; and it is that that takes time.

Now I don't think that any of these 30 steps are particularly difficult to do. What you need to do is to look at them and think what really (and I do mean really) applies to you.

With each of these steps you can apply The Dieters Scale and see where you think you are with that step.

For example:

Step 24 - Treats.

You may regularly eat treats throughout the day. This ends up replacing many of the meals that you should be eating. This means that you are going to be in the Amber or Red Zones on The Dieters Scale for eating treats.

If you only occasionally, like once a week or so, eat a small bag of crisp or something like that. Then you would be in the Green Zone for treats on The Dieters Scale.

So by applying The Dieters Scale to the different Behaviours and Actions that you undertake, you can then begin to create a Life Map to help you move your life in another direction.

A simple thing to understand is this:

> Any weight problem and its associated issues can be resolved, improved or better managed so that someone can reach their "Happy Point".
>
> Doing this requires Direction, Purpose and the Correct Application of Actions.

A Summary Of The 30 Steps

If you diet before your body is naturally stable, then all you are doing is adding to the problems. You may lose weight during that diet but I don't think you will achieve and maintain the Weight Control that you want.

Achieving natural stability means that you will need to prepare for your diet by eating 3 meals a day; regular meals, regular amounts, regular times. This helps to balance the Food Flow Rate that your body needs.

In preparation for going on a diet proper you need to begin practicing managing your food.

Look for potential problems that will affect your ability to practice the diet; and see how you can manage them better before you begin any diet proper.

Amber and Red Zone dieters need to allow about 3 months or more for their bodies to achieve natural stability. We want to achieve a natural plateau and use this as our starting point.

During that time you can Prepare your home and your workplace by practicing making small changes and practicing with reducing problems.

Before your diet proper; start practicing with ways of managing stress and anxiety that does not involve using food.

Look for "hot spots" in the coming year such as holidays, anniversaries, family visits, etc. Things that can cause you problems, issues and challenges; things that can affect your diet and behaviours.

Write down your dieting goals. Test them out. Are they really what you want?

How much pressure are your dieting goals going to put you under?

Try out different foods to see whether or not you will be able to use them and keep them in your Weight Control long term.

Work out what Practice diet you are going to use. Is it one of your own, someone else's or are you going to use a diet club?

Can your Practice diet change from being a weight loss diet, to being a weight management process that you can easily incorporate into your daily life?

Any behaviours and actions around food needs to be able to transition from the diet phase into a weight management process that fits how you want to live your life.

Should you practice losing a bit of weight and practice all this other stuff before you go on a diet proper? I would say yes!

The reality is that this can take the pressure off of you and let you practice and make mistakes at a time when you are not dieting proper. This can greatly reduce the stress and expectations that you have.

What are the other problems, issues or challenges that are part of your weight problem?

Do you understand where these fit within The Dieters Scale? Are they Red Zone issues, Amber Zone issues or Green Zone issues?

Looking at these different things; are there any that really should be addressed or managed a bit better before you begin your diet proper?

If you follow this process, what you will be doing is you will begin to deal with your weight problem at different levels. And this is actually more reflective of what a weight control problem really is.

At each Stepping Stone there needs to have been enough Preparation and Practice, in order to make it easier for you to stay on the Stepping Stone; but also so that you can lay the foundations that you need to progress to the next stage.

Part of the Preparation work and Practice that you do now, will begin to benefit you when you move on to the 2nd Stepping Stone; the Diet and Weight Control Stepping Stone. If you do the Preparation and Practice well, you will find that this automatically takes you forwards.

Part of the Preparation work and Practice that you are doing now will also benefit you when you move on to the 3rd Stepping Stone; Positive Lifestyle Management. Once again by doing the P&P well you will find that it automatically takes you forward.

And part of the P&P that you do now will also benefit you when you get to Slim Land; and it will help you to continue to live in Slim Land.

Once you have done the Preparation & Practice that you need to do; then you can move on to the next Stepping Stone.

Always remember:

> If you make a mistake or get things wrong understand that each mistake and error is an opportunity to learn and get it right next time. It's not failure; it's an opportunity for learning.

Chapter 9

Adding More Pieces To Your Life Map

Part of what we need to do with Weight Problems is to change the Attitude and Expectations that the person has developed over time. If we can't change them; then maybe we can begin the process of beginning to change them. Either way is fine.

So what we are going to do now is to use The Dieters Scale to look at some more of the Common Components of a Weight Problem. We will then be able to add these to the ones that we looked at in the first part of the book.

By combining the answers in both parts of the book, we will be increasing your Human Intelligence (**Hi**) of your weight problem.

We will also be able to add more items to your Life Map and provide a more accurate profile that you can apply that Human Intelligence (**Hi**) too.

In this part of the book we will use The Dieters Scale in the format shown below. It will be easier for you to see differences at a glance.

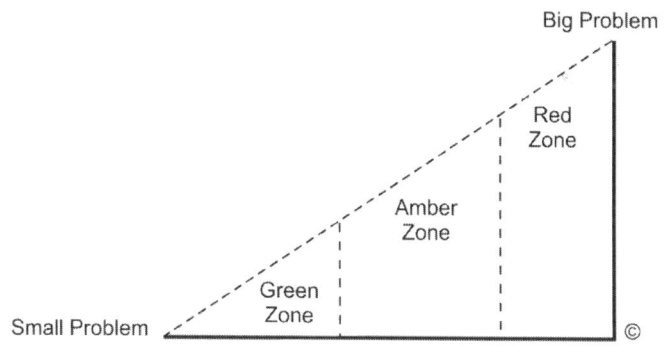

Your weight problem and any associated issues are going to fit into one of the Zones of The Dieters Scale and we only have 3 Zones:

    The Green Zone
    The Amber Zone
    The Red Zone

Each Zone represents a different level of complication and difficulty.

So this gives us 3 levels that we can use to begin to see the differences with the issues that people with weight problems experience. And we can use this to work out what we need to do to improve each issue.

Question 1

Our first question relates to your physical appearance, related to your weight and size.

How happy are you personally with your physical appearance related to your weight and size?

- Very happy = Green Zone
- Not happy , could improve, etc. = Amber Zone
- Miserable = Red Zone

So which Zone are you in? _____

Question 2

The next question relates to how easy you can move around, do things and how well your clothing fits you.

- I find it very easy to move around and to do the things that I really want to do; and my clothes fit great.= Green Zone

- I find it moderately difficult and a bit uncomfortable to move around and do things; and my clothes are uncomfortable at times.

    My weight does hinder what I want to do but it does not stop me from doing it. = Amber Zone

- I find it quite difficult to move around at times and to do things because of my weight. My clothing has been replaced by larger baggy items and things like getting in and out of chairs is difficult.

    My weight stops me from doing things that I would like or need to do. = Red Zone

So which Zone are you in? _____

Question 3

The next question relates to your social life.

Does your weight impact or affect your social life?

- No it does not impact my social life in any way. = Green Zone

- Yes my weight does affect my social life and it does stop me from doing things which I would like to do. = Amber Zone

- Yes my weight has a big impact upon my social life. I have little or no real social life. = Red Zone

So which Zone are you in? _____

Question 4

The next question relates to confidence. This question has 2 parts.

Part 1.

How does your confidence affect your weight problem?

- Not at all = Green Zone
- Quite a bit = Amber Zone
- A lot = Red Zone

So which Zone are you in? _____

Part 2.

How does your weight problem affect your confidence?

- Not at all = Green Zone
- Quite a bit = Amber Zone
- A lot = Red Zone

So which Zone are you in? _____

Question 5

The next question relates to Self-Esteem. This question has 2 parts.

Part 1.

How does your Self-Esteem affect your weight problem?

- Not at all = Green Zone
- Quite a bit = Amber Zone
- A lot = Red Zone

So which Zone are you in? _____

Part 2.

How does your weight problem affect your Self-Esteem?

- Not at all = Green Zone
- Quite a bit = Amber Zone
- A lot = Red Zone

So which Zone are you in? _____

Questions 6

The next question relates to Relationships. This question has 2 parts.

Part 1.

How do your Relationships affect your weight problem?

- Not at all = Green Zone
- Quite a bit = Amber Zone
- A lot = Red Zone

So which Zone are you in? _____

Part 2.

How does your weight problem affect your Relationships?

- Not at all = Green Zone
- Quite a bit = Amber Zone
- A lot = Red Zone

So which Zone are you in? _____

Question 7

The next question relates to: How you feel about yourself.

- I feel good about Myself all the time. = Green Zone
- I feel good about Myself a lot of the time but a fair amount of time I don't. = Amber Zone
- I rarely or never feel good about Myself. = Red Zone

So which Zone are you in? _____

Question 8

The next question relates to Control.

Overall when you look at your life and the different things which you do; how "In Control" do you feel?

- I am in control of everything that I need to be. = Green Zone.
- I am not in control of a number of things that I should be, that I need to be, that I want to be. = Amber Zone.
- I hardly control anything, I am totally out of control, I lost control a long time ago. = Red Zone.

So which Zone are you in? _____

Question 9

The next question relates to exercise.

What we are interested in here is your reality and not what you think you should say. So be honest.

- I do actually like to exercise and keep myself fit; and I do so on a regular basis. = Green Zone.
- I periodically exercise; like when I go on a diet and I think exercise will help me lose weight and look better. = Amber Zone.
- I really can't see the point in exercising and I am not interested in it at all. I don't bother. = Red Zone.

So which Zone are you in? _____

Question 10

The next question relates to your Fitness level.

What we are interested in here is your reality and not what you think you should say. So be honest.

- I am happy with my fitness level and I can do all the things with my body that I want to do without any problems or difficulties. = Green Zone.

- I am not fit and I know that I could be fitter and have a better quality of life if I was. = Amber Zone.

- I think that being fit is over rated and I have all these reasons why I cannot get fit and I have a letter from my doctor... = Red Zone.

So which Zone are you in? _____

Question 11

The next question relates to how you actually really feel about your weight.

What we are interested in here is your reality and not what you think you should say. So be honest.

- I know that I have a problem with my weight and I don't like the fact that I have a weight problem. But I am prepared to do what it takes to deal with this problem now. = Green Zone.

- I know that I have a problem with my weight and if I am being honest I have used it as an excuse for different things. If I could take a pill and my weight problem would disappear, then I would. But I realise that it is going to take more than that to fix things and I now accept that I have to do more. = Amber Zone.

- Who are you calling fat? = Red Zone.

So which Zone are you in? _____

So now let's total up the answers. This is not a competition and there are not any right or wrong answers. You should have 14 answers.

What we want to get too, is to get an idea of the problem structure that makes up and contributes to your weight problem.

- How many Green Zones? _____ / P1. _____

- How many Amber Zones? _____ / P1. _____

- How many Red Zones? _____ / P1. _____

I would expect that most people will have a mix of answers. We will use these answers and add them to the ones that you had in the first part of the book. This will add 6 more Zones; giving you a total of 20 Zones. Add your answers from the first part of the book to the P1 sections.

One reason why I developed this process was that I could see that too many people with weight problems were using dieting solutions that applied to people who fell into the Green Zone; when they themselves fell into the Amber or Red Zones.

The reality is that if you are someone who falls into the Amber or Red Zones and you use a dieting solution suited to someone in the Green Zone; then you are highly likely to fail, as they are not compatible.

This incompatibility is one of the reasons why dieters have an 84% failure rate:

> Most of the dieters who fail are going to be in the Amber and Red Zones but they will be using dieting solutions that are appropriate for the Green Zone.
>
> In reality; it is easier to sell someone the wrong solution which promises fast and easy results; than it is to sell them the right solution which involves more effort and time.
>
> When people use dieting solutions from the Green Zone, the reality is; that the demands of the weight problem that the person has, exceeds the capacity of the dieting solution being applied to it.
>
> It's a case of square pegs and round holes!

The simple process we are using, with easy to answer questions, can begin to provide us with quite a lot of useful information about the shape and nature of your weight problem.

It also begins to inform us about the journey that you need to take from Fat Land, across the Stepping Stones, and into Slim Land.

With this knowledge you can begin to focus on the right type and level of Preparation and Practice that is required for your Weight Control solution; and this will match with the Zones on The Dieters Scale.

Each Zone will require a different level of Preparation and Practice because they each need to do a different level of work, over a different amount of time, with different amounts of effort and commitment required.

But don't panic or worry about it because I am giving you the basic structure that you need to get on to the 1st Stepping Stone and to keep going.

If you fall off any of the Stepping Stones, then see what you missed; or what you forgot; or what you tried to short cut on.

Try not to rush this as doing things quickly increases your chances of making mistakes. You just won't do what you need to do, in the way that you need to do it. Rushing things is part of the Fat Land behaviour.

Remember:

> Falling off a Stepping Stone doesn't mean that you have failed.
>
> In this approach: Failure is simply another opportunity to Learn from the Experience and to go at it again.

What you need to appreciate is that when it comes to moving out of Fat Land and living in Slim Land, you need to look at the bigger picture.

Getting out of Fat Land for a little while is easy!

Diet clubs can take you out of Fat Land for a limited amount of time. What they can't do is keep you out!

What we want to do here is to keep you out of Fat Land, move you to Slim Land and help you to build a life in Slim Land. And the truth is that you can't really do this quickly; it takes time!

Currently you have a Fat Land life and lifestyle; you want to get too and begin living a Slim Land life and lifestyle.

To achieve that result takes time and things have to change and become established into new patterns of behaviour.

Now we will look at getting a foothold on the 2nd Stepping Stone and what you will do on that Stepping Stone.

Establishing A Foothold On The 2nd Stepping Stone

Weight Control The **Hi-Way** ©

"Act And Sort It Out!"

When choosing your Diet or Weight Control process you should take a note of the following:

Any Diet or Weight Control process has to be able to fit into your lifestyle.

As your lifestyle changes from a Fat Land lifestyle to a Slim Land lifestyle; your Diet or Weight Control process has to be able to do so as well.

A quick weight loss diet or fad diet lacks the structure that you need to maintain the results it may produce.

Chapter 10

Getting a foothold on the 2nd Stepping Stone

The 2nd Stepping Stone is where most dieters try to start from and where most of them actually fail.

For most of them it is not their fault as they have been lead to believe that what they are doing is the right thing to do. The reality is that they have had poor quality Human Intelligence (**Hi**) and this has worked against them.

Now, I hope, you know better!

Do you remember this from the 30 Steps?

> I want you to become so good at the Preparation & Practice that you hardly notice moving from one Stepping Stone to the next. Becoming good at the Preparation & Practice has the effect of automatically moving you forwards.

If you have been using this book as a workbook and you have been Preparing and Doing these things; then you will actually have moved to the position where you have a foothold on both the 1st and the 2nd Stepping Stones.

And when we continue with this process you will have a foothold on the 3rd Stepping Stone as well. Then you will begin to have a foothold in Slim Land.

If you continue to use this process; then you will begin living in Slim Land and you will reach your Happy Point.

To help us with that process we now need to do the next bit: Act and Sort It Out!

On this journey many things will happen and there is a high probability that you will fail with some of these things; but you won't fail with everything!

Failure can be viewed as the end or it can be viewed as an opportunity. I view failure as an opportunity and this is good **Hi**.

Failure can be avoided, it can be reduced and you can learn from it; but you can never eliminate it.

When failure does happen, you have to understand that it can provide you with a learning opportunity.

> Make a mistake and Learn; or Give up?

Successful weight loss and successful long term weight management is about working towards an achievable goal; it is not about never failing.

Think how often all the people that you admire have failed?

Athletes, actors, politicians, artist, singers, writers, film directors, business people, our parents, friends; anyone who wants to achieve anything that is difficult will experience failure; and sometime a lot of failure.

Successful people don't give up just because things get difficult or because they fail at something. They may feel like giving up at times but they don't. I know because I have been there many times myself.

They keep their eyes on the long term objectives and the goals that they have; and they persevere until they achieve those goals and objectives.

They keep working on it and they sort things out so that they can continue!

And this is what we are going to do with your journey from Fat Land to Slim Land.

We are going to persevere with being successful and not let any obstacle, challenge, issue or person get in the way and prevent you from moving on to the next Stepping Stone; and from there into Slim Land.

The thing about you being successful and overcoming adversity is that you need Preparation and Practice to do so.

The point about Practice is that when you get to the real thing; the real thing is easier to do because of all the Preparation and Practice that you have done.

This part of the book is going to provide you with more of the information, advice and support that you will need to reach Slim Land and be able to stay there.

Note

The 2nd Stepping Stone is where the dieting organisations, fad diets, diet products and quick fixes all want to have a part of their business.

Real Estate on the 2nd Stepping Stone is at a premium because so many people want to sell you their secret of successful weight loss, fast weight loss, easy weight loss, etc.

Depending upon the success of this book, I am sure that at some point someone will try to sell you the quick, easy and successful way to cross the 3 Stepping Stones.

Or, they will try to sell you the quickest route from Fat Land to Slim Land that will cut months off your journey.

What you need to understand is that if it was as easy as they make it out to be; then why do they have an 84% failure rate!

With the work that I do; I am trying to build something that actually does work and that has an above average success rate.

We can't achieve that with hype and big promises. We achieve it by being grounded in the reality of the situation and then working with it and changing it.

With all long term weight problems it takes time to fix them and to get to Slim Land. If you try to cut that time down, then all you do is that you reduce your chances of success. It is better to take a bit longer than you need; rather than trying to take less time than you need.

Regardless of how bad your weight problem is; it can be improved, resolved and better managed.

So let's get to it!

The 4 Fundamentals of Successful Weight Control!

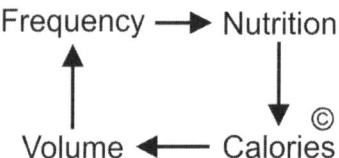

Weight Control The **Hi**-**Way** - The Dieters Scale

Chapter 11

Understanding The Difference Between A Diet & A Weight Management Process

A diet and a weight management process are not the same thing.

A diet is about losing weight and often about quick weight loss.

Weight management is about maintaining weight within a range, and if necessary, losing weight or putting on weight to get into that range.

Diets usually have a short term focus, whereas weight management would usually have a long term focus.

Weight management becomes an integrated part of your lifestyle management.

Whereas it becomes very difficult to incorporate a diet which has a focus on losing weight quickly and using diet products, into your lifestyle management. They are not compatible!

And when you look at what most dieters really need; they actually really need Weight Management and not a diet.

To live in Slim Land; you can't be reliant on diet products or prepared diet foods. Diet products and diet foods can and will have hidden ingredients that cause you to remain connected to Fat Land.

Diet products and prepared diet foods also carry a strong message that you can't really do this on your own; and they encourage you to remain in "the Fat Land mentality".

It is the Fat Land mentality that keeps you connected with Fat Land. In effect; it keeps a place open for you there for when you are ready to return from your visit to Slim Land.

To help you maintain the Fat Land mentality; you will encounter lots of subtle media pressure to compare yourself with models; that only exist as computer enhanced creations of feminine beauty.

You will see celebrities who will encourage you to use a certain diet or diet products. You will encounter teenagers with young skin who will encourage you to use certain beauty products to remain youthful and desirable.

You will see older celebrities and actors with studio lighting that hides every age line; encouraging you to buy and use certain products to keep yourself looking desirable and beautiful. However; if you actually see these people in real life you will see that they age just like you and me.

> What they are doing is that they are using your fears, your anxieties, your lack of confidence and self-esteem; and your desire to look and feel better; to seduce you to give up your control and to rely upon them for a better quality of life.

> And they cannot actually really give it to you; they can only sell you a dream!

I am not saying that you should not use beauty products and look after your body. What I am saying is don't be seduced by things which will take you off track and get you going in the wrong directions.

The same is true for diet clubs, gyms and exercise classes. Use them for your achievable goals but ask yourself whether the prize you seek is within their gift or yours?

Remember what I said about tranquilisers: Use a diet and diet club like someone would use tranquilisers; they can help you get out of a depression but they cannot keep you out of one permanently. Sooner or later you have to take over and do it under your own steam.

If you are over reliant on them; you won't be able to go it alone.

> It is likely that over the years, you will have been conditioned to think that all the problems you experience can be fixed in easy and simple ways. The diet and beauty industries have spend a great deal of money trying to make us believe that there are simple and easy ways to lose weight and look great; then they sell these ways to us.

Think of this:

> Do you find diet clubs in Fat Land or in Slim Land?

> They go where the customers are and they are all in Fat Land.

What I am going to do with this section of the book is to give you certain fundamentals which I think will help you with the dieting process and also with the weight management process. They will also help you with your Human Intelligence (**Hi**) for Weight Control.

I am hoping at this stage, you realise that on the 2nd Stepping Stone, you are going to be focused on Weight Management (Weight Control) as I described it early in this chapter and not on losing weight quickly by dieting?

There are just 4 fundamentals that you need to understand and practice with food and Weight Control; as these are the cornerstones of getting to Slim Land and living in Slim Land.

Those 4 fundamentals for Successful Weight Control are:

1. Nutrition.
2. Calories.
3. Volume
4. Frequency - Food Flow Rate

If you can understand and work with the simple process that I going to show you, then you can become successful with Weight Control.

The graphic below shows the 4 fundamentals arranged into a pattern. We will use this simple pattern with The Dieters Scale to show you how to do it.

The **Hi** Guide To Food & Weight Control

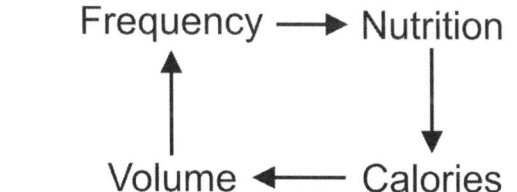

The **Hi** Common Platform - Weight Control The **Hi-Way** ©

Now you don't need to become an expert on nutrition or calorie counting or anything else. What you need to understand is the relationship and balance that exists between these four components of food and healthy nutritious eating.

> Understand how to use that balance and you will become a successful person who moves from Fat Land to Slim Land and stays there.

We will be using The Dieters Scale and the Zones to help you understand weight management in a user friendly way, which you can use regardless of any diet that you follow.

> These simple principles can be applied to any diet and any diet product.

At this stage you should have a clear idea, or be getting a clearer idea, of what diet plan, programme or self-diet that you are going to use or follow.

And you should begin to understand what the diet is promising you and what it can really deliver.

One of the things that you have to watch out for is the healthy diets and healthy foods which are not actually as healthy as you are being lead to believe. And the reality is that there are lots of them.

There are lots of false, misleading and downright outrageous claims made for foods, drinks, supplements, dieting aids, over the counter medication, exercise equipment and items that contain things such as magnets, crystals and other totems.

Remember that there is an 84% failure rate with dieting for a reason.

> Marketing promises are easy to make. Achieving a higher than average result with people who use a diet or weight control plan is much harder to achieve and maintain.
>
> This is what we are after with the **Hi-Way** Approach; higher success rates which become higher long term success rates.

Before we look at Nutrition, Calories and Volume I want you to understand and keep the following information with you.

This information relates to the fundamental of: Frequency – Food Flow Rate.

Chapter 12

Frequency – Food Flow Rate

Frequency or Food Flow Rate is actually easy to understand. It is the frequency and consistency of the flow of food and drink that goes into your body. This means:

- How often you eat.

- How often you eat what you are eating.

The Food Flow Rate is actually something that your body needs to be consistent and it needs to be within certain boundaries. If it is not consistent and not within certain boundaries; then it can throw a spanner into your dieting efforts and screw things up; big time.

> Most dieters do the wrong thing with Frequency because the right thing seems to be counter intuitive when you have a weight problem.

People with weight problems do mess up their own bodies Food Flow Rate; and this in turn messes up how their bodies manage, processes and recycles the foods that they eat and drink. *The Recycling of what you consume is something that we will look at in more detail later.*

If you are in the Amber and Red Zones on The Dieters Scale then the odds are that your bodies Food Flow Rate is out of balance and it will need to be restored or reset to a Normalised State.

Doing this is quite straightforward and this is how you can do it.

These are my own must have's for a diet. I have found that these simple things, consistently applied, do make a big different to dieters long term behaviours and their long term weight management success.

The Hi Guide To Food & Weight Control

In my view you need to:

1. Eat regular meals.

2. Of regular types.

3. At regular times.

This process helps your body to trust that it will have food at regular times, of a certain quality and at consistent volumes.

If you lose that regular pattern then your body will adjust accordingly to the irregular pattern; and you will feel the effects of chaotic and inconsistent food consumption.

In my view you should always try to eat a good breakfast and not feel hungry within at least a few hours of eating. This helps to stop mid-morning snacking.

You should have a good lunch and also not feel hungry within at least a few hours of eating. If you have snacked and don't feel like eating lunch, then what will happen is that you will snack in the afternoon and this will then have a knock on effect for your evening meal.

In the evening you should also have a good meal and not feel hungry within a few hours of eating. This helps to stop snacking during the evening; and it helps you avoid skipping breakfast the following morning; because you feel guilty about what you eat the previous evening.

Now you need to do this even if you don't really feel like it. This is because you need to establish a proper pattern of "eating consistently" which your mind and your body can trust will continue.

Eating the same amount each day but with an irregular pattern is different from eating it with a regular pattern. Although you are eating the same amount you can achieve different outcomes. This is because your body will respond differently to a consistent pattern than to an irregular pattern.

If you don't follow this simple structure then you are introducing chaos into the Weight Control process; and we know what chaos produces.

What you need to understand about this simple structure is that if you eat a main meal (breakfast, lunch and your evening meal are main meals); and you do feel hungry quickly, then there is something wrong with either the type of food or quantity of food that you are eating; or with both of these things; which you can then fix.

Personally I am not a fan of many of the breakfast cereals that have increased in number in recent years. I personally would not consider many of them to be a proper breakfast; and the small volumes you need to consume to keep calories low are beyond many people. They also have far too much sugar and other things in them from my perspective.

So what helps us with getting a regular pattern to our food consumption?

- Begin managing the food in a better way.

If you live on your own or in a household full of other people; you need to begin to manage your food. What this means is that you make simple and little changes by taking baby steps.

By the time that you actually begin the diet you have chosen, you should already have began the foundations of the diet by implementing it and practicing it.

What you need to understand is that you can stay on the preparation and practice stage for the diet proper; until you find that you can easily do it and all the other bits. Take as long as you need. Speed is not your friend at this stage so take it slowly.

If you have a family I would suggest that you try to avoid having to cook different meals for everyone, as this just creates problems long term and it's stupid.

You want to avoid creating a new generation of dieters and most people can eat good wholesome foods.

Also because you are using a diet plan, your food doesn't have to be boring. Make it interesting and enjoyable to eat; I would!

If your family is eating all the stuff that made you put on weight, then you have to ask if they should really continue with that. Having a household where eating patterns conflict can cause problems.

What you should do before you go on the diet proper, is to experiment with Slim Land food. This will help you get used to the different taste and flavours.

The reason we would practicing doing this is that when you do live in Fat Land, you have a Fat Land diet. And as a result of living in Fat Land you have developed a taste for Fat Land food.

You have to realise that many of the foods that help us to put on weight "taste great" and we become very used to the taste, flavour and texture of that type of food.

As you move out of Fat Land you don't have to lose great tasting food; but you do need to understand something.

You need to understand that you may have developed "the taste" for Fat Land foods. These are the foods that have the extra hidden sugars, fats and other things that can get you into trouble long term; and make weight management very difficult; rather than easy. As a result of this it will take time for you to lose the taste for Fat Land foods and to develop the taste for Slim Land foods.

Don't let yourself fall into the trap of thinking that low sugar and low fat foods must be good for you. The reality is that we all need fats and sugars in our diets in order to be fit and to be healthy. It's a case of finding the right balance.

Your problem is that you are taking in too many calories. Calories that may be hidden or disguised in the foods that you are eating.

It is also likely that the composition of the various fats and things you are eating may be less desirable. This then contributes to a chaotic and out of balanced weight management structure.

It's the structure that needs fixing; and the results will follow this.

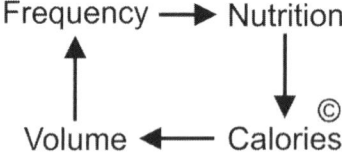

The Hi Common Platform - Weight Control The Hi-Way

Now something else that you need to understand is that the same food does exist in both Fat Land and in Slim Land. Let's use pasta as an example.

Slim Land pasta will be the same base product and it will be cooked in the same way as Fat Land pasta. It is what is added to it as it is cooked and after it is cooked that alters things.

Fat Land pasta may have a very tasty highly flavoured sauce mixed in with it. It needs to be highly flavoured because Fat Land pasta eaters have got used to highly flavoured foods.

To achieve the high flavour, additives and other ingredients will have been added into the sauce. It won't be the pasta that is the problem; it's the sauce and the other things which get added to pasta.

Slim Land pasta will also have a sauce added to it that is very tasty. But a Fat Land person has got used to a sauce that is full of other ingredients and it does not have the same punch; so by comparison it can taste bland.

So you need to allow the time for your taste to change and be able to appreciate different and more subtle taste and flavours.

Here is a fundamental truth!

> In Slim Land and in Fat Land people lie about foods.

In both places people will tell you that their food is healthy and good for you.

In both places they will tell you that their food is low fat, low sugar, low salt and so on. People and companies tell lies and practice deceptions in their marketing and in the promoting of the products that they sell and want you to buy and use.

Just because something says that it is low in fat does not mean that it is actually a "healthy food". Low fat can mean high sugar and other things that you don't want or need in your diet.

Low in sugar does not mean "healthy food" because if they are taking the sugar away they need to make it taste good by adding something else that you like; this may mean that it is high in fat and other things that you don't actually want.

What you have to remember is that Food Marketing can be like a politicians promises. It sounds good and it can get your vote; but let's see what it really does over the long term.

> So don't be seduced by someone who is telling you that they sell food to people in Slim Land and you should buy it.
>
> You need to have better quality Human Intelligence (**Hi**) with this area and this is what I am giving you with this book. Good quality **Hi**.

With all the different types of information that is around how on earth can you make sense of it all?

People will use different types of food labelling schemes, different types of healthy food labelling and different names to disguise additives that people want to avoid.

And then there is the guidance from the Government and the Medical professionals about what is and isn't good for you.

They can contradict themselves; one time they are saying that things like butter are harmful and that we should use margarine; then they say that butter is better for you than margarine???

So, I am going to show you my simple system that you can use to help you with managing your diet and getting an appropriate balanced diet for your lifestyle needs. Please don't confuse this with any other system that you may come across as this is all my own work. This is good **Hi**.

The **Hi** Guide To Food & Weight Control

If you follow the **Hi** guidelines that I am giving you, they will help you avoid a lot of the misleading and wrong information that is around. They will also help you to focus on the right things that you need.

We have already looked at one of the Fundamentals; Frequency. This helps to provide the framework that our bodies need for relying on the delivery of food.

It also helps us to develop a Pattern and Structure that we can include within our lives to help us with achieving Weight Control.

Now we are going to look at another Fundamental; Nutrition.

Chapter 13

Nutrition

In all foods Nutrition is important.

Nutrition is the collective term for all the different components that your body needs to have, in order to remain healthy and fight off infections and diseases.

All of us, without exception, need to eat fats, sugars, proteins and other nutrients, vitamins and minerals.

If we don't get enough Nutrition from our diets then we may need to supplement our dietary needs. This is where the different mineral and vitamin supplements that you see for sale come from.

What you need to understand about nutrition, is that it is possible, and it happens regularly, for someone to be very overweight and eat lots of food but suffer from a lack of Nutrition.

A lack of Nutrition would usually happen over a period of time.

Calories and Nutrition are not the same thing.

Nutrition does not exist in all foods. Some foods have a good level of Nutrition and some foods have little or no Nutrition in them.

With all food and drink the level of Nutrition is a measure of the real nutritional items that are in it; these are things like vitamins, minerals, fats, sugars, etc.

These are things which our bodies need in order to work properly.

And all of these Nutritional levels will be in the ranges from; none to low (Red Zone); low to medium (Amber Zone) or medium to high (Green Zone).

With some foods our bodies can recycle the Nutrition from the food easily and from other foods it is more difficult.

We can use The Dieters Scale to help us understand more about Nutrition.

In the following graphic, we have A Dieters Scale showing Nutrition levels.

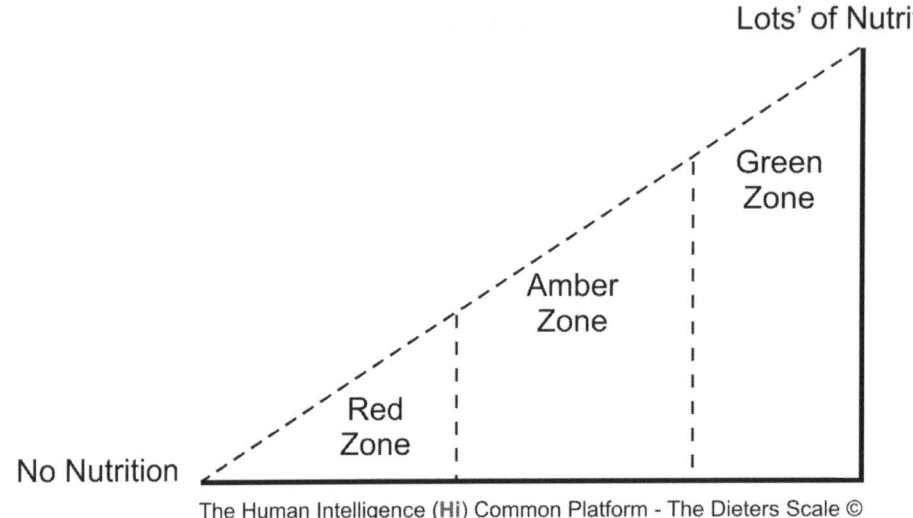

The Human Intelligence (Hi) Common Platform - The Dieters Scale ©

Green Zone Nutrition = Good nutrition levels.

Amber Zone Nutrition = Low to Medium nutrition levels.

Red Zone Nutrition = Little or no nutritional levels.

And this is how it works.

When we eat or drink foods we process that food in our digestive system. Our bodies then recycle the different minerals, vitamins and other things which it can recycle.

Our bodies are not 100% efficient and so we don't really know exactly how much of anything we do eat is actually recycled. Some of the Nutrition is recycled and some it can't be.

Also things like our overall health, the condition of our digestive system and other factors do play a part in this recycling process.

This is why it is important that we get your digestive system working better before you do go on any diet. It simply increases your chances of being successful when your body works better.

So let's look at what types of things belong in the different Zones.

As examples of what types of things go into these Zones we would have:

> Green Zone Nutrition = meats, fish, cereals, fruits, vegetables, yogurt, whole milk, cheese, eggs, etc.

When I am talking about meats, fish and cereals I am talking about unprocessed and uncooked foods. As these foods are processed and cooked the nutritional content (mixture) and nutritional level (amount) can change.

Fast frozen/flash frozen fruit and vegetables tend to be OK but these will be unprocessed and not cooked or treated.

> Amber Zone Nutrition = Bread and bread based products that are generally made quickly and in volume; yogurts that are processed beyond their natural state.
>
> Processed foods that can keep on the shelves for a long time tend to lose their nutritional level with time; they can also lose it through processing.
>
> Fruits and vegetables out of season often have different levels from those in season.

As a general guide; food that is stored for a long period of time loses it nutritional level. Fruit and vegetables that are consumed immediately or soon after picking, will have the highest levels.

> Red Zone Nutrition = Fizzy drinks, hot drinks, alcohol, processed cheese, fat free milk, processed sugar, many processed breakfast cereals, etc.

Now due to the way that the food industry works there are many, many different combinations of foods with varying degrees of nutrition. Some foods in one combination may fit into the Green Zone; others will fit into the Amber Zone and others will fit into the Red Zone.

Some food combinations, such as pizzas, may have a base which fits in one Zone and fillings which fit into another. So to avoid confusion and to make it easy; you take an overall view of the thing that you are eating.

Food Confusion

Much of the food industry thrives on confusion and a lack of clarity. This is why getting a simple universal system that is easy to understand has not happened.

The point that you need to take away from this is; that just because something can be eaten and someone is saying that it is healthy; this does not mean that it is Nutritious or that it actually has any Nutrition in it.

What you need to do it to make sure that your diet has sufficient Nutrition from the right Zones.

For example:

You may get most of your Nutrition from Amber Zone foods and make up the balance from Green Zone foods. This would probably suit most people and produce a sustainable diet with a good variety of foods.

You may also occasionally consume things from the Red Zone but they will not contribute much if anything to your Nutritional needs. However; they will normally be high in Calories and so will quickly add Calories into your diet.

> If you are eating most of your foods from the Red Zone and some from the Amber Zone; then, over time, you can become Nutritionally deficient while eating lots of Calories.
>
> *Drinking lots of alcohol, for example, would be a Red Zone activity as it is Nutritionally deficient but high in Calories. Doing thing like adding fruit to alcoholic drinks doesn't help.*

Getting the Munchies!

Becoming Nutritionally deficient may make you feel like eating more as your body will try to get the Nutritional things that it needs from what you are actually eating.

As you eat more; this in turn increases the Calories you take in, and this in turn increases your weight; and it become a vicious cycle; as is illustrated in the following graphic.

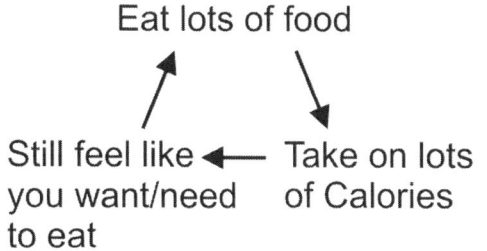

The Hi Common Platform - Weight Control The Hi-Way ©

In simple terms: The more balanced that your eating is; the less Volume of food you will need to eat to give you the necessary Nutrition that your body needs to be healthy. This is shown in the graphic below.

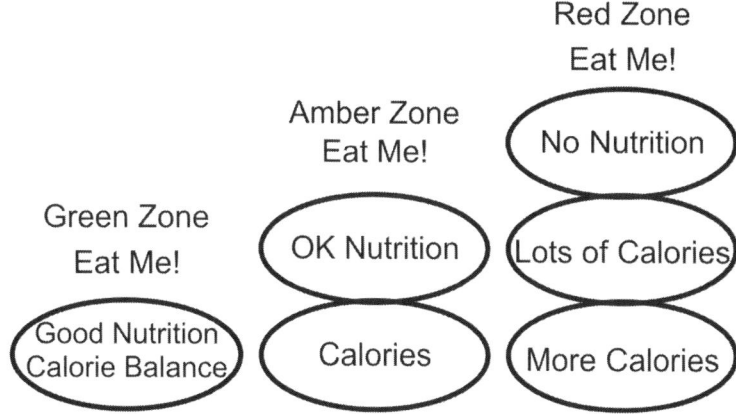

The Hi Common Platform - Weight Control The Hi-Way ©

Consuming high volumes of Nutritionally deficient foods (Red Zone) can still leave you deficient in the Nutrition that you need to be healthy.

These Nutritionally deficient foods can also leave you with thousands of Nutritionally deficient Calories as you eat lots of Red Zone foods.

And this is guaranteed to keep you in Fat Land.

What you need to understand is this:

Green Zone foods have the best levels of Nutrition. You can only get certain types of Nutrition from Green Zone foods.

To satisfy your Nutritional needs you will need to consume a higher volume of Amber Zone foods than Green Zone foods.

So if you don't eat enough Green Zone foods then the volume of food you need to eat from the Amber Zone needs to increase to try and compensate.

As the volume of food increases in the Amber Zone, Calories are likely to follow and you will consume more Calories as you try to get the Nutrition you need.

So if most of your diet is in the Amber and Red Zones (as it is for many people) then you will have to consume lots more food to try and meet your Nutritional Needs.

This is where the relationship between Nutrition, Calories and Volume comes into play. If you reduce the Volume of food that is required then this limits the amount of extra and unnecessary Calories that your body will have to process and recycle.

This in turn means that you put on less weight. I will show you how to use this process to your advantage later.

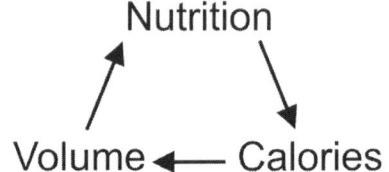

The **Hi** Common Platform - Weight Control The **Hi-Way** ©

Using Human Intelligence (**Hi**) to dispel a myth.

Contrary to the claims of many overweight people: They don't have a slow metabolism. People who are larger in size actually use more calories maintaining their larger body mass than people who are slimmer. All the different test that I have heard of, that measure metabolism in people with a larger body mass, have said that they use more calories while resting than someone who weighs less than they do.

So now let's look at Calories.

Chapter 14

Calories

Nutrition can be thought of like the lubricant in an engine; and calories can be thought of like the fuel that goes into the engine.

Basically; Calories = Energy that is stored in foods.

We use the Calories in foods to give our bodies the energy that it needs to function, remain healthy and for us to do things with it.

Calories come out of the things which we consume in liquid and solid forms. For example; milk, cheese, bread, chips, pizza, cakes, burgers, etc.

Normally Calories come as part of a package.

For example; we grill some meat and eat it. The meat has Nutrition and it will have other components which we need to survive; it will also have Calories. That's the package!

As our bodies digest the meat, it is broken down into different components by our digestive system and our body uses what it can. What it can't use straight away it will store and the waste product from the meat is pushed out of our bodies when we go to the toilet.

As we digest the Calories some will be used immediately by our bodies and some will be stored. This will be stored in our muscles and in our fat stores. We all do this and we all have these stores.

Also what our bodies do is that they take different amounts of time to digest and process the different types and parts of foods. This means that the recycling process takes longer with things like nuts than it does with things like sweets.

So when we eat; a good strategy is that we consume a mixture of things that our bodies can recycle quickly; and we also consume things which our bodies will recycle slowly.

The result of doing this is that our body recycles the energy from what we have eaten over a longer period of time; as it is digesting it over a longer period of time.

The amount of energy we need over the course of a day, a week, a month or a year; is dependent upon what activities we are doing, our climate, our lifestyles, our body type, our health; how often we eat; and what we eat. So you see that it is more than just food that is involved: It's a Package!

What processes the food and drink we have eaten and drank is our digestive system. This is quite an efficient process most of the time but it can and does go wrong.

Our digestive system is full of different materials which work together to process, recycle and manage what we consume.

Our digestive system is like our own internal factory that takes in the food and drink that we consume and it recycles the various fats, sugars, proteins, minerals, vitamins and other things which we may need.

Just like any other factory; it requires that all the materials that it needs to work with are delivered in good order, in good time and in the right way.

Just like any muscle in the body; the digestive system can be fit and toned or it can be flabby and stodgy.

If we use the digestive system in the wrong way, then it will try to adjust to cope with things. This ability to adjust means that sometimes things go out of balance and stay out of balance.

This is when we get digestion problems and other health problems.

The type, quality and volume of food and drink that we put into our digestive system, will help to determine the health of our bodies.

This will also determine the amount of Calories that are stored as fat and how well our bodies will function with the various tasks that it has to perform.

> This means that what you eat and drink determines how well your body can function and how it is constructed and looks. Understanding this is good **Hi**.

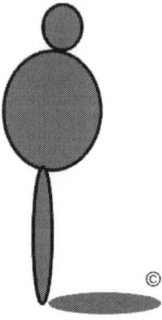

Chapter 15

Using The Dieters Scale for Calories

We will use The Dieters Scale to understand the Calorie impact different types of food have. It looks like this:

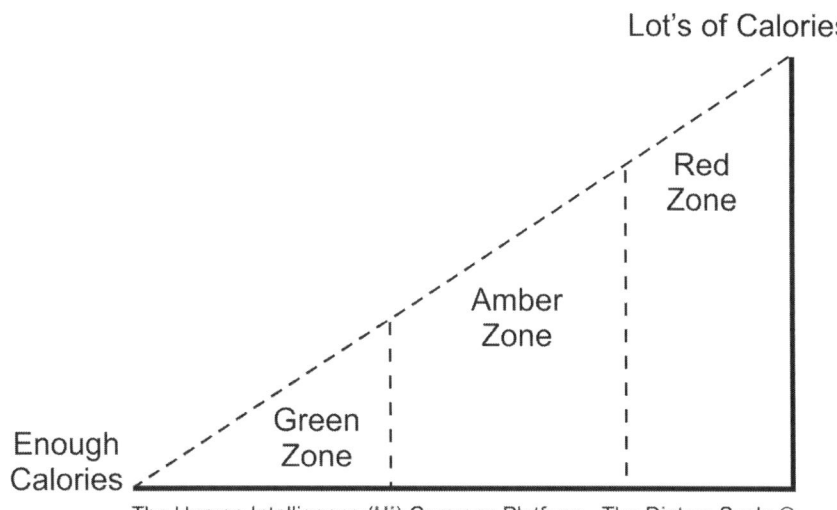

The Human Intelligence (Hi) Common Platform - The Dieters Scale ©

Green Zone Foods would be things like fruit and vegetable without any sauces on them. Natural yogurts (nothing added), milk (nothing added), etc.

Amber Zone Foods would be things like bread, pizza's (generally better quality pizza bases and ingredients), certain pasta's, meats, cheeses, nuts and many yogurts.

Many fruit based drinks such as smoothies, I would put into the Amber and the Red Zones; Along with burgers, fish & chips, fruit and vegetable with sauces, butters, creams, etc.

Personally I would include my homemade food. Things like fruit pies, bread rolls and cakes in the Amber Zone as I know exactly what is in them.

Red Zone Foods would be things like store bought cakes, deserts (generally), sweets, candy bars, chocolates, many high calorie drinks, pizza's, burgers, fish & chips, fruit and vegetable with sauces, butters, creams, etc.

You will see that I have listed certain products in more than one Zone. This is because these can be made in different ways, with different ingredients, and this makes a difference to which Zone they belong in.

Basically I am not going to be prescriptive with any of the foods here as you can eat foods from any of the Zones.

> The simple fact is that if you eat the same Volume of food from each Zone, then each Volume of food will have different amounts of Calories and other things as part of their packages.

> So a litre of apples will be different from a litre of French fries; which will be different from a litre of sweets.

Once your weight is stable you can experiment with foods from the different Zones. So no food is off limits to you and you are free to eat what you want.

However; there is always a simple reality that none of us can escape.

> If you want to eat too many Calories then this will eventually have an effect upon your body and how you look.

> If you want to eat too much of the Red Zone foods then you may end up Nutritionally deficient and this can have long term health effects.

Most people's diets will balance out with a mixture of Amber and Green Zones with an occasional Red Zone.

If your Weight Management is chaotic then this will show in how you look and how you feel.

Chapter 16

An Alternate View of Calories

My own personal view is that we have become seduced by Calories and counting Calories.

We have portioned food into packets and we label that this food has (X) Calories.

We have been lead to believe that by consuming that food, that we now have those calories in our bodies and that our bodies have taken those calories from that food.

In reality; Calorie counting is just a tool that should be used as a guide to help someone understand whether they are eating enough food. And in my view it has become misused and ineffective.

> The reality is:
>
> It is your body's ability to recover and recycle the calories from that food; and it is your body's ability to use those calories in your body; that matters.
>
> And this will be an individual thing.

How calories are measured and displayed to us on a packet can be quite different from what your body can actually recover and use from it.

For example:

A bar of chocolate may have 500 calories. If you eat the chocolate we are lead to believe that we have consumed 500 calories.

We may have consumed something that contained 500 calories but that doesn't matter. What matters is how our personal factory (our digestion) will use those materials and how much of those 500 calories we can recycle.

> We don't recycle 100% of the calories in the chocolate bar.
>
> This is one reason why Calorie Counting can be erratic and produce different results from one person to another.

In reality that chocolate bar reaches our digestive system (our factory) and it has to be broken down into ingredients that our body can process. This recycling process uses some of that energy.

What also matters is how much time our body has to work on and process the chocolate bar.

If we have a lot of other things arriving in our factory, then it will also be working on recycling those. If new things are coming into our factory then there is pressure to expel the chocolate bar and work on what else is coming through.

As a result of our "Food Flow Rate" our bodies can become more efficient at processing and recycling certain parts of the chocolate bar than others. And this is true for all sorts of foods and drinks.

What our body becomes efficient at processing may not be what we would like it to become efficient at using. Our choice over this has been removed once we put that food into our mouths and swallow it.

So if we are eating high volumes of the less desirable foods (Red Zone); then certain results are going to occur. We will continue to live in Fat Land and we will not be happy with ourselves.

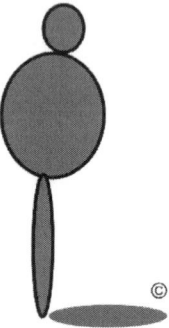

If our Food Flow Rate is erratic, then it will effect the efficiency of our recycling factory (our digestive system). This is why I keep suggesting that you take the time to let your body become stable.

If we are eating more of the desirable foods (Green Zone) and lower volumes of the less desirable foods (Amber Zone); then we can get a different result. We can live in Slim Land.

And this is what all dieting and long term weight control is about:

Getting that right balance that we can maintain, while living the life that we really want to live.

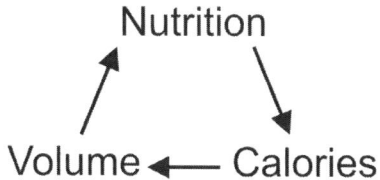

The **Hi** Common Platform - Weight Control The **Hi-Way** ©

In my view Calories should only be a guide for foods and it should not be used by people with weight problems as "the way" of losing weight and managing their weight long term.

In my view it is the wrong tool and it brings with it the wrong expectations.

The tool we should be using is The Dieters Scale and applying this to the combination of:

>Nutrition.
>Calories.
>Volume.
>Frequency – Food flow rate.

It is this simple:

If your combination of Nutrition – Calories – Volume and Frequency is in the Green Zones; then you will find that you don't have a weight problem.

If your combination of Nutrition – Calories – Volume and Frequency is in the Amber Zones; then you will find that you do have a weight problem.

If your combination of Nutrition – Calories – Volume and Frequency is in the Red Zones; then you will find that you do have a weight problem.

So this tells you that you want to be more biased towards the Green Zones than you are towards the Red Zones. This is illustrated on the following graphic.

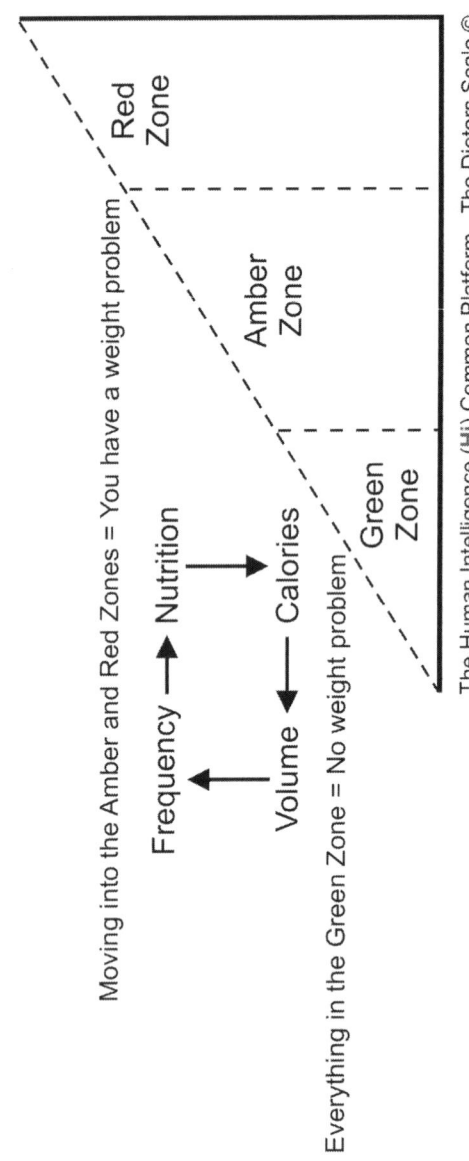

Chapter 17

Processed Foods

At this moment in time we are encountering more new combinations of foods, new structures of foods and new components of foods than we have in the past.

As a result of this people have become exposed to food and drink that is totally new to our bodies.

Because it is new, our bodies are either still adjusting to it or have not yet begun adjusting to it.

This causes problems, especially with processed foods as they can bypass our bodies' normal functions and cause us to consume more calories, faster and easier than we could have in the past.

Because of food processing; we can also consume new substances that we don't really understand; and where we don't know what the long term effects of them are on the body.

To help you to understand processed foods better we will use The Dieters Scale.

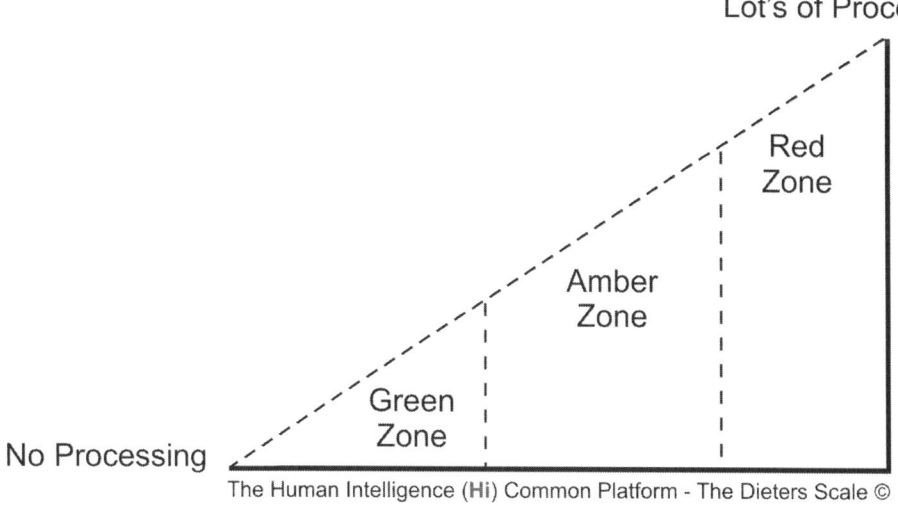

The Human Intelligence (Hi) Common Platform - The Dieters Scale ©

Green Zone = Unprocessed foods.

Amber Zone = Lightly to medium processed foods.

Red Zone = Highly processed foods.

Green Zone would be things like a whole apple, a banana with the skin still on, an unpeeled orange, vegetables that are cooked from fresh and foods which are in their natural state. I.e. Nothing has been added or done to them.

Also fresh frozen vegetables, certain olive oils, honey, meat, fish, etc.

These are foods where very little or nothing at all is added to them. So there are no added salts, sugars, water, fats, flavour enhancers, emulsifiers, etc.

It also means that there is a higher probability that any nutrition in the foods is retained.

Personally I would add certain home cooked foods to this Zone as I personally know what is in those foods when I make them.

Amber Zone would be things like certain cakes that are made by your local baker and consumed on the day of baking. Things that need to be consumed on the day tend not to have preservers added but this is not always true.

Other things that would fall into the Amber Zone are certain takeout meals, cut meats like salami, certain ice creams, certain pizzas, certain burgers, etc.

Now this is my guide and some people would disagree with me about this; but my point is:

There can be a big difference between the quality of products that are made at home, at restaurants, at shops, at factories and by food processors.

For example: One restaurant may produce good food that fits nicely into the Green and Amber Zones. Another restaurant may produce the same things but use different ingredients and ways of cooking; and their food will fit into the Amber and Red Zones.

There is no easy to understand and use guide for this. However; you can use the information and guidance in this book to help yourself get better foods; and to control foods that you didn't realise may be causing you problems.

If you eat only the cheapest and easiest foods, then you will find that a lot of what you eat will fall into the Red Zone. So what are Red Zone foods?

Red Zone foods would be things like certain burgers, certain sausages, certain pizza's, certain ice creams and many things of this type; including many sweets, chocolates, and items of this type.

Many of the cans and bottles of fizzy drinks and the so called health replenishing drinks; personally, I would put most of them into the Red Zone. This would include the sports drinks and caffeine based drinks that people use to keep awake or give themselves a boost. I don't think that most people realise what is really in these drinks and the potential long term effects of using them in quantity.

Highly processed foods which are very cheap versions of more expensive and popular foods will tend to fall into the Red Zone.

Foods where you appear to get a high volume of food in a packet, for not much money is often a guide to the quality of what is in the packet.

To be able to provide the more expensive foods at cheaper prices the main ingredients tend to be replaced by things like bulking agents. As a result you get less of the good stuff and more stuff that falls into the Amber and Red Zones.

More and more foods are being sold on the basis of "Tasting" like something or being "Flavoured" like something; rather than actually being what they are Flavoured to Taste like.

This is also a guide to how much the food and the ingredients may have been processed and changed.

So how do you balance this out?

To help you understand about balancing out your dietary requirements, with all the different foods that are out there, we will use Volume to help you do this; and we will cover this later.

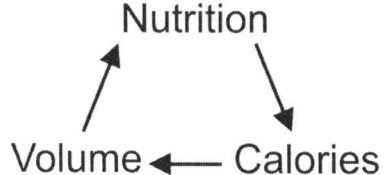

The Hi Common Platform - Weight Control The Hi-Way ©

Chapter 18

Calories and Portion Control

Just about every person that I speak to about dieting and weight control replies with:

"It's all about Calories"

Let me challenge that point of view!

In reality portion control and calorie counting is more suited towards making sure that someone gets a minimum daily amount of Nutritious food.

This is very important in countries where people have problems with the supply of foods and where people go hungry and die from starvation.

In the UK this was very important at times of war; such as during the second world war, when rationing limited the supply of food to the population. This restriction on the supply of foods continued until 1954 even though the war finished in 1945.

With potion control and calorie counting; the Government needed to understand the minimum amount of food that someone needed to have in order to remain healthy. And be able to contribute towards the war effort in their different occupations. For example: Someone doing heavy manual labour V's someone working in an office.

It was a process that was controlled by ration books and coupons. You took these to the various shops and they exchanged coupons for rations.

When someone is found not to be healthy enough, as a result of consuming the allocated rations, these could be changed by doctors. Some people would develop things like Anaemia and they would be prescribed things like Guinness and red meats or extra rations.

So this process of Calorie Counting was about the Government getting the population to a minimum level of nutrition and calories; so as to maintain a satisfactory level of health.

When it is used by Governments; you generally find that the population cannot easily supplement their diet by getting extra food. They simply can't get the extra food, so taking on extra calories is outside of their control.

In today's world the control has moved from Government to anyone with the money to buy food.

As a result of this shift, it is up to the individual now to make sure that they get sufficient food to maintain their good health. And to monitor the quality and Nutritional levels of their own foods.

> It's a case of:
>
> We are giving you the information and it's up to you make the right choices for you. We are empowering you!
>
> Therefore: You make the choice and you take the responsibility.

The problem is that people generally are not sufficiently enough educated in food management and weight management to do this.

The truth is that most people are still relying on external controls.

These external controls are the diet industry, the food industry, food regulators, Health Authorities and the Government.

If they were doing the right job, in the right way; would we have the problems with weight that we now have?

In reality we have all been given choices; but they are uneducated and uninformed choices.

I want to help you get educated and informed!

I want to help you increase your Human Intelligence (Hi) of this area and then use that Human Intelligence (Hi) to achieve better results.

How it really works recap

Calories are an essential part of being able to live a healthy life. They provide the energy that we need to live a healthy life and to do things.

Calories come as part of a package with Nutrition and other items that may be attached to those Calories.

Some Calorie Packages are better for us, than others. The Dieters Scale uses the Green, Amber and Red Zones to help you understand this.

As well as Calories we also need Nutrition to live a healthy life and do things.

To get the health balance right, we can't rely upon Calorie Counting because there are too many variables effecting our body's actual consumption and recycling of those Calories.

Over time our digestive system and our body's way of managing and processing the food and drink that we consume; can and does change.

Dieters often reach a point where their bodies digestive system and the way that they manage and process food and drink; becomes chaotic.

The result is that dieters can have a chaotic and changeable dietary system; and this impacts the way that it will manage and process the food and drink that they consume.

This is an individual process and no-one actually really knows exactly what is going on within any one else's body and how it is doing all of this.

How we find out how well someone's body is working and whether there is chaos; is we look at the result. The result is shown in their body and in their lifestyle.

So let's see how Volume fits into this and how you can use this to help you with Calorie Counting or to replace Calorie Counting and portion control.

Volume is about how much fuel you really need to put into your body engine to run the engine; and to do the things you need to do; regardless of the actual Calories that you may count on a packet.

When you put fuel into a real engine this is the only place that fuel can be taken from.

Your body is different from this because your body's engine can take fuel from other places, other than the fuel tank.

Your body will take fuel from what is being processed in your digestive system, it will take fuel from your muscles, it will take fuel from your different fat stores. It will do the same with Nutrition.

Your body will use whatever fuel and Nutrition is the easiest and most efficient for it. You can't control this.

Although you can't control this:

> What you can do is to influence it; and you can do this by your Lifestyle Management and Weight Management.

Over Time!

You can really only influence and change things like this over time. This "Over Time" approach produces sustainable results that can accurately and honestly be measured.

If you try to influence things too quickly, all you do is you introduce chaos or you increase the chaos that already exist.

When you try to do things quickly it can look as if you are achieving results in the short term but you won't be able to sustain them; and we don't want this!

So you can see how the pieces of the dieting puzzle come together and work.

With this knowledge we can change the results that you have been getting and get better results that can be sustained long term.

So how can you use Volume to help you get the right amounts and types of food?

The Hi Common Platform - Weight Control The Hi-Way ©

Chapter 19

Using Volume to Control and Manage Calories

In the graphic below there are 3 cups. Anyone can see and understand that these cups are the same shape but of different sizes.

This means that if we were to fill each cup to the exact top with rice; that each cup would contain a different Volume of rice.

If we were to then cook and eat the rice from each cup in turn, we would feel either hungry or full after eating the contents of each cup.

The Human Intelligence (Hi) Common Platform - The Dieters Scale ©

Cups of rice

If we eat from the smallest cup each day and we lost weight over time; then this would indicate that we are not eating enough. The overall Volume of food is not enough to sustain our weight, doing the activities that we are doing.

If we then eat from the second cup each day and we lost weight over time; then this would indicate that we are not eating enough. The overall Volume of food is still not enough.

If we then eat from the largest cup each day and we lost weight over time; then this would indicate that we are still not eating enough. The overall Volume of food is still not enough.

So it is not about the size of the individual cup itself; it is about how much Volume of rice that we need to maintain our weight and our health.

Now if we add something else into our diet (Let's say fish) let's see what happens.

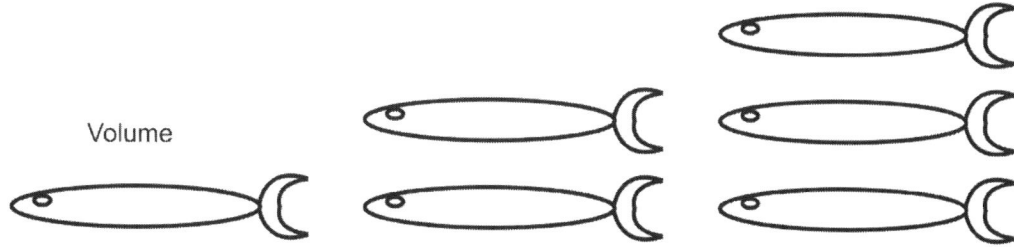

The Human Intelligence (Hi) Common Platform - The Dieters Scale ©

Now we can begin to add fish to our rice to see if we can get the volume right.

We begin by eating 1 fish and our largest cup of rice but we continue to lose weight. The overall Volume of food is still not enough.

Then we move on to eating 2 fish and our rice; and we do not lose any more weight.

We now know that we are consuming enough Volume of the rice and fish to stop losing weight. The Volume is correct!

If the volume is correct then the Calories must also be correct!

Just to be sure, we decide to check, and so we begin to eat 3 fish and the rice. Nothing happens for weeks.

As we continue to eat the 3 fish and the rice, we begin to notice that our clothes are a bit tighter. We are putting on weight because we are consuming too much Volume.

We now know that the overall Volume is now too high and we are now putting on weight. So we now know that the Calories in that Volume of food is too high for what we want.

As we don't want to put on weight, we reduce the Volume of our food to what it was before. We eat 2 fish a day with the large cup of rice.

Initially we may feel a little hungry because our body has got used to having too much food. But over a couple of weeks this feeling goes away and we gradually lose the extra weight.

We now know that when we maintain our Volume of food at the large cup of rice and the 2 fish we do not lose weight or gain weight.

The Volume of food is correct!

So for this particular food mix and the activities we are doing in our lives; this is the correct volume of food that we need.

Now let's say that we wanted to eat more fish and vary it. How would we adjust this?

Well we know that 3 fish and the large cup of rice makes us put on weight because it is too much Volume of food.

So we continue to eat the 3 fish and we change down to the middle cup of rice, which has less Volume of rice. Our weight stays the same over a period of time.

The Volume of food is correct!

To check that this is correct we decide to keep eating the 3 fish but change to the small cup of rice. Over the course of the following weeks our weight goes down.

And from this little experiment, we know that the Volume of 3 fish and 1 small cup of rice is too little.

The Volume of food is too small.

So this means that we now have a choice with the Volume and the Selection of foods. And this allows us to have more rice one time and more fish another time.

We can have the middle cup of rice and 3 fish; or we can have the large cup of rice and 2 fish.

The Human Intelligence (Hi) Common Platform - The Dieters Scale ©

Either of these combinations gives us the right Volume of this food and also the right amount of Calories.

As a result: Our weight stays stable and it neither goes up or down.

And this is the simple principle of Volume. We don't have to count Calories; we simply adjust the Volumes of the different foods that we are actually eating; until we get the right balance.

If we can't get the right balance with the volumes of food, then we simply shift our food selection from one Zone to another Zone.

For example if you are eating a large cup of Red Zone high Calorie foods and you can't get the Volume right; then shift to a large cup of lower Calorie foods in the Amber Zone and you should be able to get it right.

Don't be afraid to move your food choices around the different Zones and to experiment with different Volumes. This is how you learn what will work for you and what you have to be more careful with.

What you need to understand is this simple truth:

All successful dieting and weight management is about trial and error until you find what works for you. Then once you have found it: Apply it consistently.

Chapter 20

Burgers, Fries & Pizza

What happens if we change the food that we are looking at to a more current dieting style for many of the people who have weight problems?

Let's say that we had French fries, hamburgers, pizza, ice cream, fizzy drinks, fresh fruit, tea/coffee and water.

Now if this was all that we eat, this would not be a healthy mixture of foods. But let's see what we can do with this mixture.

Anyone who has a diet like this and who has a weight problem; is going to have a weight problem that is in the Amber and Red Zones on The Dieters Scale.

What we will do is we will follow our simple process and use The Dieters Scale to make sense of it, so that we can change a few simple things to improve this diet.

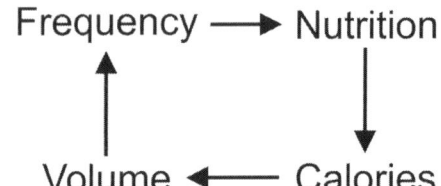

The Hi Common Platform - Weight Control The Hi-Way ©

So let's see how our Guide helps us to work with this diet, so as to manage the Calories and improve Nutrition; without major changes and without difficult changes.

Let's start with breaking the diet down into the areas shown in our graphic above.

We will begin with Nutrition and we will put things into a bar chart to make them easier to understand.

The food is: French fries, hamburgers, pizza, ice cream, fizzy drinks, tea/coffee, and water. So these would go into the Amber/Red Zones for Nutrition. This is because the Nutrition will vary and much of this food could have little or none.

It doesn't matter if you put things like pineapple, onions or olive oil on the pizzas or if you put lettuce in the burgers as this does not make it into a Green Zone item.

So even with fruit or vegetables on them they still would go into the Amber and Red Zones because it's the other ingredients that matter. We are looking at things like pizza's and burgers as a whole.

The fresh fruit would go into the Green Zone. The fruit is only a small part of the foods that are being eaten, so it has a small column. Most of the food being consumed belongs in the Amber and Red Zones, so this has a bigger column.

So the graphic following shows the relative Volumes of foods that we are eating and where we are getting our Nutrition from.

Most of it belongs in the Amber and Red Zones and a little bit is in the Green Zone.

Nutrition Volume

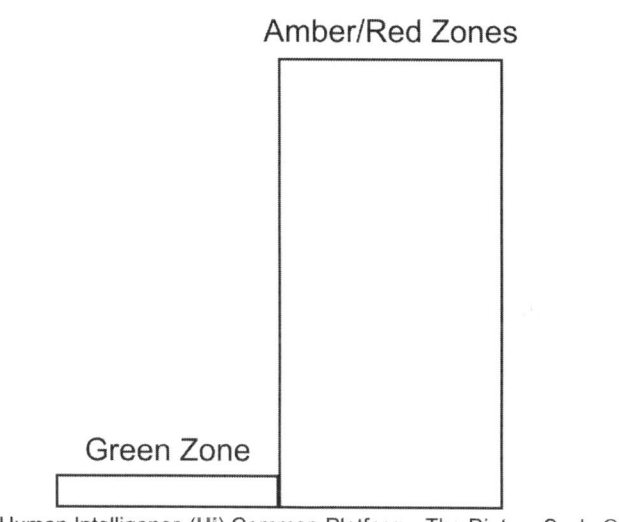

The Human Intelligence (Hi) Common Platform - The Dieters Scale ©

These are the Zones where you are getting your Nutrition from.

Let's say that this is your normal diet; and that you have had this for a long time; and that you are overweight.

A diet like this over a long time can reduce your bodies Nutrition; unless you eat a lot of it.

So to get the right level of Nutrition, in the way that this person is doing it, requires a higher Volume of these foods; which will cause them to take on more Calories and put on more weight.

Let's apply the same process to the Calories that exist in this range of foods and see what Zones they are in.

The Calories in this selection of foods are mostly in the foods that are in the Amber and Red Zones.

And we know that food in the Amber Zone is high in Calories; and that food in the Red Zone is even higher in calories.

A small amount of the food, the fruit, is in the Green Zone. And we know that when fruit is eaten normally, that it does not have large amounts of Calories.

So once again we have a large column for the Amber and Red Zones; and a small column for the Green Zone.

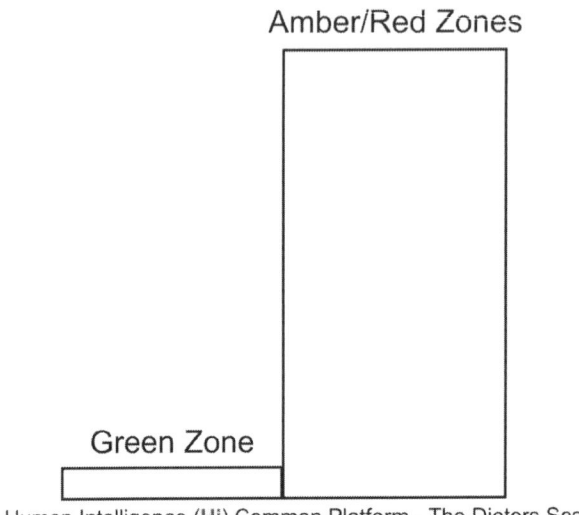

The Human Intelligence (Hi) Common Platform - The Dieters Scale ©

These are the Zones where you are getting your Calories from.

And the next part of our guide was Volume. If we ask about the food that is actually being consumed; and we ask:

> Which Zones are we consuming our foods from and which Zones are we consuming most off?

We can see that our Nutrition is mostly from Amber and Red Zones.

We can see that our Calories are mostly from Amber and Red Zones.

So we then know that our Volumes are also going to be mostly in the Amber and Red Zones with a little in the Green Zone. This is illustrated in the following graphic.

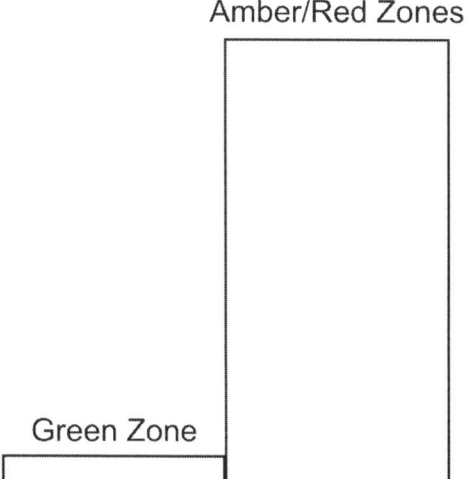

Volume of Food Eaten

Most of the Volume of food that is being consumed is in the Amber/Red Zones.

And if we confirm where the person's weight problem would be on The Dieters Scale; where would they be?

In the Amber or Red Zone!

So you can see that The Dieters Scale helps us to begin to understand the structure of a weight problem.

It also helps us to begin to understand our own weight problem in another way.

Once we have this understanding and knowledge we can then begin to do something different.

We can begin to see how we can influence that structure to achieve the results we want!

So how can you use Volume to help you "Manage Your Calories", even with a diet like this?

Let's see what we could do if you were following the Fat Land to Slim Land journey.

Chapter 21

Improving The Burger, Fries And Pizza's Diet

To refresh your memory the diet we are working with is: French fries, hamburgers, pizza, ice cream, fizzy drinks, fresh fruit, tea/coffee and water.

And we know that this diet is out of balance; and that the person who has this diet is overweight and in the Amber or Red Zone on The Dieters Scale.

So how would we use our simple graphic and our process to help us change and improve this?

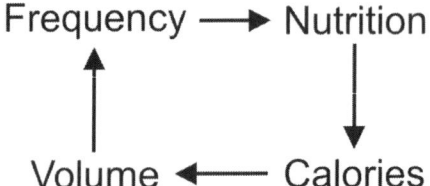

The Hi Common Platform - Weight Control The Hi-Way ©

For the purpose of this exercise we will assume that the person is overweight; that their weight is stable; but that it can vary a little. We will also say that they have a regular routine for eating; that can vary a little. So Frequency is stable.

We know that their Nutrition is mostly from the Amber and Red Zones; with some from the Green Zone.

If they were to increase the Volume of Green Zone Nutrition, this would be a good start and it would help them move in the right direction. So let's do that!

1. Increase the Volume of Green Zone Nutrition and maintain this increase.

So this would be an increase in the fresh fruit and perhaps introducing fresh vegetables. It could be as simple as eating 1 more item of proper fruit each day or every other day. Proper fruit would be a good sized whole apple for example.

They would maintain this level until it became Normal.

Once it became Normal they could then repeat it.

This should be an easy thing to do as they are not being asked to change much.

If this is then repeated a number of times over the course of a year, then the effects are cumulative and it shifts their Nutritional balance.

They want to Avoid switching to things like smoothies as a replacement because these are Amber and Red Zone foods.

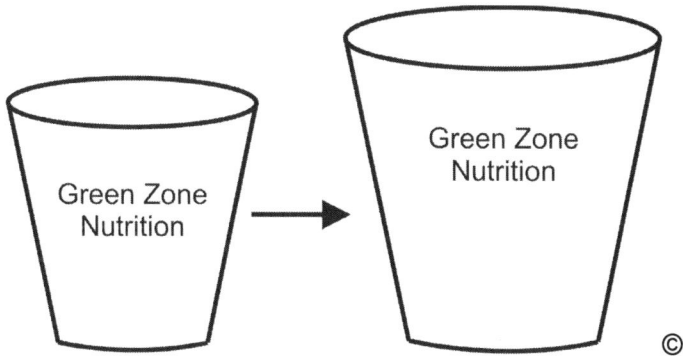

Step 1. Increase the Volume of Green Zone Nutrition.

The next thing to do, would be something that they could probably do easily, without really noticing it at all or very much.

2. Decrease the Volume of Red Zone food and drink they are consuming and move this Volume to the Amber Zone; instead of the Red Zone.

Just by making slight shifts from the Red Zone to the Amber Zone, regularly over a period of weeks, it will make a difference to the Calories that they are consuming and potentially to the Nutrition.

Things like fizzy drinks are an easy thing to reduce, as many people just get in the habit of drinking them. They provide you with fluids but they often have lots of sugar in them; and other things are often added that you really don't want or need to consume. I personally would include Sports drinks in this.

Studies from the major producers of fizzy drinks have shown that when people switch to smaller cans; that they actually consume more and end up paying more. So avoid switching to smaller cans.

See if you can switch more to the tea/coffee or water. Try putting things like lemons, peaches and other fruits into water to give it different flavours. Watch out that you don't add lots of sweeteners or cream to your hot drinks.

Try things like changing pizza toppings and having better quality ingredients; try reducing the amount of olive oil and other oils (pizza's don't really need oils - I know because I make my own). Try freshly made pizza bases rather than factory made ones; or switch to a better quality base, or switch to another better supplier.

Try changing to a higher quality proper dairy ice cream (In the UK ice cream has to have real dairy produce in it only if it claims to be Real Dairy Ice-cream).

So cheaper ice cream can have many different ingredients to create the taste and texture of an ice cream. As a result you can end up eating a chemistry lesson rather than ice cream.

Try removing and reducing things like mayonnaise from burgers. Changing or leaving out sauces can all make a difference as many of these are hidden Red Zone foods with high amounts of sugar.

Personally I am not a fan of many of the buns that are used for burgers and hot dogs. To me they are not real bread and many could improve quality. The reality is that large bakeries need to make their produce to a budget and they have to bake quickly. Could you improve the buns you are eating?

So shifting the Volume from one Zone to another Zone has the effect of Reducing the Calories that someone is consuming while maintaining the Volume of food.

By increasing the Nutrition and reducing the Calories, while maintaining the Volume; it is less likely that they would notice any real difference when they eat it.

This is because we are making gradual shift and not big shifts. It's like going from number 9 to number 8; it's just next door.

The Red Zone food that we are replacing will have little or no Nutrition but lots of Calories, so switching to the Amber Zone food potentially increases their Nutrition while reducing their extra Calories.

This process makes it easier for someone and it lets them adjust things slowly.

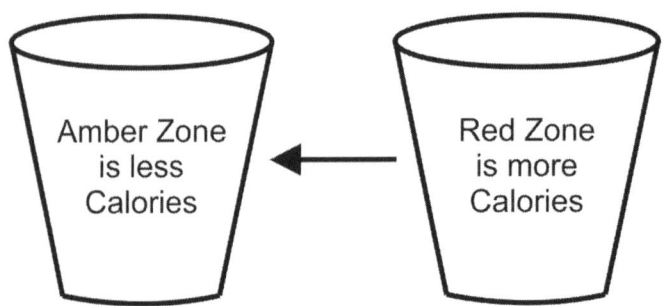

The Human Intelligence (Hi) Common Platform - The Dieters Scale ©

Step 2. Shift Volume from the Red Zone to the Amber Zone.

Doing these 2 simple things would begin to make a difference. It would be slow but this is what we want as their body has not had a chance to settle yet.

Now imagine if we repeated this process again once they got used to the first change?

Then we repeated it again, and again until they got to the point where everything related to their diet and how their body worked was more balanced.

They would achieve a better quality diet because they were gradually altering the quality and shifting the volume of their diet from the Red Zone to the Amber Zone. This would have an impact on Calories by reducing the amount of Calories that they consumed.

The result is that they would get to where they wanted to get to, without all the stress and drama that a conventional diet has; and they would achieve more.

They would also find it much easier to maintain the results as we have not asked them to go on a diet proper; we have just asked them to Practice changing a few simple things!

This simple process is sustainable, whereas the normal way that people approach dieting, with large sudden changes, is much less sustainable.

If people adopt this simple approach we can increase the number of people who successfully manage their weight problem and improve their lives. The number of people who live in Fat Land will reduce and the number of people who live in Slim Land will increase.

If you were to practice this stuff before you began your diet proper; how much easier would the diet proper be once you began doing it; or would you even need to begin the diet proper?

In this exercise we dealt with 3 parts of the process. I left out Frequency because we were doing a simple example. If we were doing a real world case then Frequency would come back into the picture. This is because Frequency helps us achieve stability in the body and predictability with food consumption.

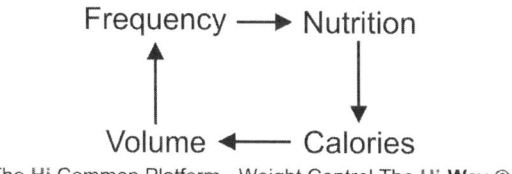

The Hi Common Platform - Weight Control The Hi-Way ©

Chapter 22

Getting The Body Stable
And Prepared To Go On The Diet Proper

If you follow the guidance that I am giving you in this book, you will get to the point where your body becomes stable. You will reach the natural Plateau.

While you are waiting for this to happen, you will be able to begin adjusting the other aspects of your life that also need to be improved; to help your dieting experience be better and more sustainable.

My own experience is that it takes about 3 months for someone's body to become naturally stable; and maybe longer for some other people who are more chaotic.

Getting your body stable (reaching that natural plateau) is a part of the process that you can't actually rush. If you try to rush it then you will find that you just fall off the Stepping Stones and end up back in Fat Land.

If you get impatient and you try to push things to go faster; all you do is that you introduce chaos into a process that requires stability. When you do this all that happens is that you have to start the 3 month clock again.

> Remember that it's your body that determines when it's ready; not a diary or a deadline.

If it was me doing this, then I would put a note in my diary of when I began the 3 month stability stage and then review how I was feeling and whether I was ready to diet proper at that time.

If I wasn't, I would diary more time and just continue to practice the necessary diet things to get and keep my body stable. And I would continue to practice the other lifestyle management things; like stress control that we talked about earlier in the book.

This in itself will usually begin to produce positive results for many people.

When you have a problem or hit a challenge; you have to remind yourself of what it is that we are going to achieve here:

> What we are going to do here is to get you out of Fat Land and help you across the Stepping Stones and into Slim Land. Once you are in Slim Land

we want you to be able to continue to live there.

To achieve this, enough things need to alter within your life and with your weight management processes for you to be able to get to Slim Land in the first place.

Remember this:

> A diet can be thought of as a form of rehabilitation of habits. And if that rehabilitation does not go far enough, it will prove ineffective. And this tends to prove true for many people with weight control problems. The rehabilitation of their weight control does not go far enough.
>
> Remembering this is good Hi.

While you are waiting for your body to become stable there will be plenty of other things for you to prepare and practice.

Take this time to begin to practice and even change the way that you are actually doing and managing things.

This really is the best time to do this because you haven't gone on the diet proper yet and so you haven't got all that stress and those expectations of dieting.

When it comes to the diet proper; I often think that people would be better off just continuing to Practice Weight Control, rather than actually going on the diet proper. Doing this reduces the pressure and makes it easier to incorporate simple changes into your life without having to explain or justify it.

Once all the necessary changes have been incorporated it then becomes easier to transit the Stepping Stones, move into Slim Land and find your Happy Point.

Chapter 23

Achieving Stability And Moving On To The 3rd Stepping Stone

Let's move forward in time and say that you are now 3 months or more into your preparations and practices for the diet proper.

Well done!

If you have done the things that I suggested then you will have prepared yourself in a great way to be successful with this.

If you have been doing what I suggested and you are following and using the information; then you should be feeling better than you did at the beginning.

I would strongly suggest that you keep reading through this book and taking note of the different pieces of information and guidance.

When you read this book at the start of the process you will understand some things better than others.

As you progress through your Weight Control and Life Improvement, and you read it again; then you will understand more and in different ways. This book has been designed for this to happen.

As you move on to the diet proper (or you continue with Practicing the diet) it is important that you don't put yourself under pressure to achieve fast and consistent results.

If you do put yourself under pressure to achieve fast and consistent results, then all you are going to do is to reserve your place in Fat Land and make sure that you get back there quite fast.

Just take it one day at a time and do the things that you need to do on this journey.

If you have prepared in the right way, you will have practiced what to do when you have a bad day. So when a bad day happens, and it will happen at some point, then you will know what to do and how to handle it – Follow your plan when things go wrong as this will help you.

Whatever happens once you are on the diet proper, it is important that when something does go wrong (and it will) that you take a step back and manage it.

You might feel the compulsion to revert to what you would normally have done in the past; but take a step back and manage it.

If you can't take a step back and manage it and things go horribly wrong; don't worry - Learn!

Look at what happened and how it happened. What could you have changed in order to achieve a different result? Then remember that the next time.

Remember that you did not get into Fat Land and take up residence in Fat Land by just making one or two little mistakes over a weekend.

Getting into Fat Land was a process that you worked on, diligently, over a long period of time.

That process had a lot of little steps that took you there over a long period of time.

The following diagram illustrates this.

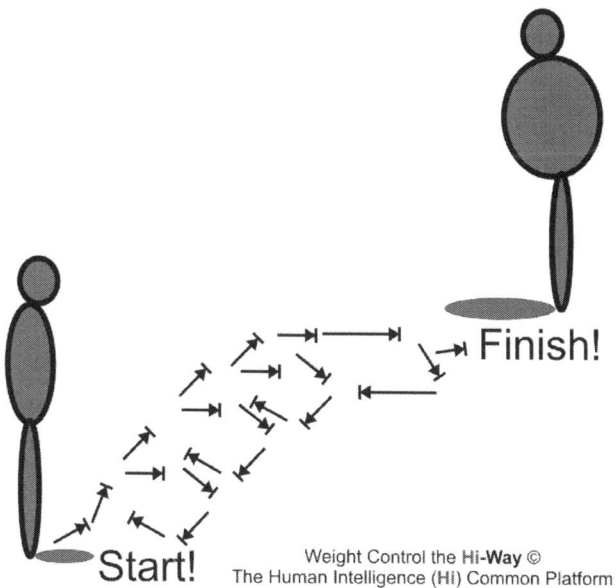

And what we want to do is to reverse that process and take a lot of little steps, over time, to get you out of Fat Land and into Slim Land. The following diagram illustrates this.

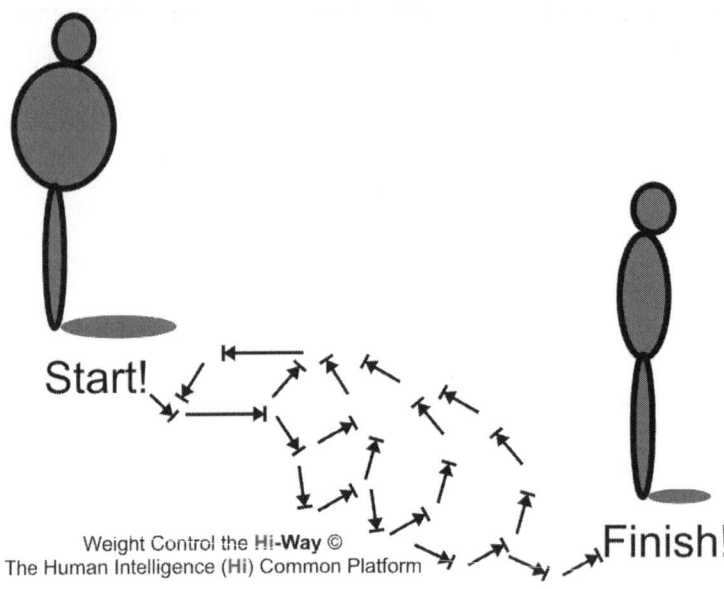

A major mistake that most dieters make is that they have been educated to think of weight loss as a straight line process. As shown below.

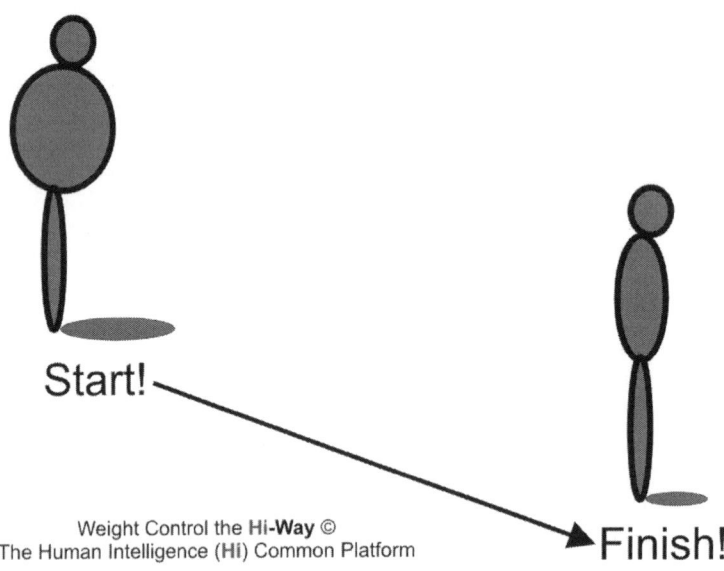

The truth is that it's a false belief system that says you can lose (X) lb's a week until you reach your target weight.

Trying to work with that false belief is bad **Hi**.

The real truth about Weight control is that you can influence how your body works "Over Time"; and you can influence this in positive ways; if you do the right things, in the right way, at the right time, for the right reasons.

If you work with your natural processes, then you can coax them to begin to do what you want them to do.

If you do it the right way then your body will begin to produce the positive results that you want. And you will be able to maintain those results.

You just need to make sure that you are on the right Journey.

Understanding this is good **Hi**.

Chapter 24

Weighing Yourself – How Often?

Before we move on to the 3rd Stepping Stone I want to give you another little warning about weighing yourself.

So many people twist themselves into knots weighing themselves daily or weekly. And for most of them this is unnecessary and counter productive!

My view is that you should not weight yourself daily. Perhaps do it once a month and use other methods to give yourself a better guide to how you are really doing.

Let me explain.

Your body and how it behaves and responds to different situations is all Dynamic.

This means that it may be stable in one set of circumstances and conditions but it can change and alter as those circumstances and conditions change.

Your weight and physical dimensions will vary throughout the day, week and month. Eating, drinking, moving around, the weather, going to the toilet and your choice of clothing all effect your weight and your body mass.

As you get hot or cold, and as you move around, your body moves fluid into and out of your muscles and towards and away from your skin.

Because of this Dynamic behaviour you can only measure things like your weight, body mass, physical dimensions, body fat, and any other way; by doing so over time and seeing what the Trend in measurements are.

That is:

Over time, is the trend that your weight is going up; is it holding steady; is it going down?

> Over time, are you feeling better than you did when you began this?
>
> Over time, are you looking better than you did when you began this?
>
> Over time, are you managing your Lifestyle better than you did when you began this?
>
> Over time, are you managing your food better than you did when you began this?

Over time, is your weight management better than it was when you began this?

Over time, is your weight more stable than it was when you began this?

Over time, are you feeling happier, more in control and more positive about your future?

These are the types of ways that you should really be judging how you are progressing and what you are achieving.

That little indicator on the weighing scales is not the way that I would choose and it may well be your short cut back to Fat Land.

I would suggest that you go back to Step 29 in the 1st Stepping Stone section and read that again.

Now we are going to move on to the 3rd Stepping Stone: Positive Lifestyle Management and begin to establish a foothold on that Stepping Stone.

Establishing A Foothold On The 3rd Stepping Stone

Positive Lifestyle Management

Weight Control The **Hi-Way** ©

"Consolidate And Put It Behind You!"

Chapter 25

The Common Purpose

If you have done the things which I suggested and you have taken the time to do them properly; then you will have already begun the process of establishing a foothold on the 3rd Stepping Stone, and begun the process of establishing a foothold in Slim Land.

Part of what I have been attempting to do with this book and The **Hi-Way** Weight Control Approach is to get you properly focused. I have been attempting to give you a Common Purpose that you can use to achieve successful results.

What is a Common Purpose and why is it a useful thing for Weight Control?

A Common Purpose is when your actions, motives and desires all share something which is the same.

> Successful long term weight control and having the life that you want to have; is achieved by a series of things all coming together with a common purpose.
>
> That common purpose is to get you from Fat Land to Slim Land. And for you to be able to take up residence in Slim Land.
>
> The ultimate place that you want to get to in Slim Land is your Happy Point.
>
> The Place where you are happy to be and where you can comfortably live.

This is the Common Purpose for everything that I have been telling you in this book.

With this Common Purpose you will use the new skills and knowledge that you have been developing; and the new strategies that you have been putting in place. This is applying the new Human Intelligence (**Hi**) that you have.

I am hoping that you will have been doing all the Preparation & Practice that I have been encouraging you to do.

It is all these simple things from the 1st Stepping Stone that begin to create "The Common Purpose" that you need for the journey from Fat Land to Slim Land.

As you moved on to the 2nd Stepping Stone you should have continued to practice them and used them. And you should continue to Prepare & Practice with any new challenge, issue or problem that arises.

By doing this, you embed that Common Purpose into your actions and your thoughts; and it then influences how you begin to manage and control the things that happen to you and around you.

And by going on to the 3rd Stepping Stone, and then going on into Slim Land, you will continue to use and develop that Common Purpose as it becomes Your Common Purpose.

Hold on to your dreams and work towards making them a reality.

Chapter 26

Locking Things In Place

On the 3rd Stepping Stone you will begin a process of locking things in place and leaving old habits and practices behind.

One of those things you will lock in place is your new weight management process; and one of those things you will leave behind is dieting and going on a diet.

Remember that going on a diet and weight management are not one and the same. If you confuse these two things you will find it difficult, and be wondering why things are not working out for you.

This is because a diet tends to be something that people do for a period of time and then stop; and sooner or later they revert back to their previous normal eating habits which have not had time to change.

Weight management is a process that you use to manage your weight to a level; and then you continue to use those same processes to maintain your weight at about that level. So there is no sudden change with dietary practices, food, behaviours, etc.

Also as you use and develop the weight management process, you will gradually change your eating habits and practices; and these become your new and sustainable eating habits and practices. These are the new Special Chapters that you will write into Your Life Profile and use on a daily basis; making them stronger each day.

If you find that your weight and eating habits begin to drift, you can reassert your weight management process and re-establish your new eating habits and practices. You simply re-enforce them.

When this is done properly you find that you do not have to diet at all. What happens is that you notice that you have put on or lost weight and you want to adjust things back to the right weight level.

Because we are looking at weight in a different way; you avoid any sudden over reactions and you simply adjust your weight management process so that over the coming weeks and months you move back to the right level.

This type of adjustment does not throw your body structures out of balance and it does not interfere with your digestive system or your bodies recycling processes.

As a result we avoid the chaos and it becomes a simple, easy and constantly achievable process. And this is exactly what you want.

Positive Weight Management is a part of Positive Lifestyle Management.

It is about being Pro-Active and dealing with problems as you see them coming or as they occur.

Positive Weight Management is about taking responsibility for what goes into your mouth and the effects of that consumption upon your body.

Positive Weight Management is also about taking control of how you use food in different situations when you are feeling vulnerable, scared or unsure about what to do.

Remember:

> It's not about what you eat or drink. It's about what you put into your mouth in the first place!
>
> If it never goes into your mouth, you never give your power away to food and drink.
>
> This simple process gives you the power to influence how your body works, how it looks and how it behaves; by what you put into it.
>
> You can use that influence to achieve the long term control over how you look and how you feel.

Positive Lifestyle Management is how you move away from a life focused on your weight and the problems that this causes in your life.

Positive Lifestyle Management is about making some positive choices about your life; and then making those positive choices into a reality.

It can be challenging if you are not used to doing this but it is something that everyone is capable of doing.

To achieve successful results with your Positive Lifestyle Management we will use the same processes that we have been talking about and using throughout this book.

Once again we can use The Dieters Scale to help us in this process as it is something that you are familiar with. This can help you to achieve better quality Human Intelligence (**Hi**) that you can then use in positive ways.

To help you to achieve the life changes that you want, we will use The Dieters Scale and apply the Green, Amber and Red Zones to the different issues, problems and challenges that life naturally brings to us.

As your starting point, you could consider the issues, problems and challenges that the questions in this book asked you to consider.

Those are potentially things that impact your weight problem, impact your life and impact how you feel about and view yourself.

Managing these different things is like managing a weight problem; there are right ways to go about it and wrong ways.

And what we want to do is to get more things right than we get wrong.

By applying The Dieters Scale we can see that other problems have different degrees of complication and difficulty attached to them; just like dieting does. And just like dieting they need to be worked with so that they can be moved from one Zone to another; and then to where we want them to be within the final Zone.

For example: If we were looking at Self-Esteem, Confidence and Motivation; we would recognise that some issues are small and easy to address, and some are difficult and hard to address.

The simple ones belong in the Green Zone and the difficult ones belong in the Amber and Red Zones.

And when we want to sort these things out and begin to achieve positive results, we don't want to make the mistake of apply a Green Zone solution to a Red Zone problem.

Because now that we have better Human Intelligence (Hi) we now know that if the Zone of the problem and the Zone of the solution do not match; then this has a very high probability that it won't work and that we are just setting ourselves up to experience failure.

To break all these different problems down into manageable bits that we can easily work with; we will combine the help that The Dieters Scale can give us with The Stepping Stones approach. So let's recap them.

If a problem is in the Red Zone we know that we are unlikely to be able to jump from the Red Zone into the Green Zone and maintain those results.

So we begin a process of moving out of the Red Zone and into the Amber Zone.

Then we move out of the Amber Zone into the Green Zone.

Then we move to where we want to be in the Green Zone. We move to our Happy Point.

So we achieve this by taking a series of baby steps which have a Common Purpose: To take us in the direction of the positive result we want to achieve and maintain.

Exactly like we did with Weight Control; we focus on achieving and Maintaining the result; not just on achieving it.

If we make an error and we put the problem in the wrong Zone, then we go up a Zone rather than down a Zone.

> It is better to apply an Amber Zone solution to a Green Zone problem; than it is to try and apply a Green Zone solution to an Amber Zone problem.

This simple tactic applies to all the different types of problems that you may experience and want to deal with.

Once we have Identified the problem that we want to deal with or work with. We will then use The Stepping Stones approach to understand, work with and then achieve the outcomes that we want.

> This simple process can help you achieve positive results again and again.

The Stepping Stones that you can use again and again are:

- Identify the Problem to be dealt with.
1. Preparation & Practice.
2. Act and Sort It Out.
3. Consolidate and put it behind you.

Just like with your weight problem; if you fall off a Stepping Stone, you simply begin the process again and learn from falling off the Stepping Stone.

And just like I suggested with your weight problem; you can take baby steps and you can tackle any problem by degrees. Small steps usually work better than big steps.

If you make a mistake and get things wrong; then simply do what I told you to do with your weight problem. Use failure to show you what you need to do to achieve success.

So all of this becomes a simple process that you can incorporate into your life and it is simple to follow.

It will not always be easy but by being consistent you can achieve positive results that you never thought you would be able to achieve.

When a problem, issue or challenge occurs; always take a step back and take another look at what is happening and why.

Avoid knee-jerk reactions.

If you need a little space and time; then take it.

Don't let others push you into making the wrong decisions or taking the actions that you will regret later. They will and can walk away but you will end up having to live with it.

Learn to say No! Practice saying No and get used to hearing yourself say it. This can be very Empowering!

In any situation you may not know the positive end result that you would want from that situation. That is OK; because you probably will know the negative result that you don't want. If you can't work towards something clear and positive; then work away from something until you can do something better.

I have helped people to deal with some very bad situations in their lives. I have always found that Preparation and dealing with things in manageable pieces, without over reacting, is the best way. Its' not always the easiest but it is the best.

You may not always be able to do this but the work that we are doing here will provide you with the foundations that you need to successfully do this in the future.

Chapter 27

Creating Your Slim Land Identity

Well, we are moving towards the end of this book but not the end of the wonderful things which you and I can create and achieve.

Regardless of how difficult, complicated or bad life gets; life is a golden opportunity that we need to take and enjoy.

To help you with this I am going to give you another piece of the dieters puzzle.

If you are someone who has a weight problem, a number of things would have changed in your life as that weight problem developed and became established.

One of those things is that Your Life Profile will have changed and you will have developed a Fat Land Identity.

Once someone has developed a Fat Land Identity it begins to define who they are, what they do, how they do it, what you can expect from them; and how they respect and value themselves.

Now at this point I know that there are some people who will want to give me an argument about this.

I have noticed that there is a trend for people saying that we should not recognise or see someone's weight; in the same way that we should not see or recognise the colour of someone's skin.

> "We should see the person inside."

My view on this is simple!

I have <u>not</u> come across many people who have weight problems who are really and genuinely happy with being overweight; and living with the effects and affects that this has upon themselves and the lives that they have.

I have come across a lot of people who <u>begin</u> by claiming that this is the case, but when we have got beneath the surface the rhetoric changes. They stop lying to me and to themselves and they admit the truth. They are not at their Happy Point.

If you want to be overweight and live a happy life, I don't have a problem with that. I am not going to waste a single breath telling you any different.

I am interested in the people who are not happy having a weight problem and who want to really do something about it; so that they can feel better about themselves and have happier and more fulfilling lives.

So let's get back to those people who do want to change and improve their lives and leave the people alone who don't want to change and improve their lives.

As I said before:

Their Fat Land Identity begins to define who they are, what they do, how they do it, what you can expect from them; and how they respect and value themselves.

Changing this is something that we do in baby steps; and we began that process back in the first part of this book when I began working on your Human Intelligence (Hi).

With some things you will find that it is easy to leave your Fat Land identity behind and to embrace your Slim Land identity.

With other things it may be more difficult.

The things that are more difficult just require you to do them in stages. Moving a little bit at a time; taking time to Prepare and Practice and move across the Stepping Stones again and again until you reach the final time that you cross the stones.

One major reason people have a problem with the difficult bits is this:

They shy away from changing or dealing with certain parts of the problem. They want the Spiders Web to change but they don't want to change certain parts of it.

Now when you do this you are, in effect, trying to be in two place at once. You are trying to be in Slim Land but without leaving Fat Land.

The more that you try to do this, the more challenging and difficult it becomes.

This then results in you having increased stress and anxiety which leads on to things becoming more difficult and chaotic.

And the reality is that it is not unusual for someone to be taken back to Fat Land from their journey into Slim Land because of things like this: Issues that need to be dealt with but which are not being dealt with.

> You can't develop your Slim Land Identity while you are also trying to maintain your Fat Land Identity. It's just too difficult.

I have helped people to finally move on and let go of their connections to Fat Land a number of times; and it is always the same.

Once they have dealt with things properly and not compromised themselves; they can then move into Slim Land and begin to get to the right place in Slim Land for them.

> They become free to find their Happy Point.

The more time that you spend in Slim Land without having a foothold in Fat Land; the easier it will get for you.

Allow your weight to change, allow your life to change and allow yourself to change.

We continued with the baby steps approach when we moved on to the 2nd Stepping Stone: Diet & Weight Management.

We will continue with those baby steps as you consolidate your position and positive weight management becomes a part of your normal everyday life.

On the 3rd Stepping Stone you combined everything you have done so far and you continue to use The Dieters Scale and the 3 Stepping Stones Approach.

If you continue with this, then you will find that you gradually become established in Slim Land. It happens slowly, so you tend not to notice it happening.

One day you will realise that life has changed and you may not quite realise exactly when it happened and how it happened; but it has happened.

You will find yourself in Slim Land and in order to stay there you just need to continue to do what you have done; and use the same tools and processes that I have given you.

If you find that you need extra help at any time you can always send me an email to the address at the back of this book or through my website.

Chapter 28

Moving Into Slim Land

At this stage of your Quest, you have crossed the Stepping Stones and you have reached Slim Land. This is a great achievement; well done!

Over the coming months you will move deeper and deeper into Slim Land.

You will see that Slim Land also has Green, Amber and Red Zones.

This is because reaching Slim Land is a great achievement; but now you need to find your Happy Point in Slim Land.

This is your Happy Point with your weight control and the other challenges, issues and problems that helped to develop and maintain your weight control problem.

As you reach your Happy Point with these different things, you will gradually move through the different Zones in Slim Land and begin taking up residence and living in the right Zone.

The Common Purpose that you want to take with you is to reach and establish your Slim Land identity in the Green Zone. This means that your real Happy Point will be your place in the Green Zone.

Each person will have their own unique Life Map as they enter into Slim Land.

As they move towards and into the Green Zone, more of their Life Map should become Green Zones.

Some aspects of life may remain in the Amber Zones; the truth is that this is real life and things are seldom perfect.

However; through the skills and the new Human Intelligence (Hi) that they will have developed; they will be better able to manage and work on those Amber Zones.

If you find that you still have Red Zones, then you had better start working on them and sorting them out. It may be that you can't resolve them but you can usually improve them. Moving things from the Red Zone to the Amber Zone can make them easier to manage.

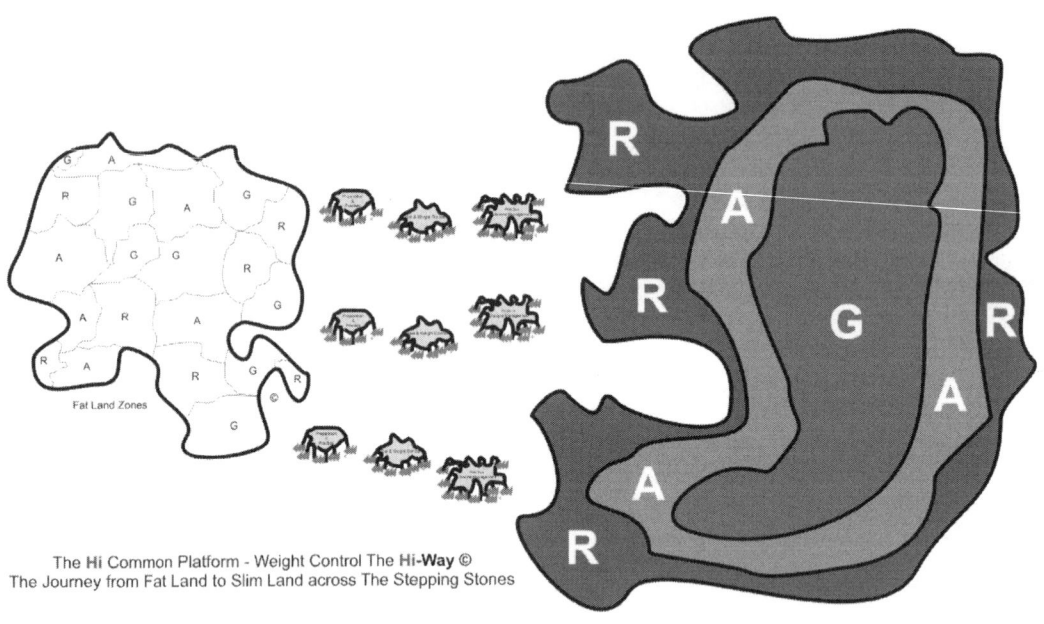

The Hi Common Platform - Weight Control The **Hi-Way** ©
The Journey from Fat Land to Slim Land across The Stepping Stones

Chapter 29

Don't Get Mugged By Poor Hi

Once you have taken up residence in Slim Land and you have attained your Happy Point in the Green Zone; you still need to be aware of Fat Land.

The reason for this is that you have a connection with Fat Land that will gradually diminish and become a distant memory; but that connection will still continue to exist like a scar.

There will be times in Slim Land when things become difficult. It is at times like this that you need to reaffirm your Slim Land practices and Positive Lifestyle Management skills.

If you begin to stray and lose your firm foundations then you may become vulnerable to poor Hi.

Poor Hi can often come with a smiling face. It may be the commercials for beauty products, the new super slim food products, the new diet product that means that you can eat lots of fast food and not put of weight, the friend who keeps telling you to trust them about how good a product or new service is, etc.

All of this is stuff that preys upon vulnerabilities; and it tries to create and increase vulnerabilities.

By being aware and using your own Hi and Positive Lifestyle Management skills; you can avoid being mugged by poor Hi.

If you do find that you do get mugged; then all is not lost. Simply get yourself back on track by using what you have already learned.

So now this is the end of this book.

I wish you the very best of wishes on your journey and I hope that I hear from you with tales of your Quest from Fat Land to Slim Land.

David John Sheridan

About the Author

David John Sheridan has spent many years understanding the fundamentals of different disciplines, social structures, financial management systems, business structures, personal interactions, human nature, innovation, social control and management, nature, theoretical thinking and understanding the true nature of things with a philosophical perspective.

David has also spent many years developing new products, systems and solutions to problems as an independent developer and free thinker. This is in a self-funding environment without the support and protection of a larger organisation.

David has worked with commodity markets, with consumer products and developed new products intended to break the commodity market dynamic.

David became a therapist in the early 1990's and spent a number of years working in the area of addictions and challenging behaviour with alcohol and drugs. At the same time he developed his own clinic working with long term weight problems, obesity and other issues.

David has spent many years involved in martial arts and achieved a number of black belts in traditional weapon systems and taught and trained in martial arts for many years.

David believes that one man can make a difference; albeit not in his own time or in his own country.

David is a believer in positive thinking in a real context.

All the material in this book is based on David's own experiences, observations and understanding of the processes involved. The different Concepts, Definitions and Explanations are all the work of David John Sheridan.

Hello Readers!

You can find more information about the things that I am doing such as Lifestyle Management Programmes, seminars, workshops, public speaking, books, etc. by visiting the following websites:

www.GlobalWeightControl.com

www.PalmSolutions.co.uk

You can email me; David John Sheridan with any comments or inquiries at: david@GlobalWeightControl.com

This material is Licensed

Thank you for buying this book.

I hope that you found this book very useful and beneficial but please remember that this is not a license for anyone to use the material from this book.

If you want to use any of this material you will need to have permission to do so as years of work have gone into the creation and development of this material.

I am happy to hear from anyone who would like to have authorised use of this material and to discuss the terms of such use.

All Commercial use will be subject to licensing. Please see our website for more information.

www.GlobalWeightControl.com

Our Intellectual Property includes the following which is protected by Copyright, Trade Marks, Registered Trade Marks, Design Rights and Trade Secrets.

The Human Algorithm® Project

The Human Intelligence (Hi) Common Platform

Weight Control The Hi-Way

The Dieters Scale and its various concepts and applications

The PALM Solutions Lifestyle Management Platform

Hi-Way lite

The Hi-Way Stepping Stones Approach

The Fat Land and Slim Land concepts

The Fat Land and Slim Land Identity concepts

The Slim Land Quest & The Stepping Stones Quest

The 3 Steps Approach to dealing with the Weight Control problem and the different Common Components.

The Common Components, the Basket of Common Components, the Spiders Web

*Hi-Way*lite Is part of The Human Intelligence (Hi) Common Platform; The Human Algorithm® Project; and is subject to Copyright © and other Intellectual Property Rights.

As is PALM Solutions and their Strategic Lifestyle Management Solutions; Lifestyle Management Platforms and other material.

These were created and developed by David John Sheridan – Lifestyle Services Corporation Ltd (UK)

Printed in Great Britain
by Amazon.co.uk, Ltd.,
Marston Gate.